# The Watercolor Artist's Guide to COLOR

A visual guide to choosing and using color to bring your paintings to life

RICHARD TAYLOR

DAVID & CHARLES

www.davidandcharles.com

# Contents

A WORLD OF COLOR.....4

**PART 1:** WATERCOLOR BASICS.....6

Pigment & Water.....8

Creating Dimension.....10

**PART 2:** PAINTS & COLORS.....14

Paint Types.....16

Grays & Neutrals.....22

Color Families.....28

- Yellows.....34
- Reds.....48
- Blues.....62

**PART 3:** LIGHT & SHADE.....76

The Three Stages.....78

Reflected Color.....80

Still Life Studies.....82

**PART 4:** WARM & COLD.....90

The Theory.....92

Still Life Studies.....94

**PART 5:** COLOR IN ACTION.....102

Sketchbook Studies.....104

- Irises.....106
- Sunflowers.....114

FINAL THOUGHTS.....124

ABOUT THE AUTHOR.....126

THANKS.....126

INDEX.....127

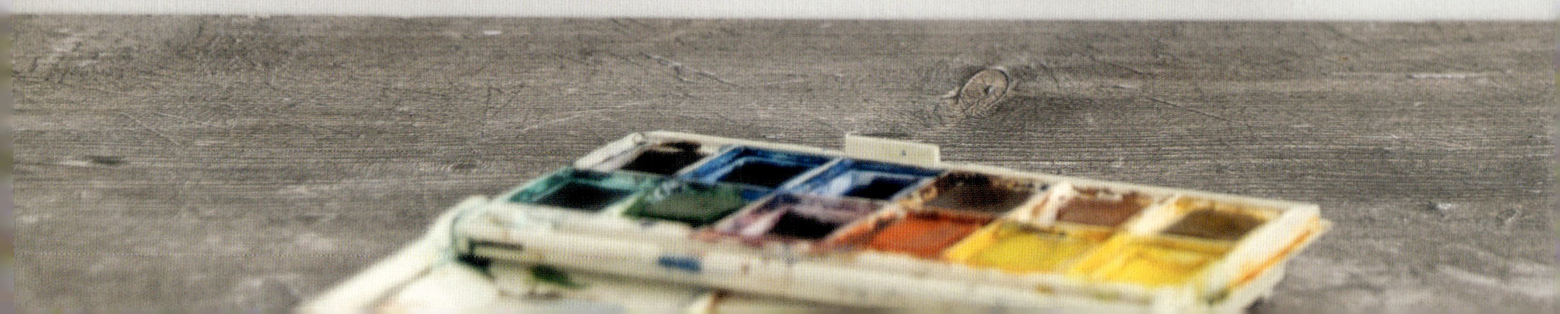

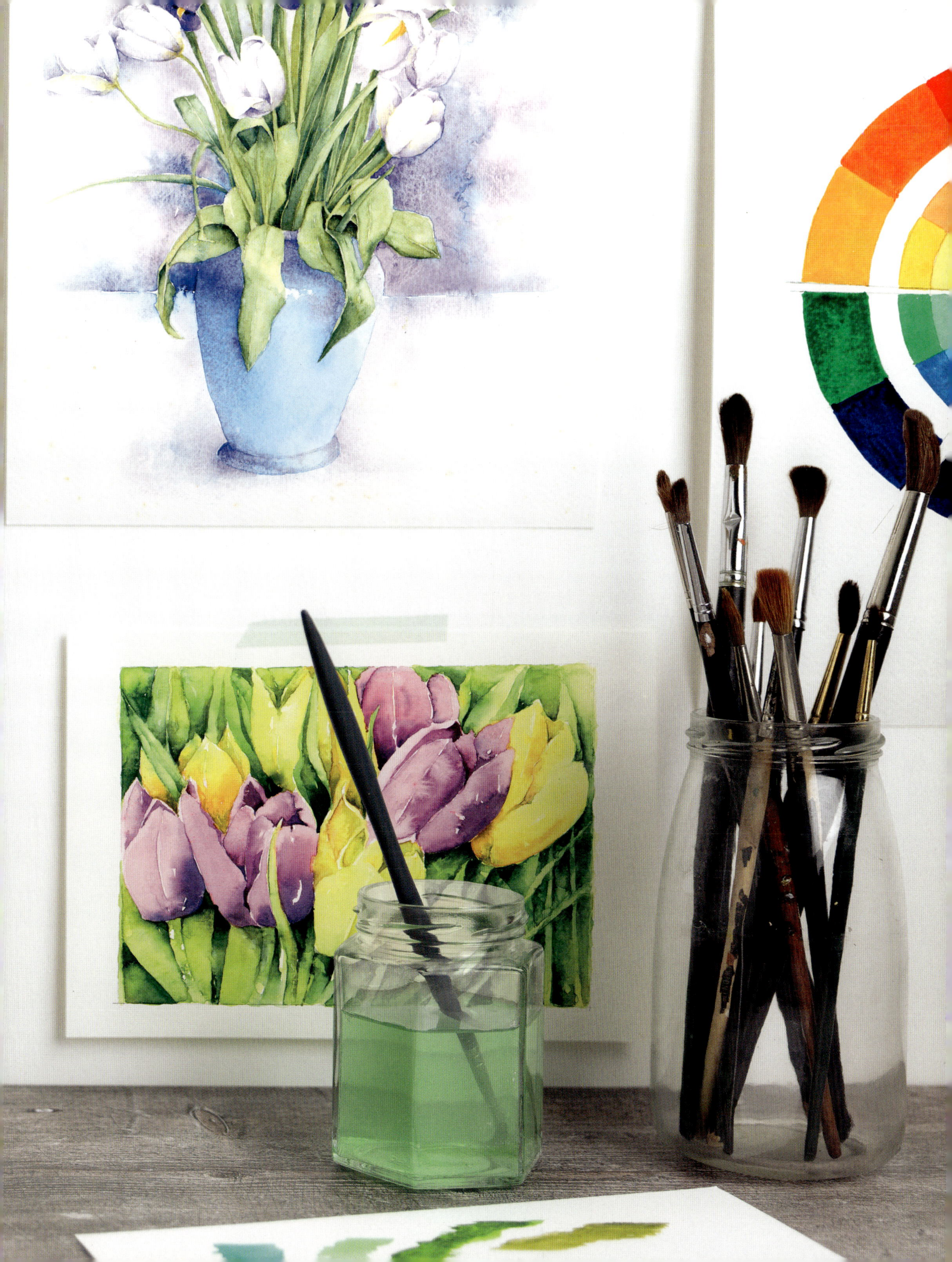

# A World of Color

Since the beginning of time, people on all continents across the globe have sought to use the magic and beauty of color to record the world they inhabit. We are still using color today for exactly the same purpose.

## COLOR IN HISTORY

The prehistoric peoples of Europe discovered the ochres, siennas and umbers in the clays of the Alpine regions, making hand prints and colored drawings of their everyday lives – most famously in the caves at Lascaux. Meanwhile, the Native Americans created a wealth of imagery using the same methods on cave walls in Alabama, Minnesota and across California. For these people, however, personal adornment was more important than creating pictures, and took the explorations of color in different directions. The ancient Egyptians were great innovators and may well be credited with the discovery of the heating processes which allowed them to make a synthetic blue pigment by mixing copper and calcium. They soon began to produce some of the most stunning colored jewelry and clothing for their leaders to confirm and assert their status. Color clearly mattered.

Civilizations that followed attempted, usually in vain, to capture the colors of their surroundings by crushing or distilling the actual subjects they wished to paint – green from grasses and leaves, and red from berries and seeds. These efforts usually failed as the colors created were fugitive, their very short lives causing the color to fade to near invisibility within minutes. Some, however, did succeed – madder root was successful in producing a purple, and a dark blue color called indigo was created from indigenous Asian plants. Production knowledge and techniques were developing.

By the mid 1500s, the studios of the Italian Renaissance painters were filled with apprentices grinding pigments then blending them with oils to create colors with such wonderful names as Sinoper, Cinabrese and Orpiment. Many of these pigments came from a more refined method of extracting color from the natural rocks and clays found in the foothills of the Alpine regions than those of their prehistoric ancestors.

## THE INDUSTRIAL REVOLUTION

But it was the arrival of the industrial chemists in the eighteenth century that created an explosion of experiments and developments while seeking new and better colors for the dye industry. Coal was the driving force of the emerging industries and the waste product, coal tar, was in no short supply. It was discovered that it contained the compound aniline, which held a wealth of color making properties. Soon, rich, radiant purples and blues were being extracted from this black slime that formed the basis of many of the colors that we know today. Color production was in the hands of the industrial scientists, and inquiry and experimentation continued at some pace, through to the polymers and plastics of the 1950s and '60s, when a new type of industry required a new set of colors for new purposes.

## MODERN COLOR

Today, art stores can be overwhelming places with vast arrays of paints arranged on their shelves, often with little or no explanation of their purpose. Sometimes the names of the paints will give you a clue: Lemon Yellow, for example, will offer a visual clue about the color of the paint in the tube. It's not too hard to imagine how this might look on paper. But exactly what would you expect from Caput Mortuum, and what is the difference between Light Red and Burnt Sienna as the colors in the tube look exactly the same?

*"I personally find the world of color both fascinating and still exciting after nearly 50 years of engagement and struggle with it."*

## ABOUT THIS BOOK

The purpose of this book is to help you navigate your way through all the siennas, umbers, phthalocyanines and dioxazines. It is not possible to explore all of the many paints that are in production, so I have made a selection of the most common paints found in art stores and those that I use most frequently in my painting. I have concentrated chiefly on the color of the paints, rather than any other qualities they may have, to allow you to step off on your voyage of color discovery. Personally, I use a fairly limited palette of around six paints and dip into others when necessary. I also often use ready-made secondary colors – oranges, greens and purples – but only as a starting point, adding whichever color I feel is required to change the tone according to my needs.

The question "Do red and yellow always make orange?" has never been far from my mind in creating this book. Yes, they will create an orange when mixed, but that orange will be entirely dependent upon the particular red and yellow that you start with – is this the orange that you were looking for? Sometimes they will create the color you are seeking, but sometimes they won't. For this reason, I often start the color mixing process with a pre-mixed tube of orange paint and add other colors to it in small quantities until I have reached the desired result (stopping before I create a muddy brown instead of a dark orange). This will all be explored in the coming pages with examples and suggestions for you to try. These can only, however, be the solutions to the problems of color mixing that I personally have found. You will most certainly find others through experimentation and, maybe, a little risk taking with your paints.

I have chosen easily sourced subjects as examples for you to paint in the comfort of your own home where the light is constant and the wind isn't blowing your paper across the landscape. You don't need a studio – a kitchen table will do nicely.

I personally find the world of color both fascinating and still exciting after nearly 50 years of engagement and struggle with it. I do hope that this book will help you to feel the same. Of course, an understanding of the origins and qualities of paints helps greatly, but a passion for their application is what really counts. Enjoy using it!

*Part 1:*

# WATERCOLOR BASICS

Before we go any further with the color mixing process, it will be useful to examine the basics of the process of watercolor painting. At its most fundamental level watercolor painting involves adding wet paint to paper. It will help, however, to explore exactly what happens to the paint and paper when they meet.

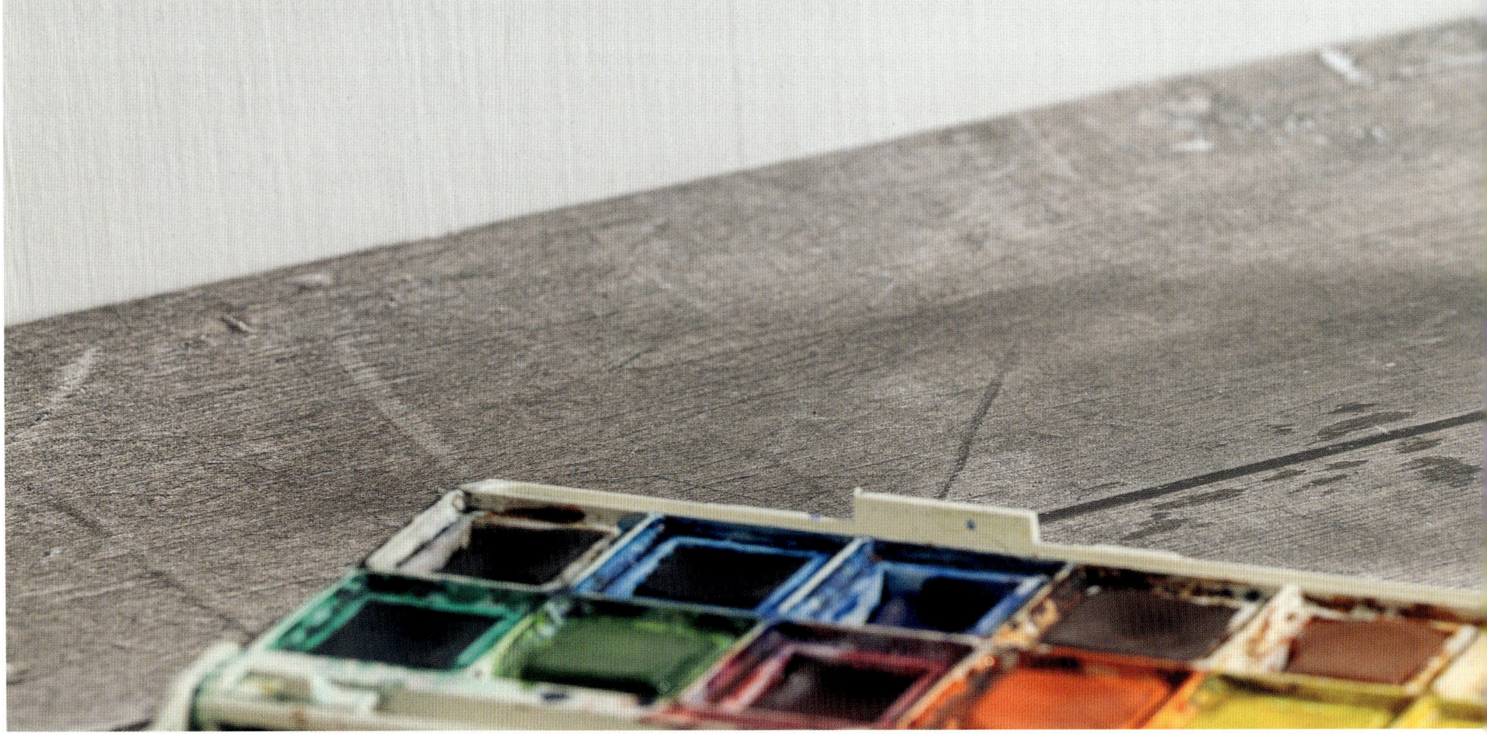

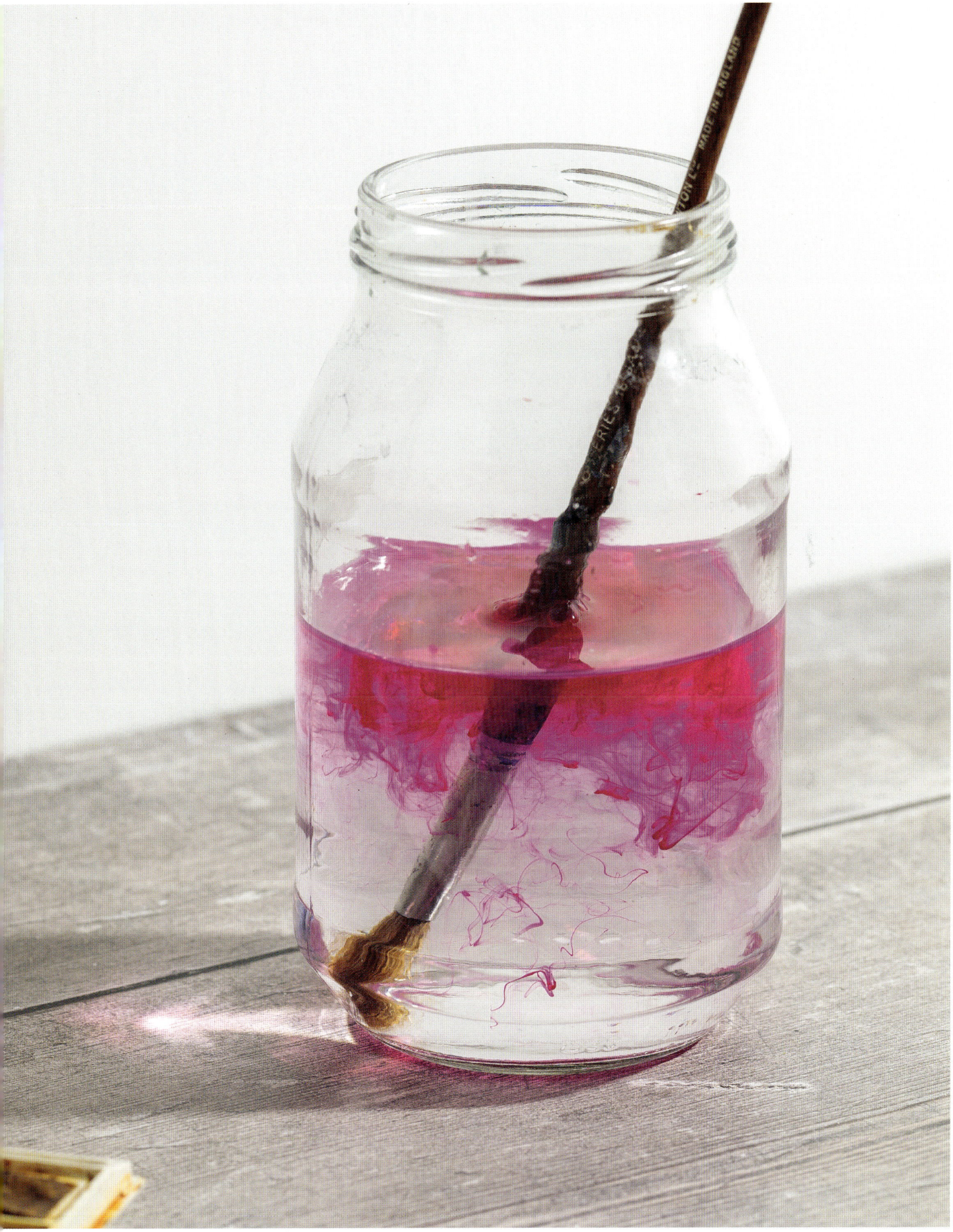

# Pigment & Water

One of the most important features of our craft is that, unlike most other mediums, watercolor paints can only be made lighter by the addition of water, not of other paints. The reason is physical, not optical, requiring a brief explanation of the relationship between the key elements of watercolor painting – paper, gum arabic, pigment and water.

## PAINT PIGMENTS

The simple act of brushing wet watercolor paint onto watercolor paper sets off a series of physical processes that determines the way the paint will eventually look. First, the water activates the glue or "size" with which manufacturers coat their paper. You will find that the amount of size will vary between different types of paper and different manufacturers.

Watercolor paint is made by combining pigment with gum arabic solution, and usually a medium to aid flow such as glycerine. When added to the paper, the paint will initially appear strong, vibrant and shimmering. This is because the eye is seeing light reflected from the white of the paper, through the wet size and the diluted gum arabic. Imagine looking at a bead of rain water or morning dew on a leaf and how intense the reflected light appears. The principle is the same.

As the pigment is absorbed into the fibers of the paper, so the size will begin to dry and any remaining surface water will evaporate. When this simple process is complete, the color is viewed through the dried pigment, dried gum arabic and dried size. The passage of light is no longer enhanced or amplified by water. So, it is vital that you bear in mind that the color you see when you first apply the paint to paper will probably not be the color you will see when everything has dried.

The thinner the initial wash, the lighter the color will appear as less pigment obstructs the passage of light. Adding another layer of paint increases the amount of pigment, further restricting the flow of light, reducing the translucency and making the color appear darker. So, the only way to lighten watercolors effectively is to dilute them.

## TONAL DIAGRAMS

The tonal diagrams throughout the book illustrate the ways in which watercolor paints react when diluted and applied to paper. In these circular diagrams, the raw, straight-out-of-the-tube paint is on the outside (only a touch of water will have been added to loosen the paint). Then, when you try it for yourself, you will get a feel for the quality of the paint and its potential for flow and coverage. Some paints are quite thick and even glutinous, needing to be vigorously "worked up" on the palette before use to eliminate lumps and irregular coverage. Others lose intensity as soon as a drop or two of water is added. Others flow freely and evenly, and give a good account of themselves in terms of maintaining their color when diluted.

## READING THE RINGS

The inner rings of the tonal diagrams show the diluted color. This is important as many paints change appearance noticeably once water is added. I use three levels of dilution, a technique that I urge you to try. First, a little water is added, creating a barely diluted paint, but different from the original. Next, a little more water is added to create a mid-tone. Then, even more – the initial color is discernible, but shows how light of a color you can achieve.

You will find that different paints have their own unique appearance once diluted and, once again, using this technique to get to know your paints will allow you to make informed decisions about the colors you choose and how you use them.

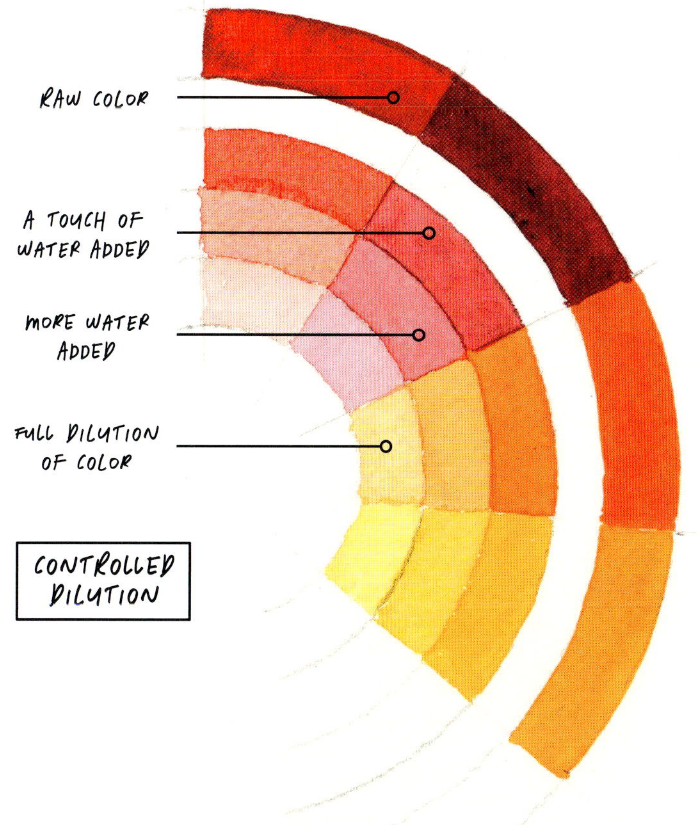
RAW COLOR
A TOUCH OF WATER ADDED
MORE WATER ADDED
FULL DILUTION OF COLOR
CONTROLLED DILUTION

## THE COLOR WHEEL

I will go on to expand on this in much more detail, but for now, here is how the color wheel works. The three primary colors sit in a neat central triangle. When mixed with their neighbors, they create secondary colors. A primary color will always sit opposite a secondary color on the wheel. Because of the visual effect that these colors have on each other (more on this later) they are referred to as "complementary" colors. The importance of this is that complementary colors are particularly useful in creating tones – that is, making a color darker. So, let's put all of this into practice.

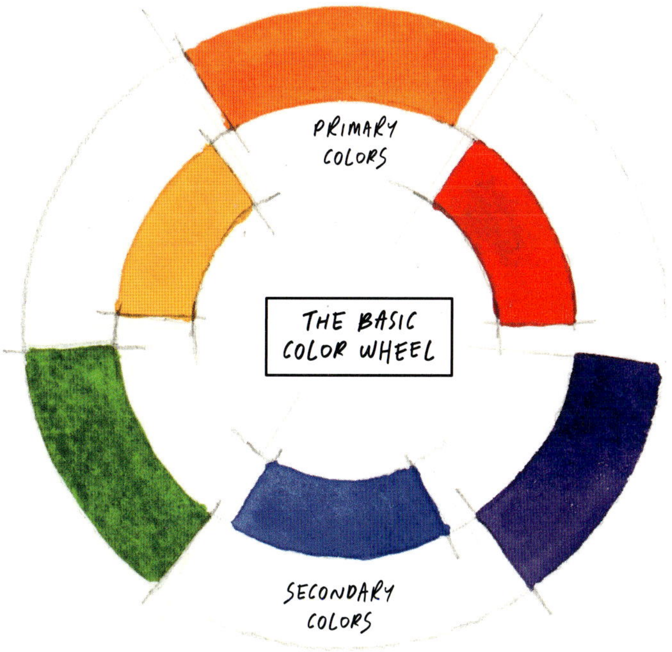
PRIMARY COLORS
THE BASIC COLOR WHEEL
SECONDARY COLORS

### A NOTE ON VOCABULARY:

Much has been written about art terminology. For clarity, in this book, "tone" refers to how light or dark a color is.

# Creating Dimension

Having dealt with the technical aspects of watercolor, or the "why" element, we can spend a little time on the "how" part of the process. So, how do you use color to make your painting appear three-dimensional on a two-dimensional surface?

## PUSH-PULL

Throughout this book, I have used a three-stage process to create paintings. The first stage – creating highlights – has just been considered in Pigment & Water. When dried, the lightest sections appear as the highlights. They cannot be made lighter, but can be made to *look* lighter by adding mid-tones. This is the "essential" color of the object, unaffected by shadows or reflected colors. Finally, shadows are added to the darker section that is furthest from the light. This process is often referred to as the "push-pull" technique. Placing a dark color next to a light one creates the illusion of the lighter color being visually "pushed" forward, and the darker color being "pulled" into the background.

## THE LIGHT SOURCE

The three spheres illustrate the process. The highlighted section is where the light source hits directly on the top right-hand side. These are the lightest sections in terms of color. Next, the mid-tones are gradually applied, working carefully around the highlights and deepening the intensity of the color as it moves away from the light. A three-dimensional look begins to appear. For added volume, and to complete the dynamic illusion, a series of dark tones is added, making the side furthest from the light appear to be in shadow.

HIGHLIGHTS

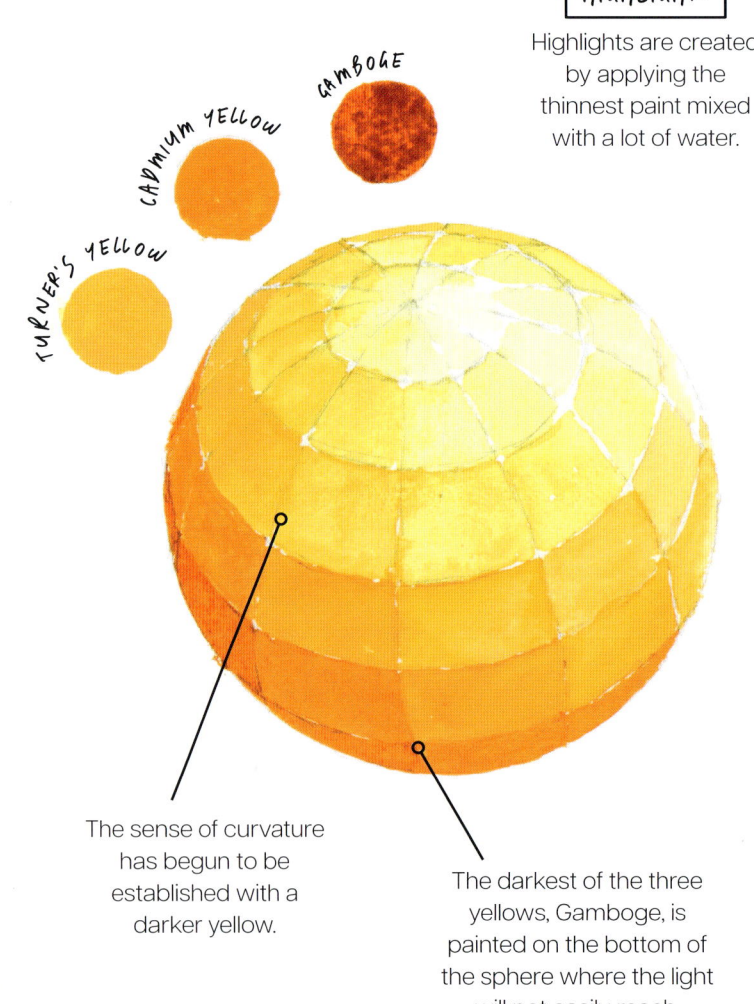

Highlights are created by applying the thinnest paint mixed with a lot of water.

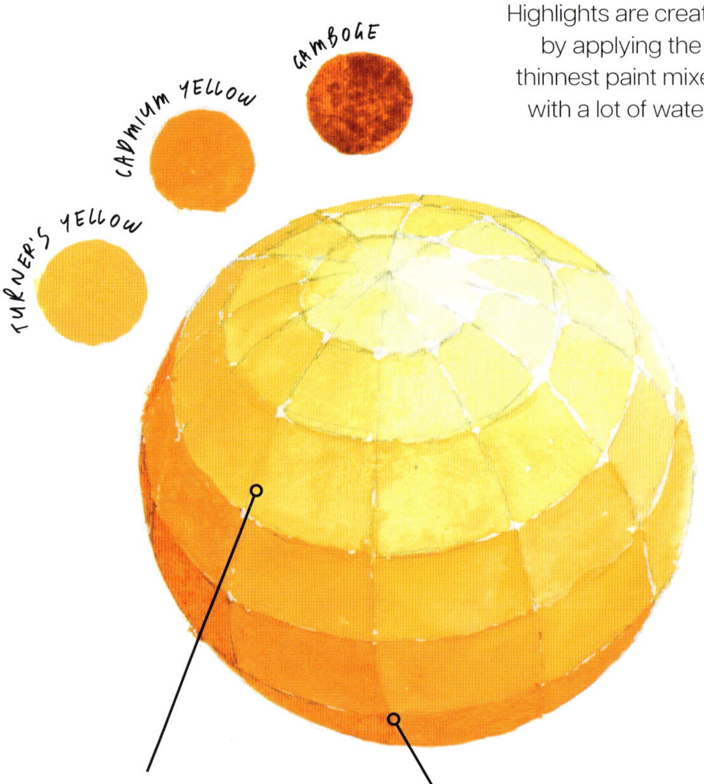
GAMBOGE
CADMIUM YELLOW
TURNER'S YELLOW

The sense of curvature has begun to be established with a darker yellow.

The darkest of the three yellows, Gamboge, is painted on the bottom of the sphere where the light will not easily reach.

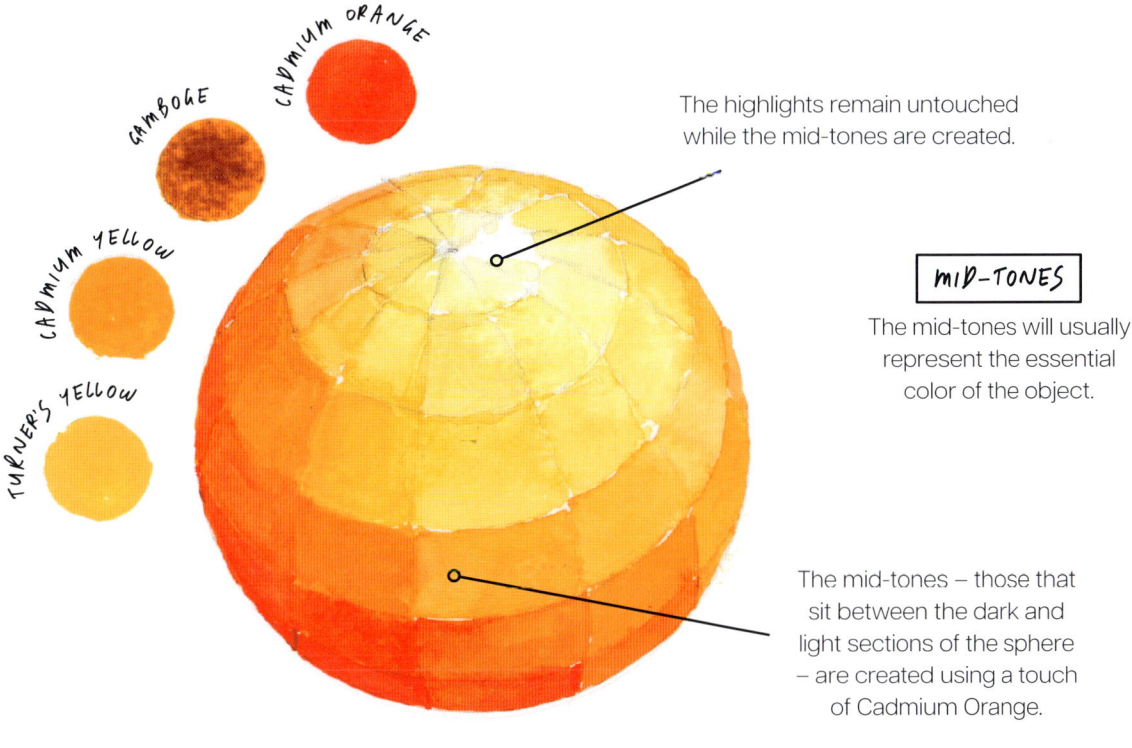

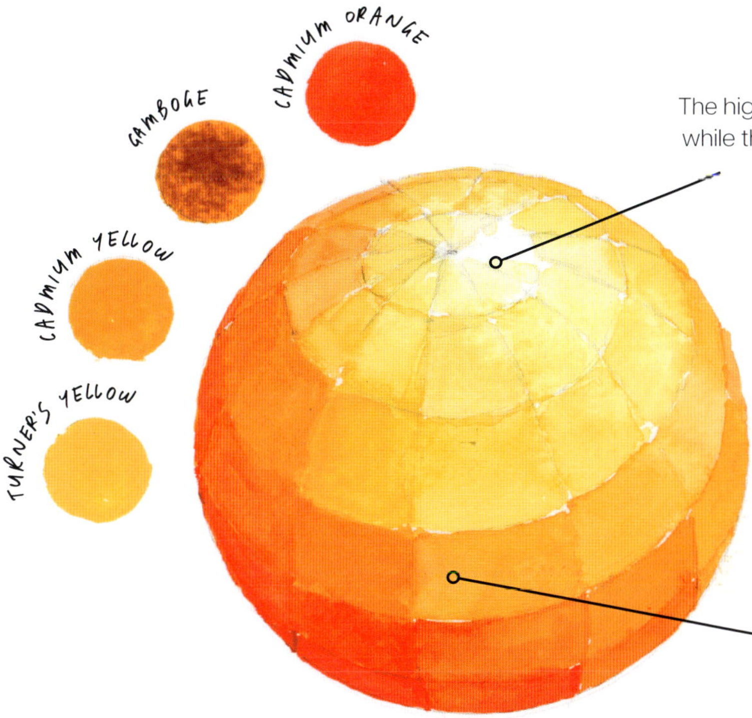
CADMIUM ORANGE
GAMBOGE
CADMIUM YELLOW
TURNER'S YELLOW

The highlights remain untouched while the mid-tones are created.

MID-TONES

The mid-tones will usually represent the essential color of the object.

The mid-tones – those that sit between the dark and light sections of the sphere – are created using a touch of Cadmium Orange.

SHADOWS

Shadows are a collection of reflected colors cast onto a surface, and involve mixing several colors together – they are not black!

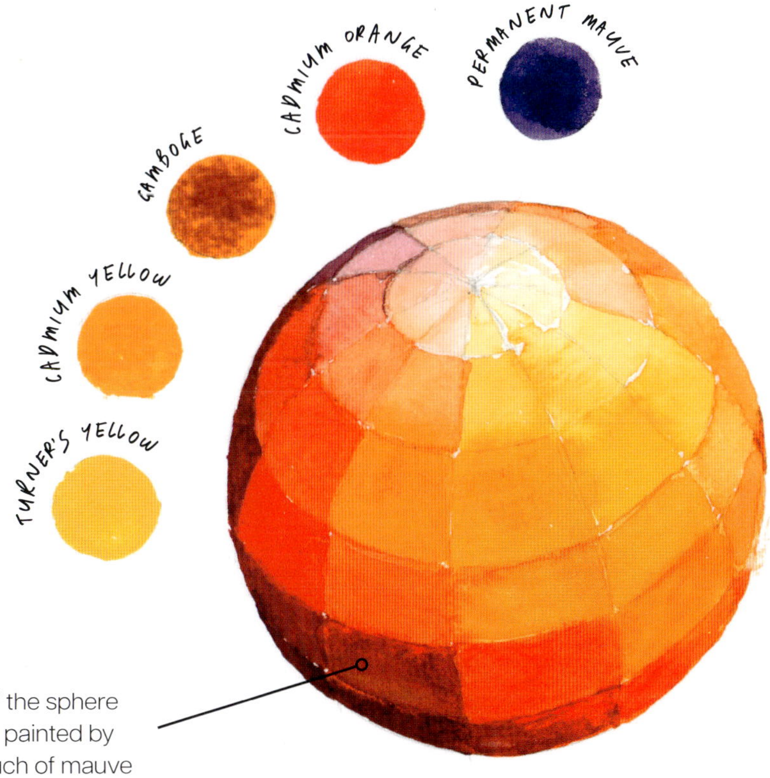
CADMIUM ORANGE
PERMANENT MAUVE
GAMBOGE
CADMIUM YELLOW
TURNER'S YELLOW

The part of the sphere in shade is painted by adding a touch of mauve to the orange mix.

***The push-pull theory is explored further and put into practice in this still life painting. You can start to get a feel for the fun that you can have in using color!***

## PUSH-PULL IN PRACTICE

First, the lightest and wettest colors are washed onto the paper. The colors have been allowed to bleed a little, as these bleeds will help to create the shadows. Next, the main colors, using less water, are applied. They are also allowed to bleed a little, enhancing the physical and visual connections between the group, while starting the process of creating a sense of form from previously flat shapes. Finally, the colors used are mixed together to create a range of tones within the shadows, which are visually pulled back. This technique will be explored further in Part 3: Light & Shade.

BUILDING THE TONES

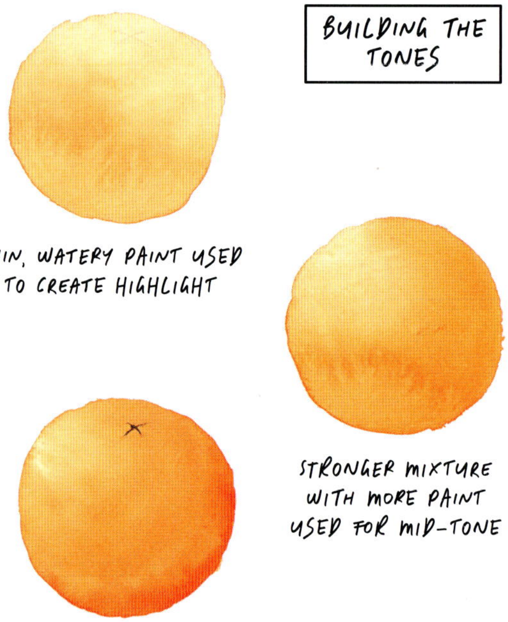

THIN, WATERY PAINT USED TO CREATE HIGHLIGHT

STRONGER MIXTURE WITH MORE PAINT USED FOR MID-TONE

THE DEEPEST, DARKEST TONES ARE ADDED AT THE END OF THE PROCESS

STAGE 1

In the first stage of this painting only thin, watery colors are applied and allowed to dry freely.

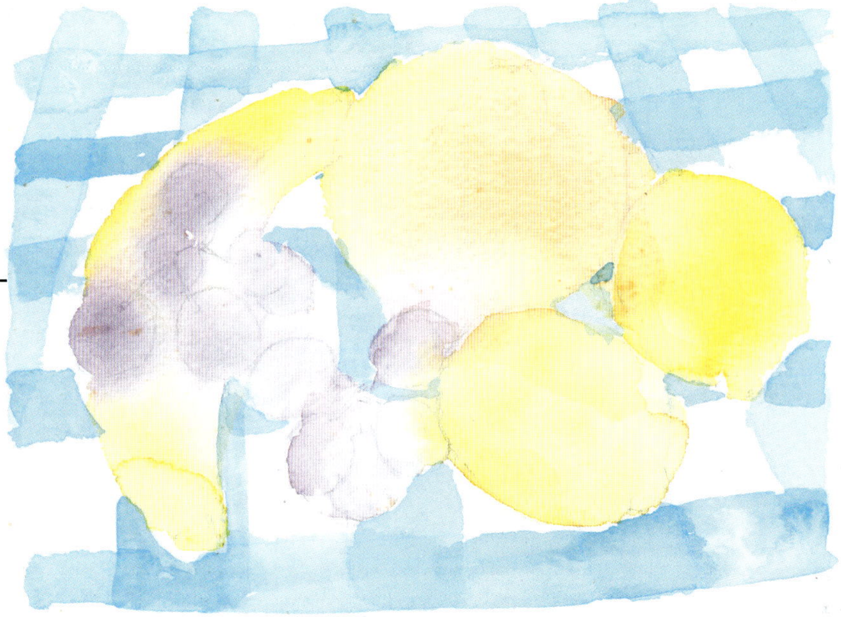

### STAGE 2

The essential color is applied around the highlights, pushing them forward. This is the main color of the fruits – the oranges, yellows and purples.

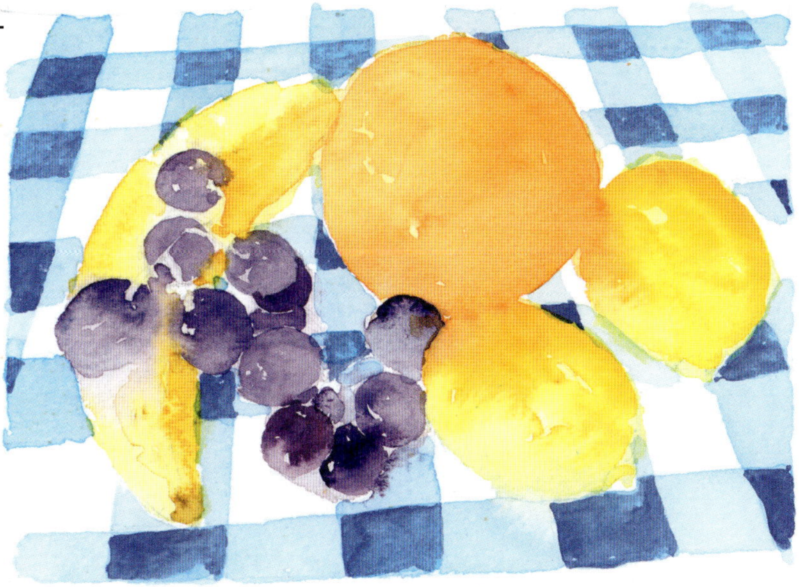

### FINAL PAINTING

In this stage, the darkest colors are painted, creating shade and shadows and visually pushing the lighter colors forward. The shadow colors are a mixture of all the colors used in the composition.

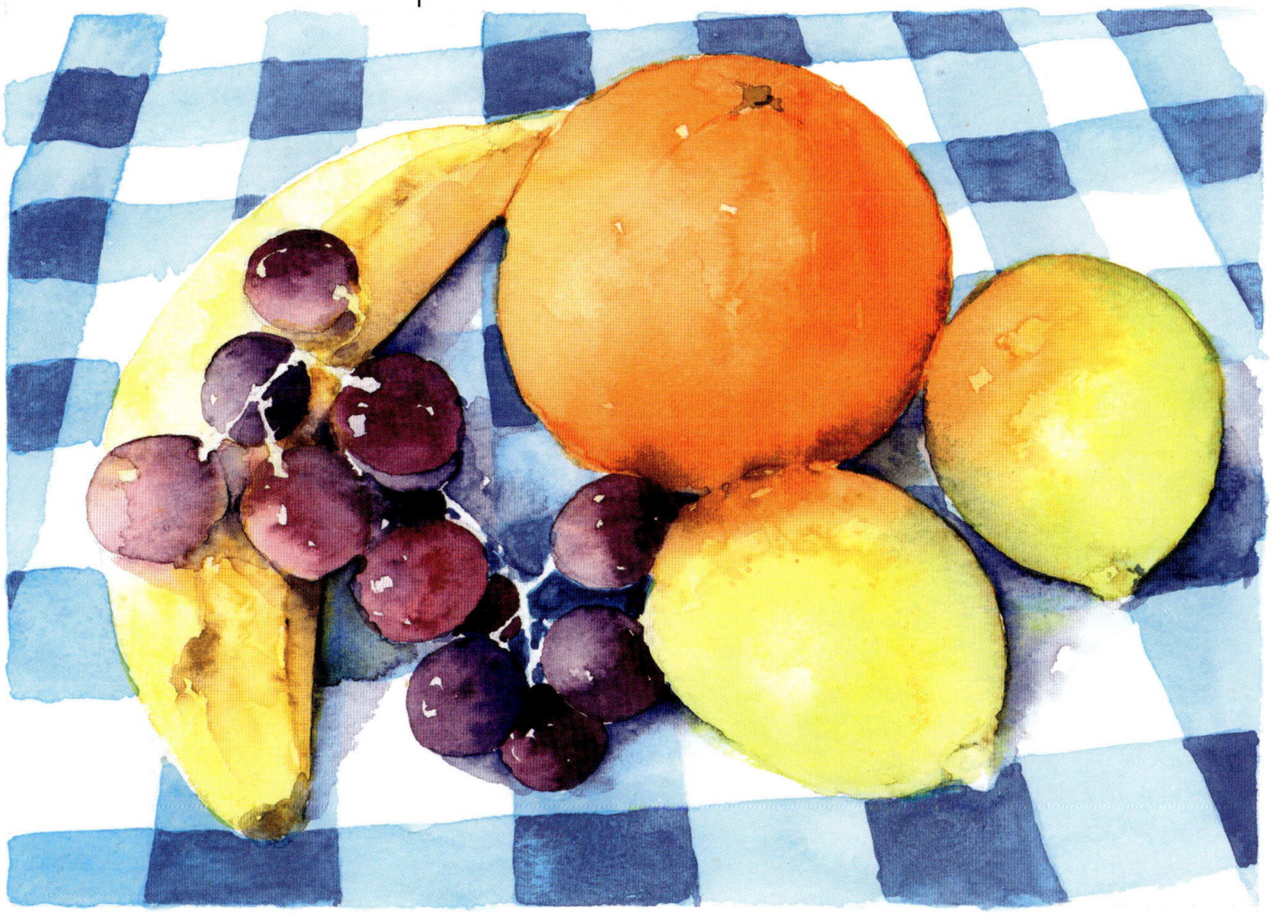

# *Part 2:*

# PAINTS & COLORS

As I mentioned in the introduction, a wealth of watercolor paints can be found in art stores and catalogs with only a tiny flash of the color contained in the tube or pan available for you to make a judgment about.

Although it is not essential to understand the origins of these paints, a little knowledge and awareness of their origins and methods of production can help you to make some better informed decisions about which paints to use for which subjects.

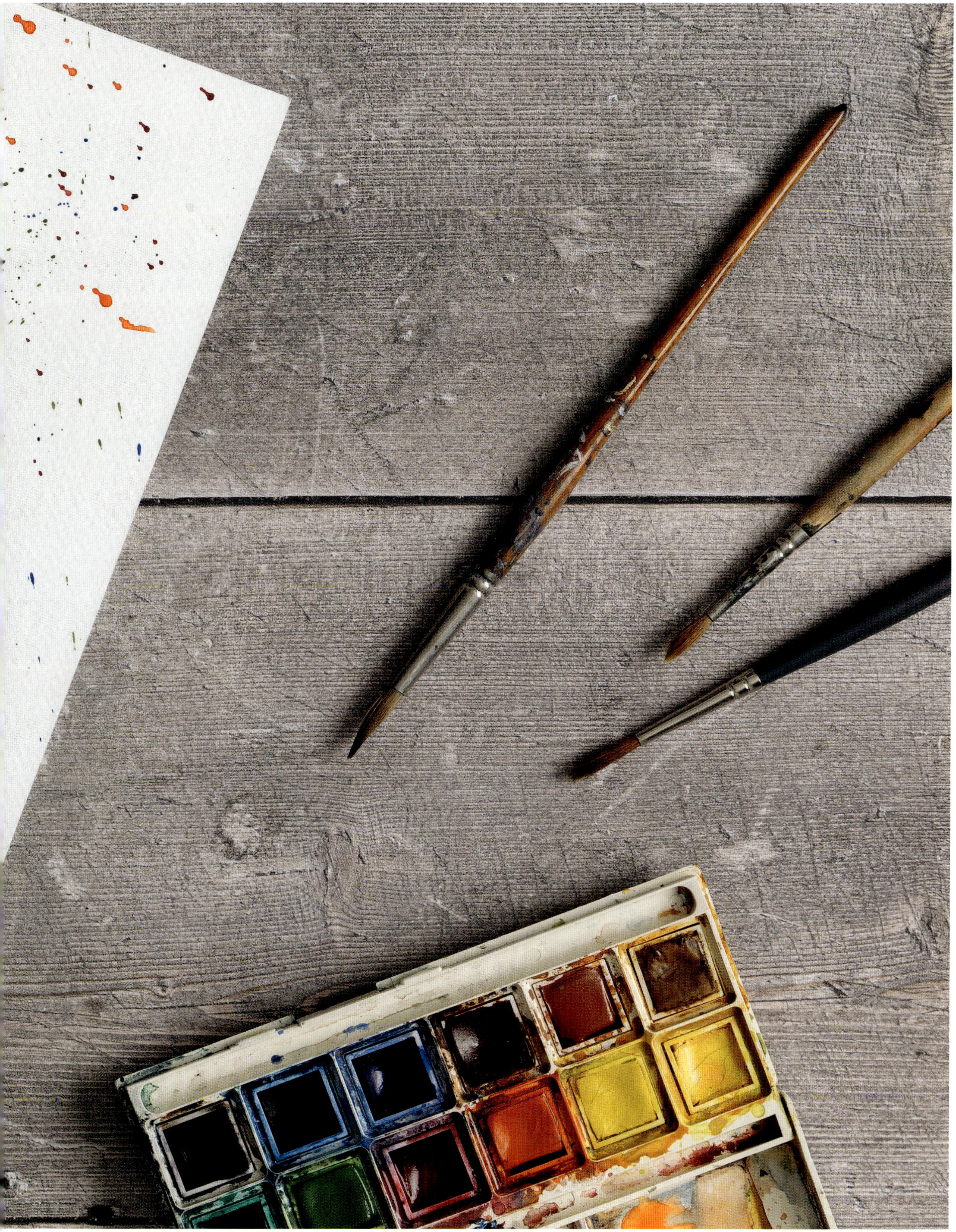

# Paint Types

I am an artist and this is a book about art, not chemistry. Modern paints are synthetic, in that an element or pigment has been transformed into paint through an industrial process. It might, however, be interesting to look at the origins of some of the paints that I have chosen from the wealth of colors available to us.

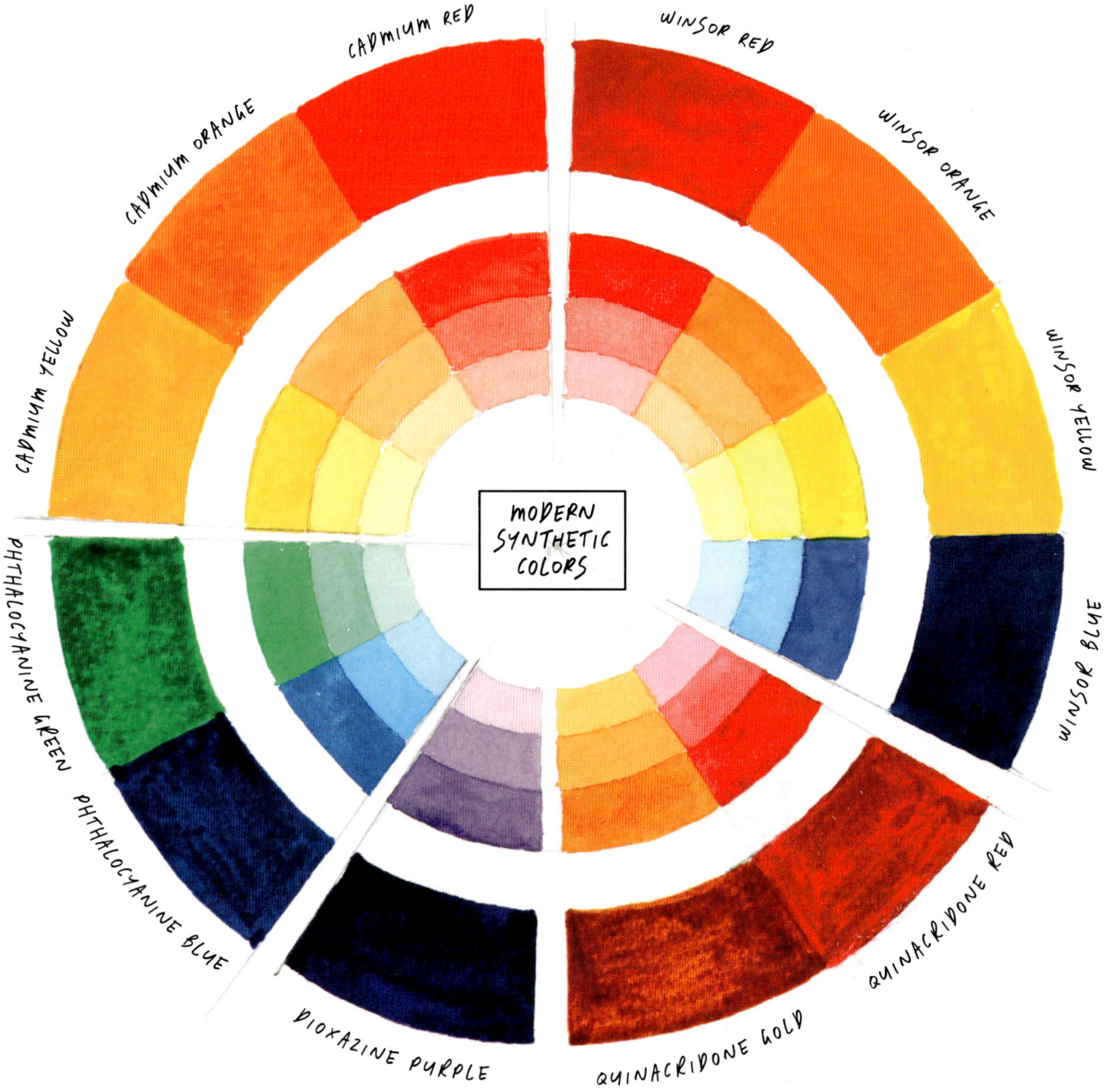

MODERN SYNTHETIC COLORS
CADMIUM RED
CADMIUM ORANGE
CADMIUM YELLOW
WINSOR RED
WINSOR ORANGE
WINSOR YELLOW
WINSOR BLUE
QUINACRIDONE RED
QUINACRIDONE GOLD
DIOXAZINE PURPLE
PHTHALOCYANINE BLUE
PHTHALOCYANINE GREEN

# MODERN SYNTHETIC COLORS

We have briefly explored how the production of coal tar led to a whole new range of pigments for artists. The dye industry was expanding exponentially as demand for colored fabrics grew. Artists quickly became the accidental beneficiaries of the chemists who fed the needs of the dyers. The chemists' laboratories became the center of paint production – soon colors were produced that were "synthetic" even though they were derived from coal tar and other petrochemicals. They had taken something from outside their laboratories, often organic with the exception of cadmiums, and created something special inside – usable color.

From the artist's perspective, it's worth knowing that several of these synthetic colors are essentially dyes. They work by staining the paper. Once applied, they are difficult to remove – attempts at washing out will lighten but spread the stain. They are wonderful colors to look at as they are usually intense and vibrant. But a little will go a long way, so make your judgments well in advance. Of course, if you experiment with these colors beforehand by simply testing a few swatches on a small piece of your chosen paper, your knowledge will be considerably enhanced and your judgments more effective.

The key synthetic colors that I have selected here come under the following headings:

**QUINACRIDONES** really came to prominence in the 1950s for industrial use, so you can expect a real intensity of color. The rich red, golds and oranges are on the "warm" end of the spectrum. They are, however, best used with some caution due to their potential strength.

**DIOXAZINES** are purple/violet paints and tend towards the blue rather than the red side of the color spectrum. These dilute well and spread evenly.

**PHTHALOCYANINES** have "cool" qualities. The blue paint often has a bias towards green and the Phthalocyanine Green paint itself is closer to the old emerald. They are particularly strong, intense paints and can very easily overwhelm any other paint or paint mixture to which they are added. So, again, use with pleasure, but a little caution.

**CADMIUMS** are a range of paints that have been the staple of my personal palette for many years now. They are consistent, reliable and really are excellent blenders when used with other colors. They dilute and wash well and will not dominate any color mixture to which they are added. They are mostly within the yellow to red range of the color spectrum – you can find Cadmium Green, but you can easily mix Cadmium Yellow with Viridian yourself to achieve a similar color. Yes, they are inorganic but are included on this page to show the full visual power of the modern synthetic paints and to offer a valuable comparison between the cadmium and Winsor ranges.

**WINSORS** have very similar qualities to the cadmium range, but they do, in my opinion, have a slight edge in terms of their luminosity. The difference, initially, might not be glaringly obvious, but when you start to use these paints, you may find some subtle variations. The reds, yellows and oranges are warm, deep tones which dilute and mix particularly well. Winsor Blue is close to Phthalocyanine Blue with just a hint of green. Winsor Green is also close to Phthalocyanine Green.

So, this is my choice of modern synthetic colors. They are great colors, uncomplicated in their behaviour on the palette and paper, but do come with a warning about using too much too quickly. Enjoy them, but do approach with care.

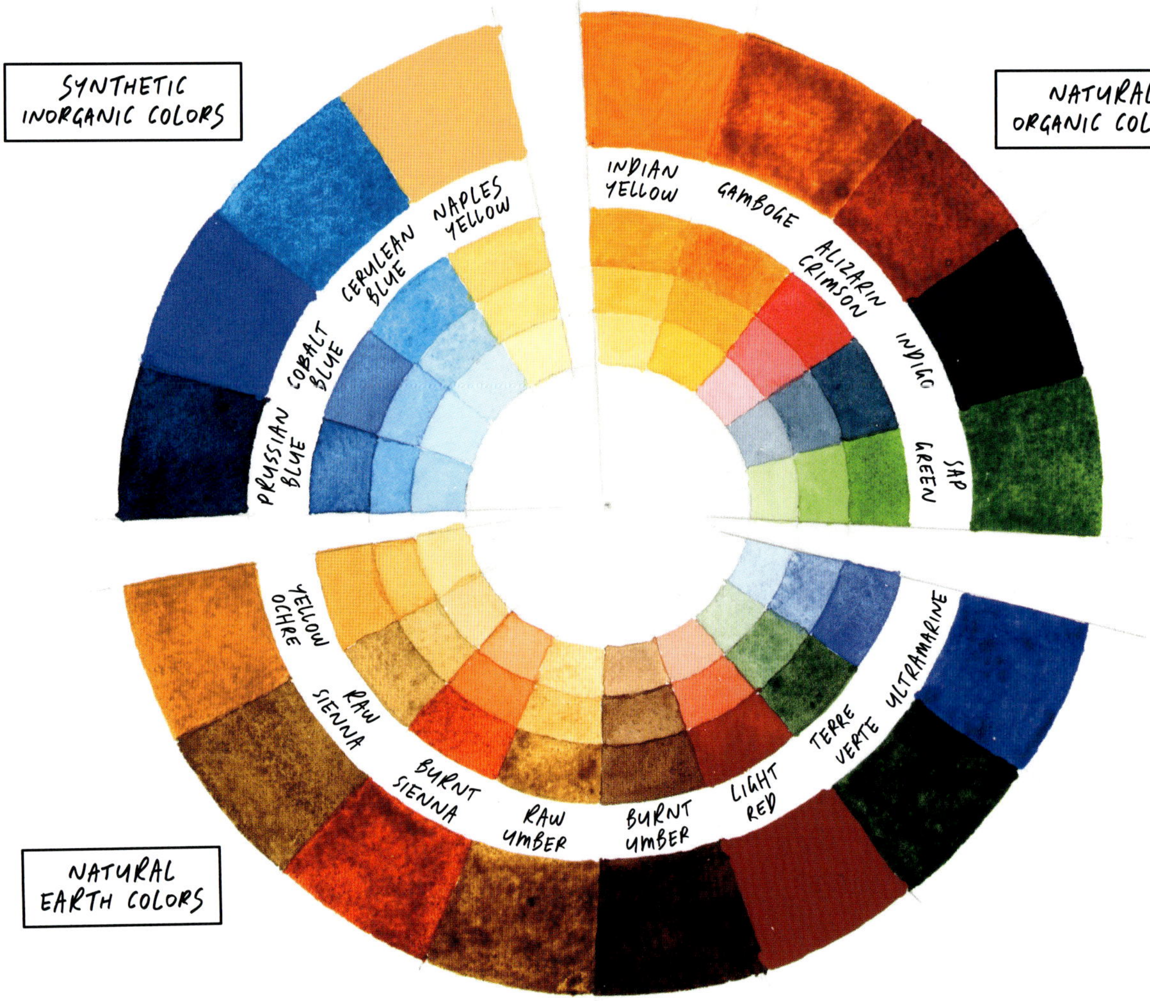
SYNTHETIC INORGANIC COLORS
NATURAL ORGANIC COLORS
NATURAL EARTH COLORS
PRUSSIAN BLUE
COBALT BLUE
CERULEAN BLUE
NAPLES YELLOW
INDIAN YELLOW
GAMBOGE
ALIZARIN CRIMSON
INDIGO
SAP GREEN
ULTRAMARINE
TERRE VERTE
LIGHT RED
BURNT UMBER
RAW UMBER
BURNT SIENNA
RAW SIENNA
YELLOW OCHRE

***All modern paints are synthetic in that they have been processed in a factory. They all, however, in one way or another, have a strong connection with the natural world.***

## SYNTHETIC INORGANIC COLORS

These paints are inorganic in that they have never been a part of living things and are not carbon compounds but come, after several processes, from naturally occurring metals – usually through relatively simple chemical reactions. The following paints are types of colors that fall within this category.

**PRUSSIAN BLUE** is a very strong, deep and cold blue that has slightly limited uses as it can overpower and change the nature of any color to which it is applied.

**COBALT BLUE** also comes from a metallic compound. This is one of those colors that looks quite appealing in the tube or pan but can be a little disappointing when diluted. I find that it has a tendency to "flatten" colors it is added to.

**CERULEAN BLUE** is a bright blue which is particularly useful when painting skies.

**NAPLES YELLOW** is one of the oldest known pigments. It dries as a flat, pastel-type color useful for portraiture.

## NATURAL ORGANIC COLORS

These paints are carbon compounds and have their origins in either vegetables or animals.

**INDIAN YELLOW** is another thick, strong yellow which borders on light orange. It is a bright color with very strong covering power and, intriguingly, originally came from the urine of cows fed on mango leaves.

**GAMBOGE** is a strong, thick yellowish-brown paint that can be difficult to use given its consistency. It is made from the resin of the Garcinia tree and this shows. It is glutinous and difficult to dilute and apply evenly, but can offer some warm, autumnal tones to trees and foliage.

**ALIZARIN CRIMSON** comes from the roots of the madder plant. It is a particularly strong color which I often use in combination with Ultramarine to create deep Mediterranean shadows.

**INDIGO** was made originally as a dark blue dye from plants found in the tropics. It is a flat gray-blue color which will vanish quickly once diluted. Its main use is usually in storm-laden skies.

**SAP GREEN** was originally made with the juice of buckthorn berries and has multiple uses as a paint. It dilutes well and has excellent covering power. It is my first choice of color as a base to add other colors to in order to create varied tones of warm greens.

## NATURAL EARTH COLORS

These paints have their origins in the colored minerals found in rocks and clays.

**YELLOW OCHRE** can appear to be a rather flat color but maintains a warm glow and can be particularly useful for creating underwashes for pots and paths.

**RAW SIENNA** is a darker pigment than Yellow Ochre, although similar in dilution. It can be quite tricky to tell one from the other when wet – that is, until they dry when the differences become clear. It is particularly valuable as an underwash to paint on top of.

**BURNT SIENNA** is a rich, reddish-brown pigment created by roasting Raw Sienna. It dilutes well and can usually be relied upon to granulate with ease.

**RAW UMBER** has a greenish-yellow cast and tends towards the cooler end of the spectrum when diluted.

**BURNT UMBER** is a rich chocolate-brown pigment created by roasting Raw Umber. It is a good paint to choose for painting any type of wood or woodwork.

**LIGHT RED** is similar to Red Ochre in appearance. It can be a difficult color to use as it can have a slightly sticky feel in tube form, but it is an excellent granulator and is a really valuable asset when painting crumbling brickwork.

**TERRE VERTE** is sometimes known as Green Earth. It is a cold, thin color that does have its uses in creating distance in landscape painting.

**ULTRAMARINE** is a warm, deep blue pigment which was originally made from the valuable mineral lapis lazuli discovered during the fifteenth century in the mines of Afghanistan. It is my personal favorite of all the blues and can be used for many purposes which will be explored throughout the book. But don't forget – it is a granular paint and will, accordingly, granulate.

***I have given the natural earth colors space as they have some particularly valuable elements in their make-up. Although they hold some unique qualities, they can cross all classification boundaries and mix very easily with almost any color I can think of.***

## MORE ABOUT NATURAL EARTH COLORS

These paints originally came from the colored minerals found amongst the rocks and clays of the Alpine regions of Europe. The volcanic rocks containing naturally occurring metals were dried and ground to make pigments, usually by the apprentices of the Renaissance painters. To create these paints, ochrous sand is dug from the ground and then suspended in water. The impurities float to the top and are then abandoned, while the clay and colored oxides remain in suspension. This solution is allowed to evaporate, leaving only the colored pigment to be ground. These are not particularly strong or vibrant colors and are best used for brickwork, terracotta pots and wooden structures. They are also valuable for creating "earthy" colors in general landscapes.

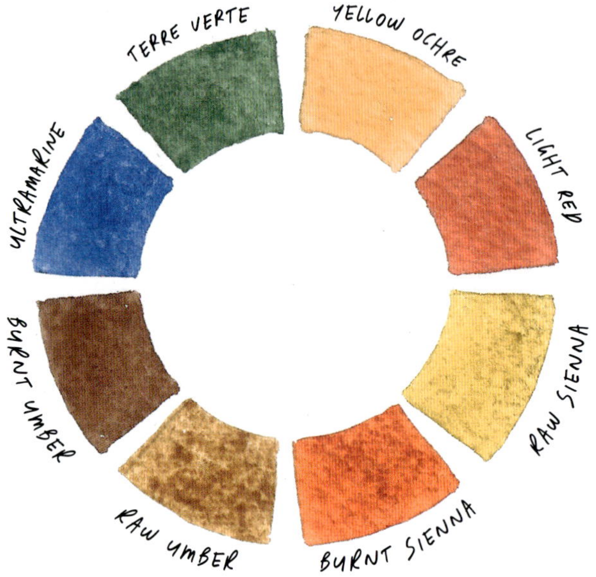
TERRE VERTE
YELLOW OCHRE
LIGHT RED
RAW SIENNA
BURNT SIENNA
RAW UMBER
BURNT UMBER
ULTRAMARINE

## CREATING TEXTURE

The natural earth colors, however, are at their best when texture and granulation are required. As the paints are made from pigments that are themselves granular, as opposed to dyes, the granules start to separate as they dry. If they are drying with a regular granulation, drop a small amount of water onto the surface of the paper in irregular patches as it dries. This disturbs the drying process and scatters the granules into patches, enhancing the ageing effect.

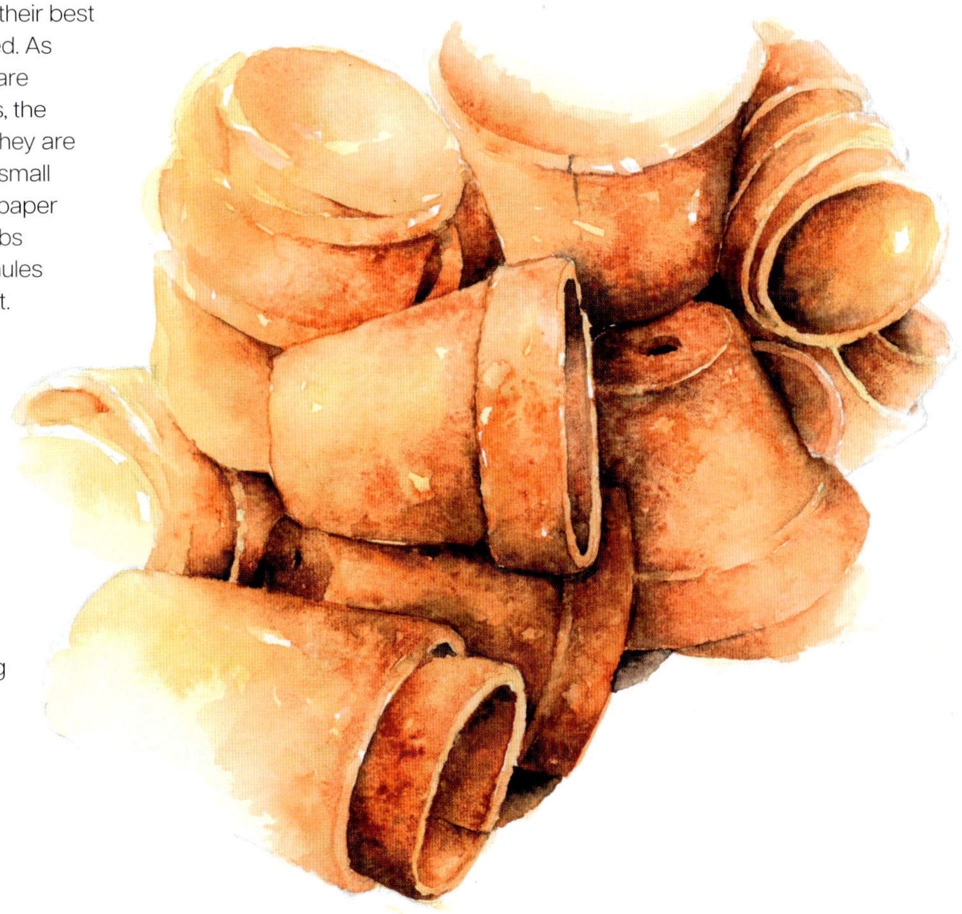

USING GRANULATION:
Old bricks and garden pots are ideal subjects for experimenting with these colors. The paints granulate with ease, creating a strong sense of texture.

**LIGHT TO DARK:** This column shows the tonal range that can be created by mixing a small selection of natural earth paints: from light Raw Sienna, down through the mid-range Burnt Sienna then the darker Burnt Umber. The color is darkened further using Ultramarine, with the darkest tone at the base.

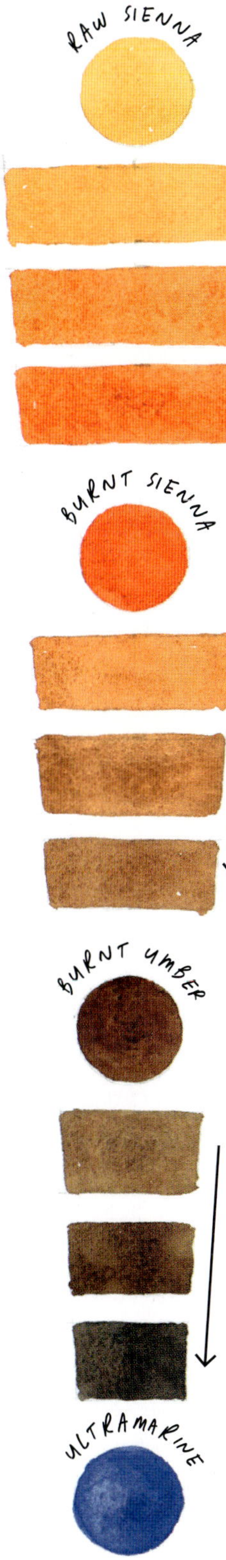
RAW SIENNA
BURNT SIENNA
BURNT UMBER
ULTRAMARINE

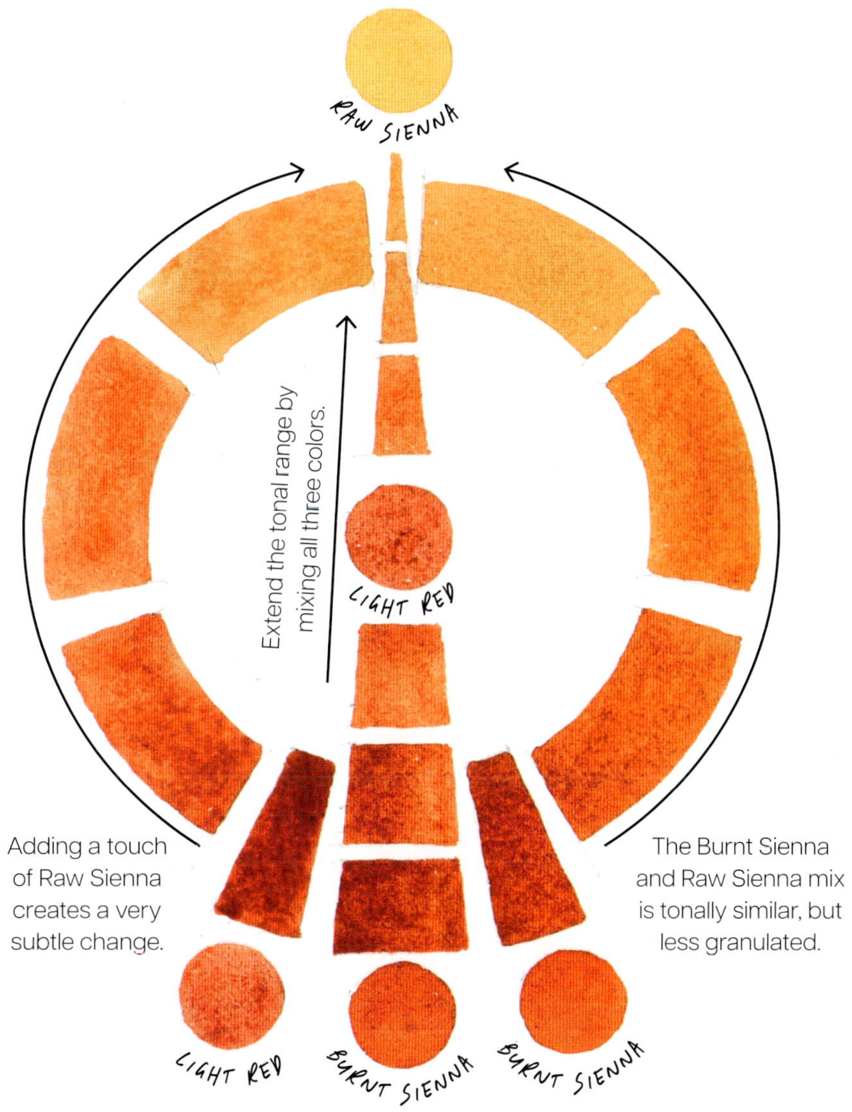
RAW SIENNA
Extend the tonal range by mixing all three colors.
LIGHT RED
Adding a touch of Raw Sienna creates a very subtle change.
The Burnt Sienna and Raw Sienna mix is tonally similar, but less granulated.
LIGHT RED
BURNT SIENNA
BURNT SIENNA

**TONES & TEXTURE:** This chart explores the range of tones that can be achieved with only three natural earth paints. The differences between Light Red and Burnt Sienna are not so much in tone, but in texture.

# Grays & Neutrals

From the late 1700s towards the middle of the 1800s, academic training taught painters that shadows, either indoors or out, were brown or black. Then, a gradual awareness developed of the science of the ways in which we perceive light and the way in which light and color work together. Artists began to think differently about the ways in which light and shade were represented.

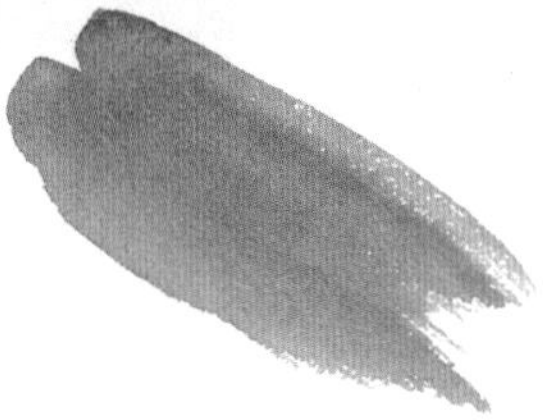

### NEUTRAL TINT

Neutral Tint is classified as a "gray" – that means that it holds no specific color of its own and, when added to a colored paint, will create a darker version of it while maintaining the essential quality or integrity of that color.

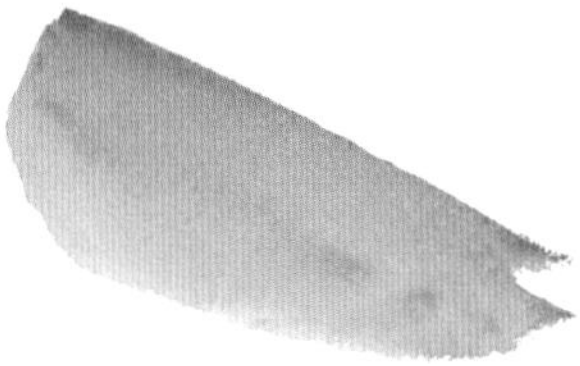

### PAYNE'S GRAY

Payne's Gray was developed during the eighteenth century by William Payne as an alternative to the blacks traditionally used to paint shadows. Payne sought a fresher way of creating shadows, rather than the "tobacco stained" shadows of the academic artists. This paint does hold a slightly blue tint.

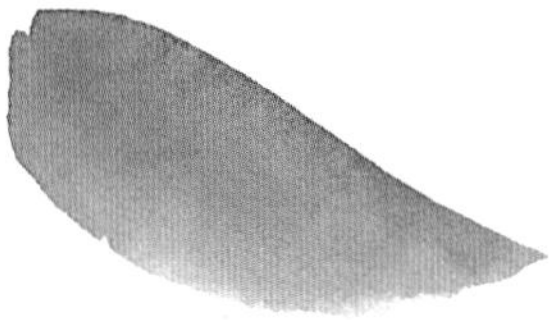

### DAVY'S GRAY

Henry Davy was a student of the watercolor painter John Cotman when he developed this paint. He, too, was seeking an alternative that could be used instead of flat black shadows. The result is a soft, transparent gray paint with a distinctive green tint.

## FIRST IMPRESSIONS

The main paints that we will explore here are grayish in nature and traditionally neutral in tone. They are designed to allow the tonal range of colored paints to be altered without changing their essential nature. For this to happen, grays and neutrals should sit somewhere on the tonal scale between black and white, completely free from any color at all.

These paints are not, however, a panacea for solving all our tonal mixing problems. It is, in fact, very difficult to alter the tone without making noticeable changes to the nature of that color. This is not always a bad thing, especially when using "fragile" colors such as Lemon Yellow. The addition of Payne's Gray to Lemon Yellow will create an acidic, cool green, ideal for recording spring foliage. But for others, a closer examination is required.

## RETAINING INTEGRITY

The following pages illustrate some of the effects that these paints can have on colors. I have chosen a small selection of colors with which to try these "neutral" paints. The darker colors, such as the purples, are more amenable to tonal change using these neutral paints. As a general rule, the darker the color, the more success you are likely to have in using either Neutral Tint, Payne's Gray or Davy's Gray to change their tone. The integrity is not altered so noticeably. The lighter colors, however, do not fare so well.

We will explore the differences between using gray paints versus the complementary color to make a darker shade. You will see how Payne's Gray can influence the tones of Lemon Yellow and Permanent Mauve, in comparison to the effects of Davy's Gray. Then we explore three different yellows – light colors that are susceptible to rapid change. The blue/black composition of the gray paints soon turns the yellow to green, whereas the complementary purple creates a more authentic set of tones.

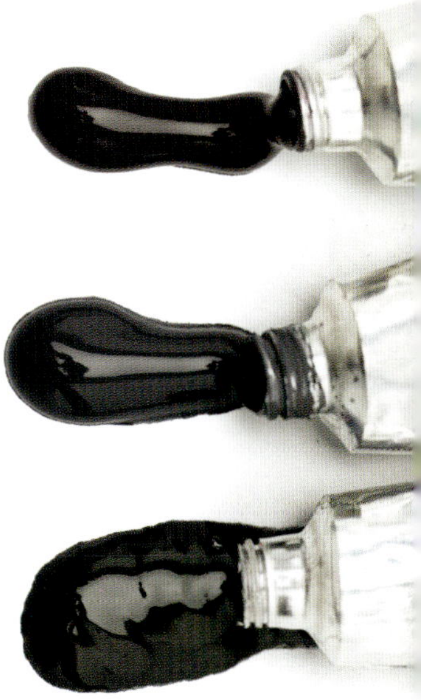

*"...don't settle for any one convenient color when you can create your own mixes. Payne's Gray is a useful base, but alone would be very dull."*

**Now that we have explored the tonal features of grays and neutrals, this exercise will help you to make decisions about the effectiveness of their qualities when used for mixing.**

1. Lemon Yellow gradually added to Payne's Gray
2. Permanent Mauve gradually added to Payne's Gray
3. Permanent Mauve gradually added to Davy's Gray
4. Lemon Yellow gradually added to Davy's Gray
5. Water added to raw Payne's Gray in three stages
6. Water added to raw Davy's Gray in three stages

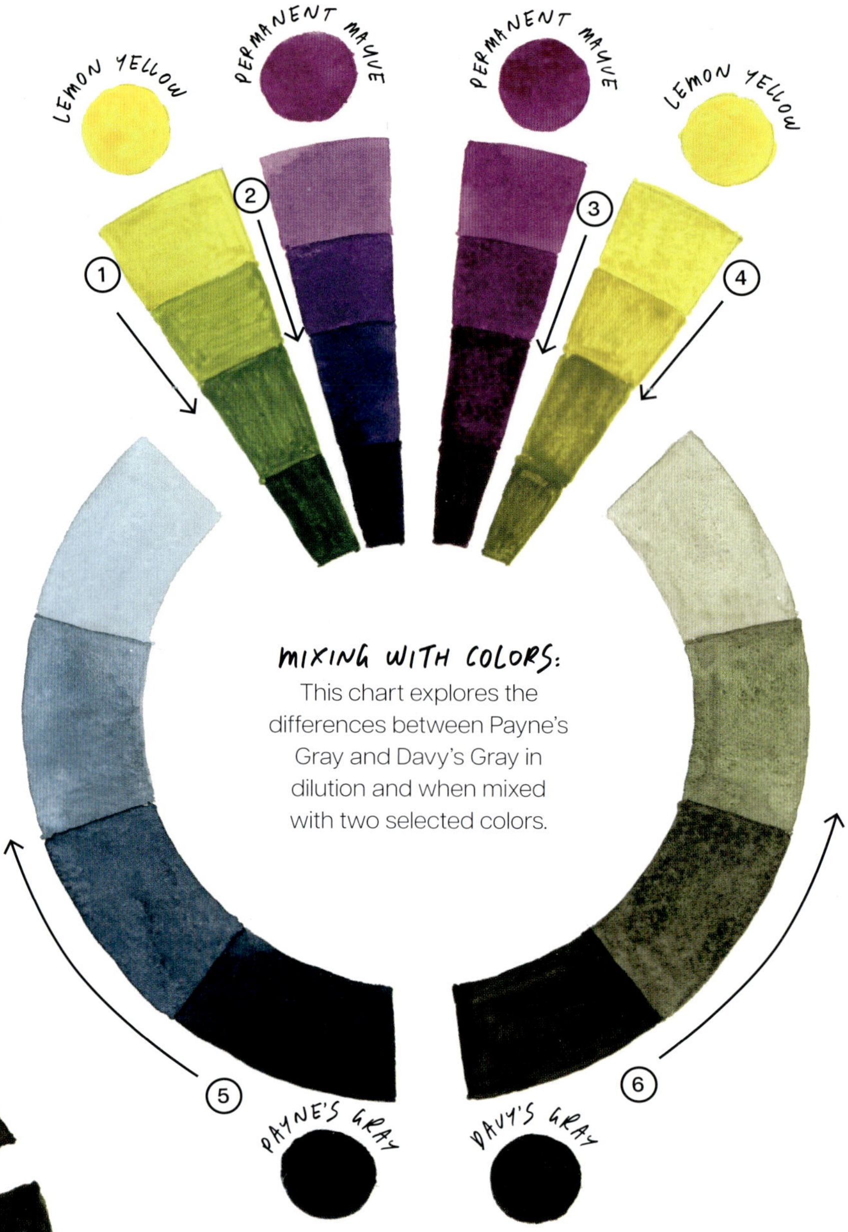

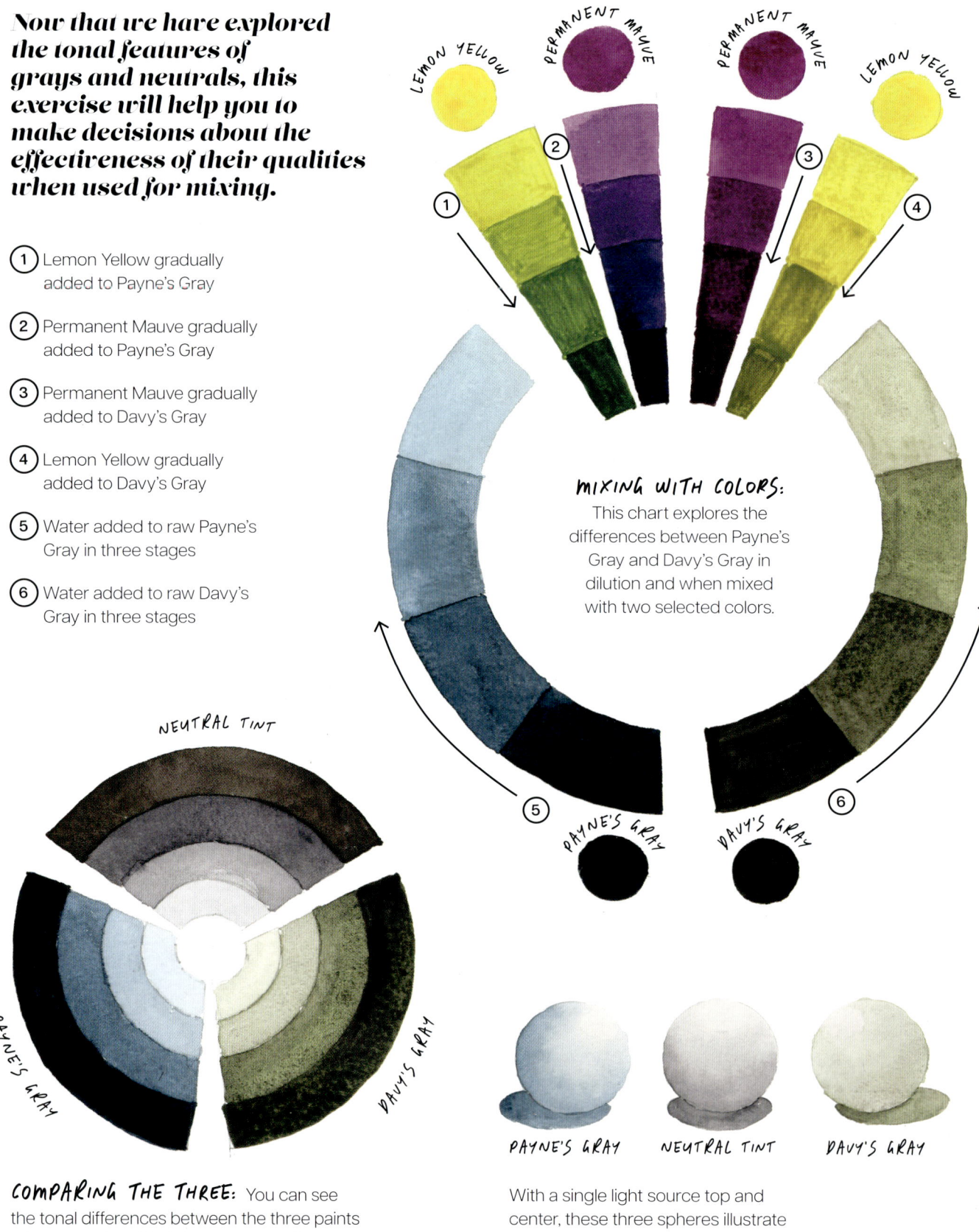

LEMON YELLOW
PERMANENT MAUVE
PERMANENT MAUVE
LEMON YELLOW
1
2
3
4
5
6
PAYNE'S GRAY
DAVY'S GRAY


**MIXING WITH COLORS:** This chart explores the differences between Payne's Gray and Davy's Gray in dilution and when mixed with two selected colors.

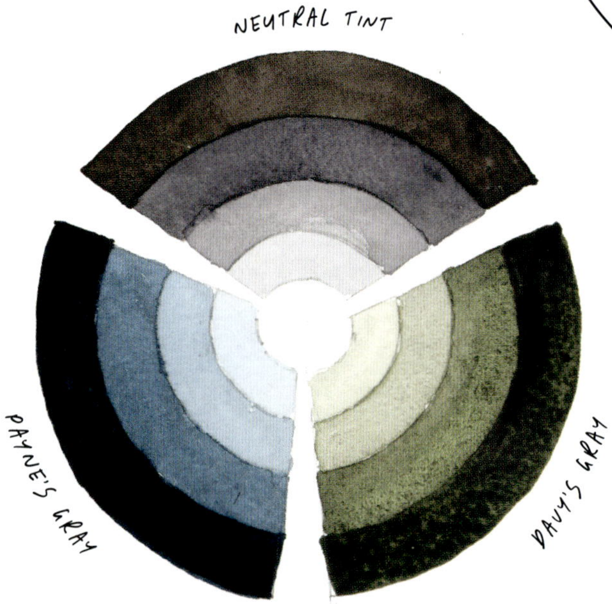

NEUTRAL TINT
PAYNE'S GRAY
DAVY'S GRAY


**COMPARING THE THREE:** You can see the tonal differences between the three paints when water is added, one stage at a time.

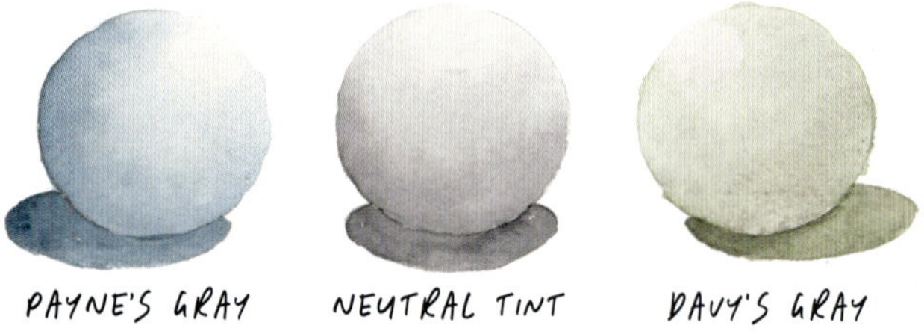

PAYNE'S GRAY
NEUTRAL TINT
DAVY'S GRAY


With a single light source top and center, these three spheres illustrate the full tonal range of the gray and neutral paints in dilution..

**USING NEUTRAL TINT:** I have mixed the Neutral Tint with three different yellows, and compared this to mixes of the same yellows with different purples (yellow's complementary color).

(7) Neutral Tint gradually added to Cadmium Yellow

(8) Dioxazine Purple gradually added to Cadmium Yellow

(9) Neutral Tint gradually added to Naples Yellow

(10) Permanent Mauve gradually added to Naples Yellow

(11) Neutral Tint gradually added to Indian Yellow

(12) Purple Lake gradually added to Indian Yellow

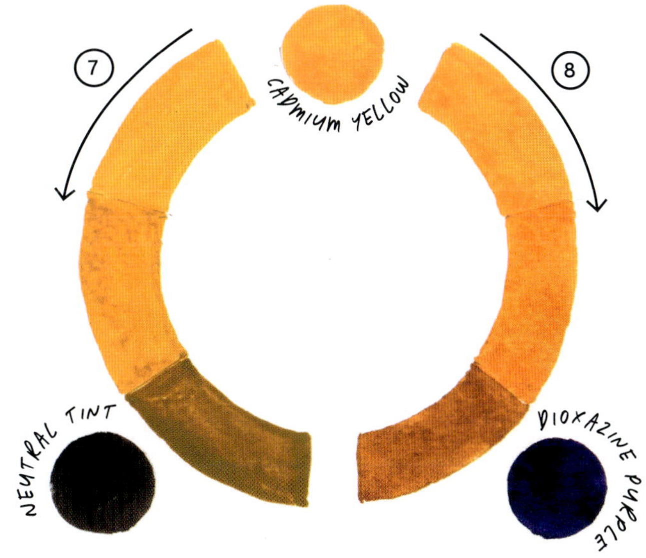
7
8
CADMIUM YELLOW
NEUTRAL TINT
DIOXAZINE PURPLE

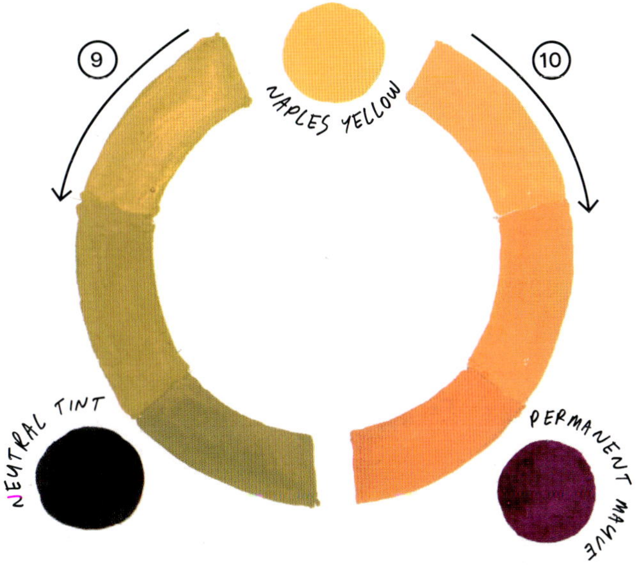
9
10
NAPLES YELLOW
NEUTRAL TINT
PERMANENT MAUVE

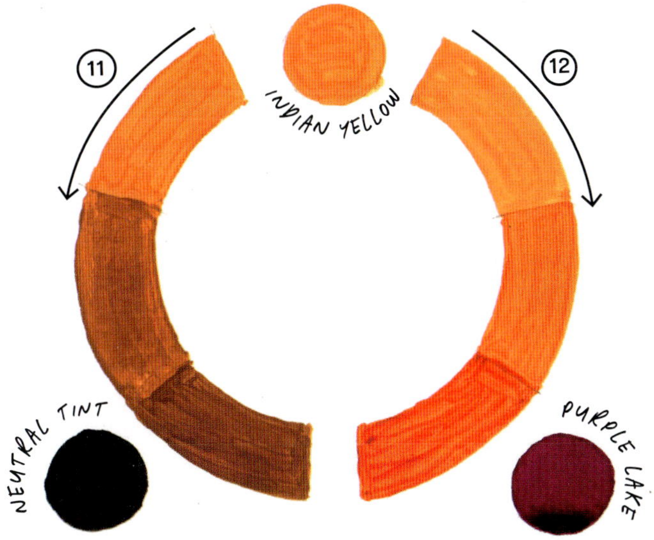
11
12
INDIAN YELLOW
NEUTRAL TINT
PURPLE LAKE

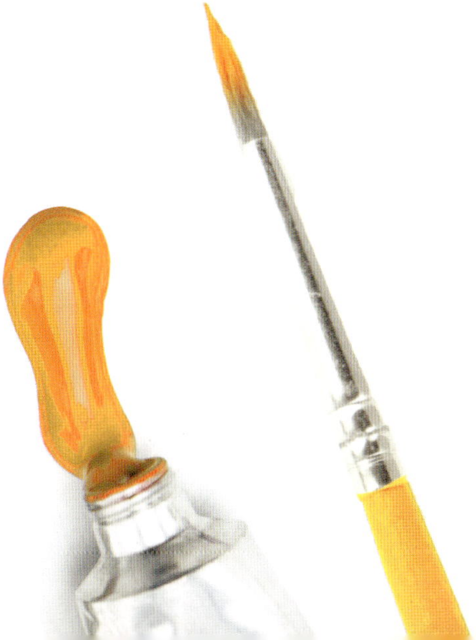

***Here I have mixed my own "gray" paints to create different neutral tints, choosing different sets of colors to assess which combinations might be the most effective.***

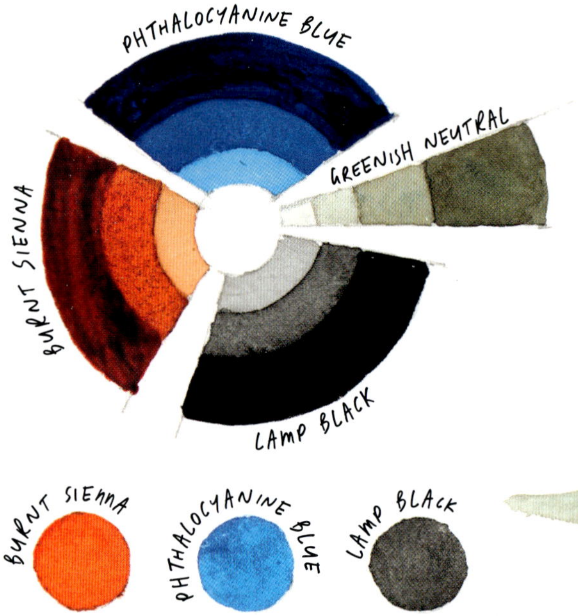
PHTHALOCYANINE BLUE
GREENISH NEUTRAL
BURNT SIENNA
LAMP BLACK
BURNT SIENNA
PHTHALOCYANINE BLUE
LAMP BLACK

**TINT 1:** Greenish tones are the result of using blue and black.

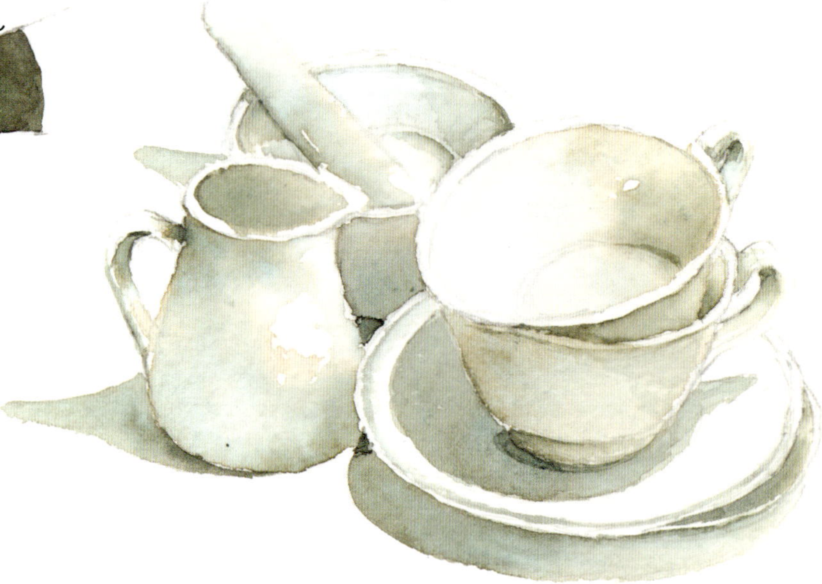

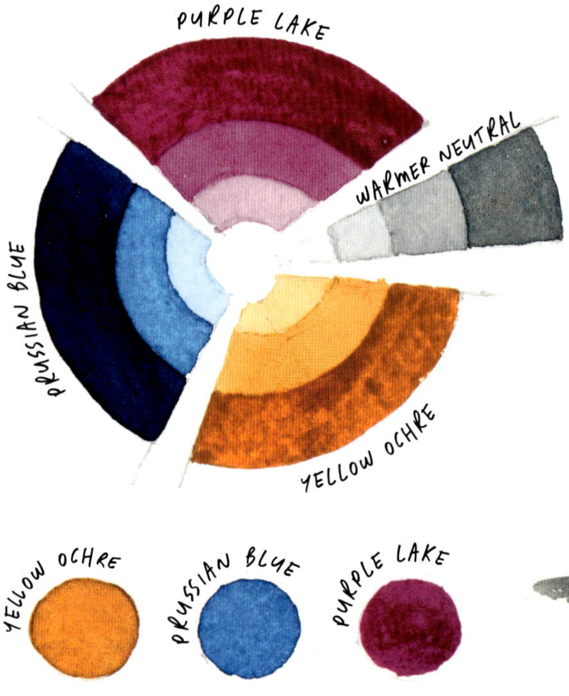
PURPLE LAKE
WARMER NEUTRAL
PRUSSIAN BLUE
YELLOW OCHRE
YELLOW OCHRE
PRUSSIAN BLUE
PURPLE LAKE

**TINT 2:** Warmer tones result from the influence of purple.

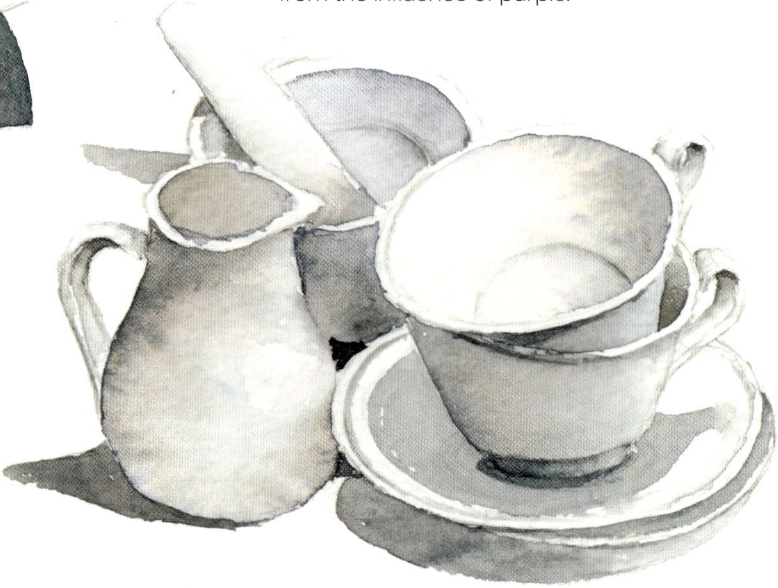

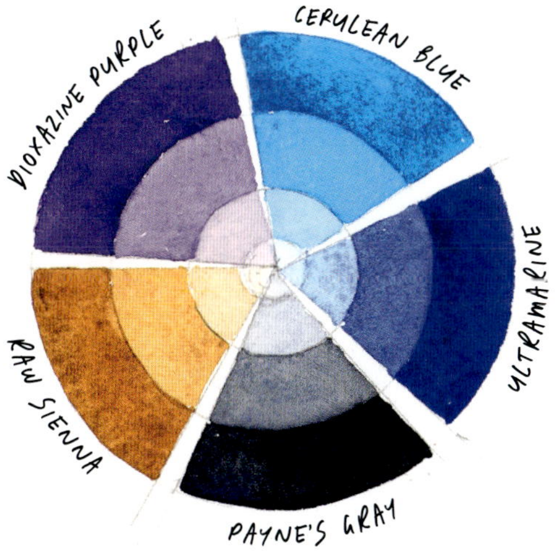
CERULEAN BLUE
ULTRAMARINE
PAYNE'S GRAY
RAW SIENNA
DIOXAZINE PURPLE

**TINT 3:** By adding a selection of colors to Payne's Gray, it is possible to influence the color range. A warmer gray could be mixed with Dioxazine Purple, while a cooler gray could be achieved by using Cerulean Blue. This will give you more choices – especially when painting white against white.

## EXPERIMENT WITH TINTS

White objects viewed together are tricky as they hold very few, if any, colors to "bounce off" each other. We, therefore, have to invent them as can be seen in the three mixes in the illustration groupings here.

There is a noticeable difference between the first and second mixes. Black and blue create a greenish tone, while purple slightly warms up the tone. I then mixed my desired tone. This third mix really captures the central theme of this book. That is, don't settle for any one convenient color when you can create your own mixes.

Payne's Gray is a useful base, but alone would be very dull. The addition of other colors to influence the tones helps considerably to create a more authentic and interesting looking painting.

Mix your own neutral tints using one, or a combination, of these formulas. Painting is not a precise science. The quantities of each paint need to be discovered by gradually adding one to the other. Once the colors are mixed, see what you think – that's what really counts!

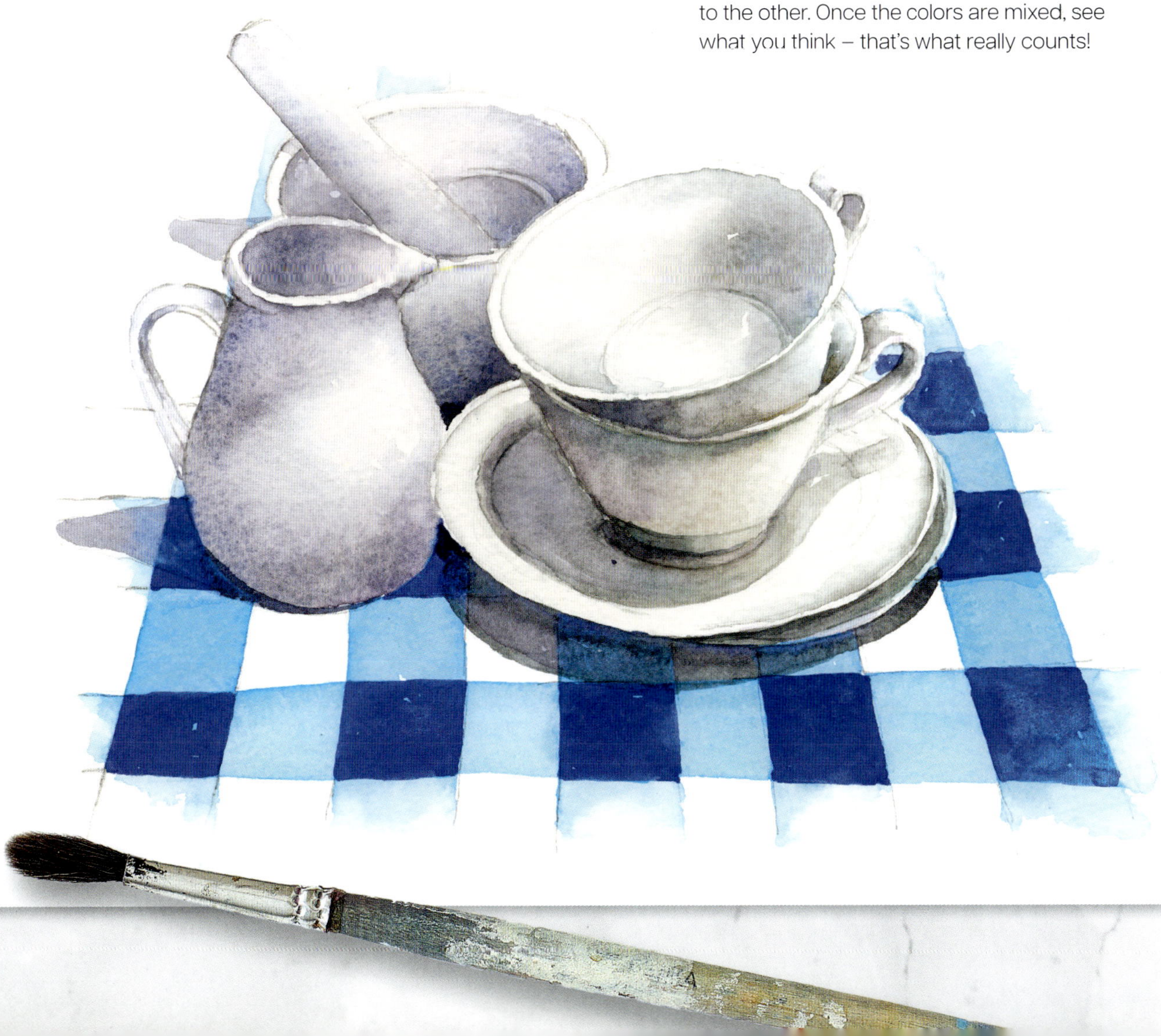

# Color Families

In this chapter, I have created a type of artists' "filing system," linking all paints, whatever their origins and labels, into families of color. Initially, I have used the standard system of primary colors, but this is followed by secondary colors. So, why only three primaries as a starting point?

## THE THEORY

The "primary colors" that we know today date back to the late seventeenth century. Scientists who were experimenting with color and ways of seeing discovered that only three colors, red, yellow and blue, were required, alongside black and white, to create a full range of tones. The entire color spectrum could be built around these.

I believe that the system I have used here makes color classification easier. On the following pages I have linked together a set of commonly used paints and placed them together in what I believe to be their rightful "families" – reds, blues and yellows.

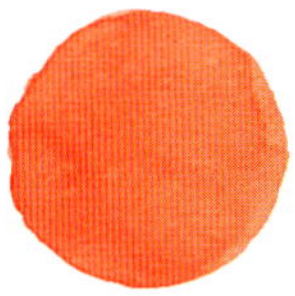

### REDS

The natural earth colors Light Red and Burnt Sienna are filed as reds along with the synthetics – Winsors and cadmiums – as well as Alizarin Crimson from the natural organics.

### BLUES

Indigo from the natural organics is filed along with Prussian Blue, Cobalt Blue and Cerulean Blue, combined with the synthetics Phthalocyanine Blue and Winsor Blue to create the blue family.



### YELLOWS

All paint types are represented in this family: Yellow Ochre and Raw Sienna are natural earth colors, Indian Yellow and Gamboge are natural organics, Naples Yellow is a synthetic inorganic, and Cadmium Yellow and Winsor Yellow are synthetics.

## BASIC THEORIES

Next, I have explored two groups of colors. The first group is known as "secondary" colors. The next group of colors is more fluid. The distinction between the two can be a little convoluted, so I'll try to simplify the terminology.

First, the color wheel itself. The color wheel can only work one way. Red, yellow and blue will always sit in a set order no matter how you might try to rearrange them. But what about the colors that are created on mixing the three primaries? These are the secondary colors. Secondary colors are the pure colors that you might expect to sit exactly between the primaries if you were allowed to imagine one orange only, one green only and one purple only. Try to remember the art trolley at your primary/elementary school and the bright, ready- mixed colors in the tubes. These would usually have been the three primaries – red, yellow and blue – alongside the brightest greens, oranges and purples. So, orange will sit next to yellow, but the more you extend your color mixing range, the more different the range of tones that you will have.

## MIXING IN ACTION

So, where does yellow end and orange begin and, at the other end of the scale, where does orange begin and red end? This is something that we can try to discover for ourselves by pushing the colors we have to their tonal limits through mixing them together in stages.

The next consideration is this: we have identified the fact that orange, for example, is created when red and yellow are mixed – but what type of orange? How much red and how much yellow? Again, this will be explored in much more depth throughout the coming pages of this book, but for now I have divided the three secondary colors into five tones.

## CREATING DYNAMICS

When set into the color wheel, these new colors which sit between the primaries expand the wheel and create another category – complementary (or opposite) colors. Now, the structure of the color wheel will ensure that a primary color will always sit opposite a secondary color. Blue will always be opposite orange, red will always be opposite green, and yellow will always be opposite purple. The reason for the introduction of the term "complementary" refers to the way in which these colors react when placed immediately next to each other – the use and value of this system will be explored in more depth in Part 3: Light & Shade. But for now it is worth viewing a primary and its complementary secondary color together to get a feel for the visual dynamics that these combinations can create.

So, now it's time to think beyond the colors in your paint boxes and really get to work on starting to create your own.

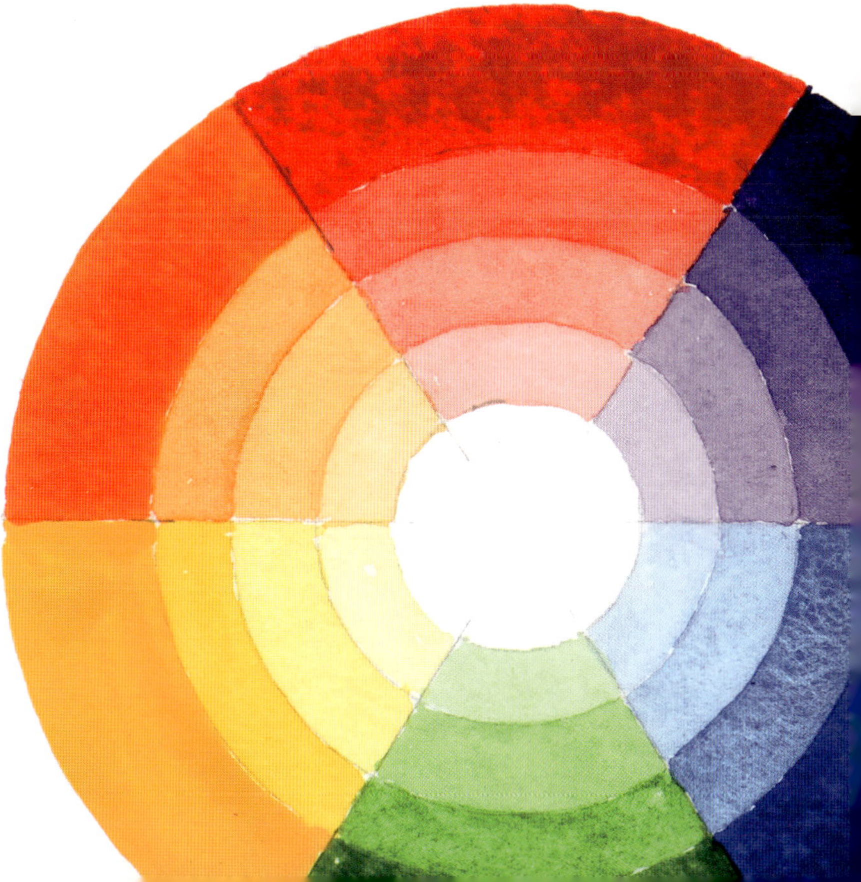

THE COLOR WHEEL SHOWING PRIMARY AND SECONDARY COLORS

**Here, I have gathered some of the most readily available paints and grouped them into their primary color families. You can compare their qualities, both in their raw states and their tonal values.**

It is interesting to compare paints within each color family. How, for example, does Yellow Ochre differ from Lemon Yellow? Or, how do Scarlet Lake and Light Red, or Prussian Blue and Cerulean Blue, appear when viewed side by side?

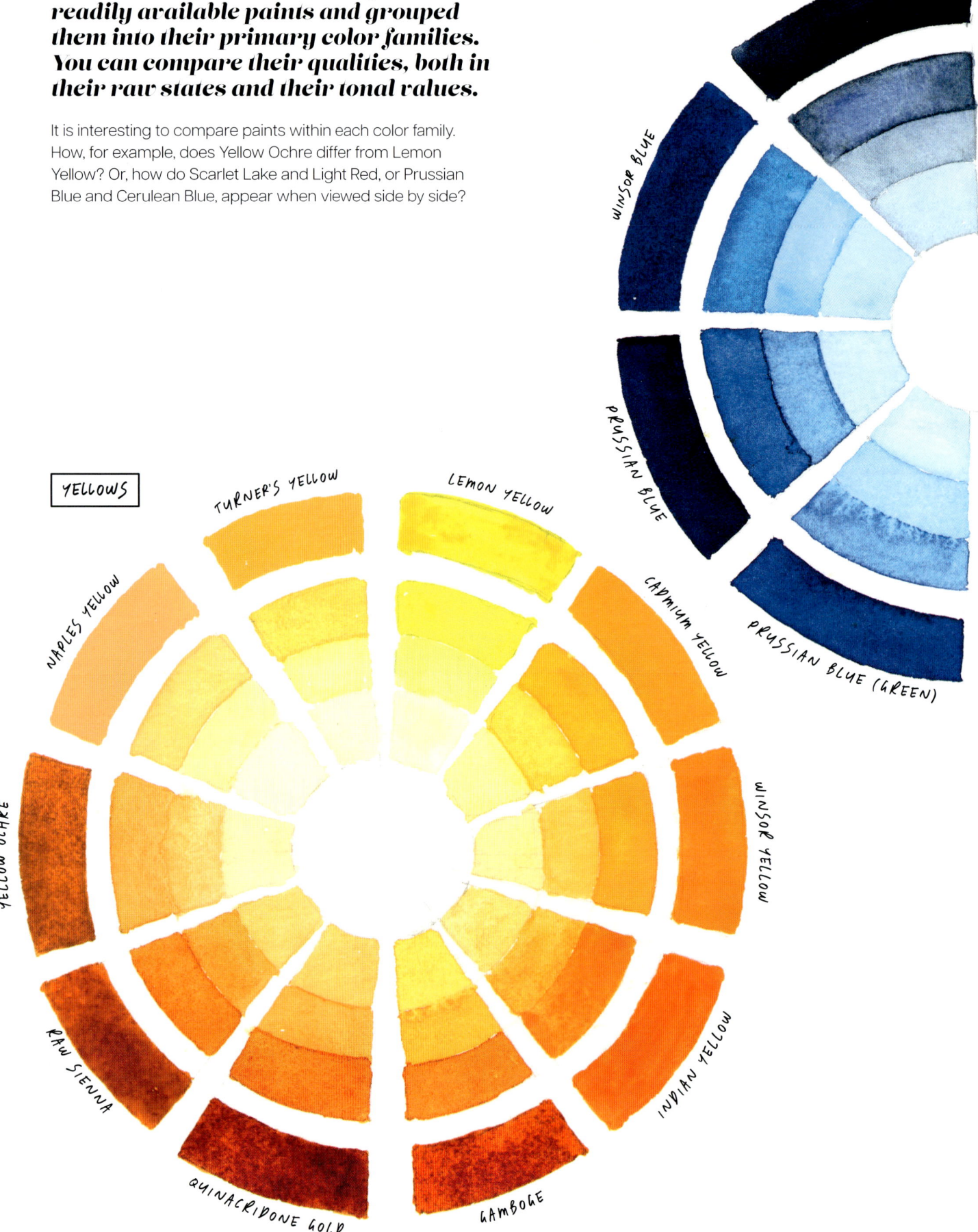

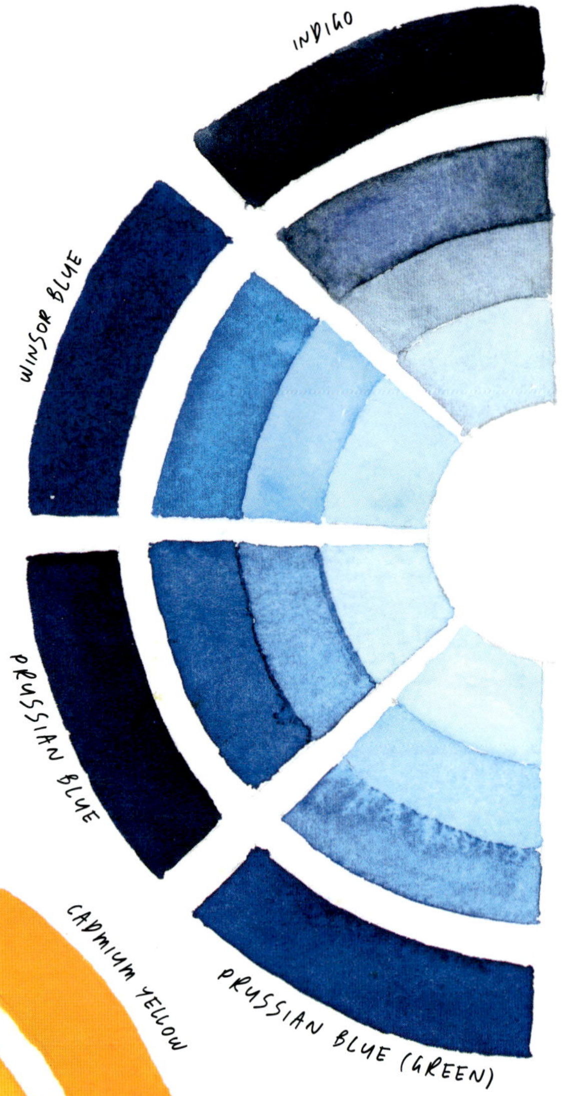
INDIGO
WINSOR BLUE
PRUSSIAN BLUE
PRUSSIAN BLUE (GREEN)

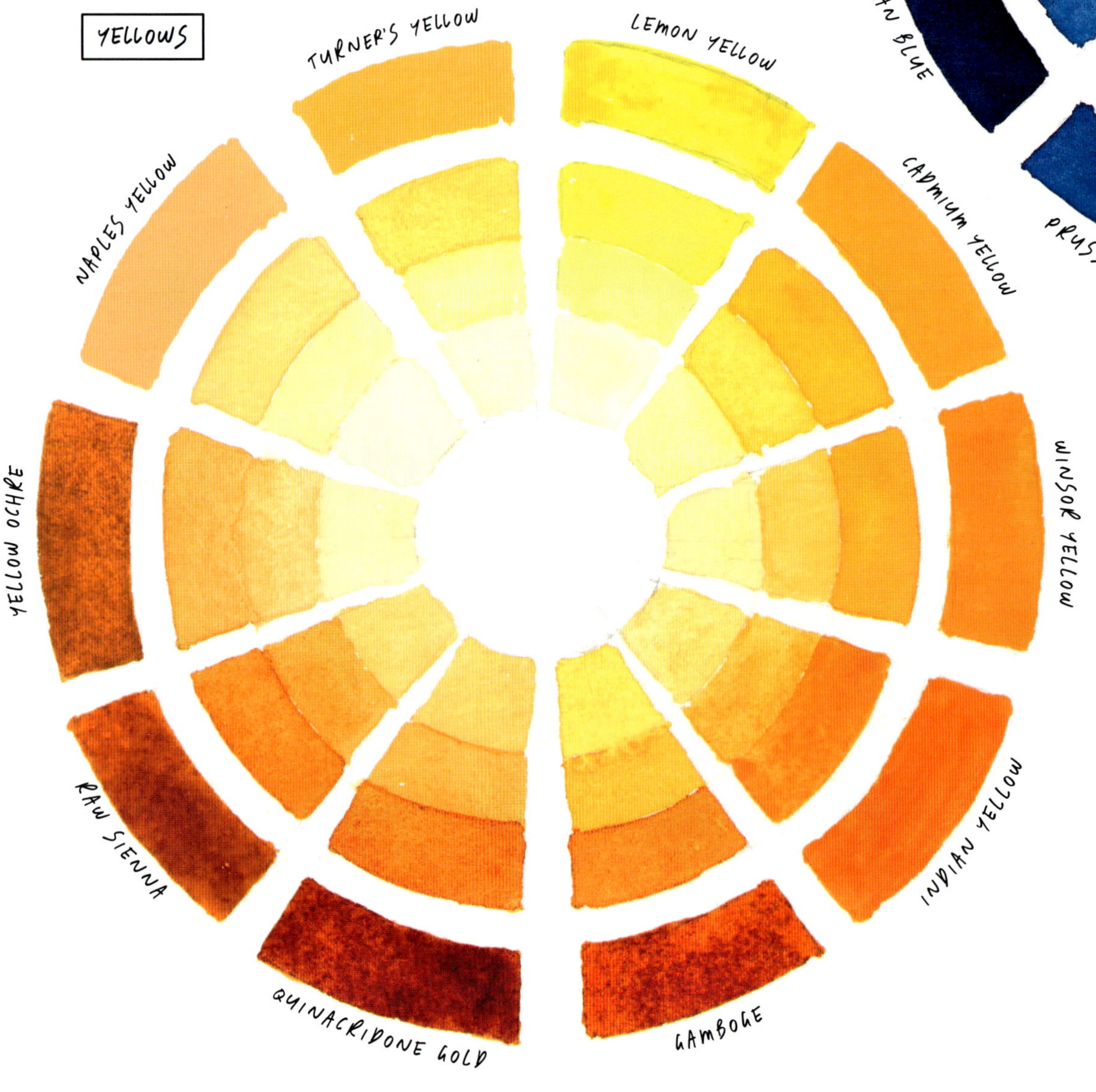
YELLOWS
TURNER'S YELLOW
LEMON YELLOW
NAPLES YELLOW
CADMIUM YELLOW
YELLOW OCHRE
WINSOR YELLOW
RAW SIENNA
INDIAN YELLOW
QUINACRIDONE GOLD
GAMBOGE

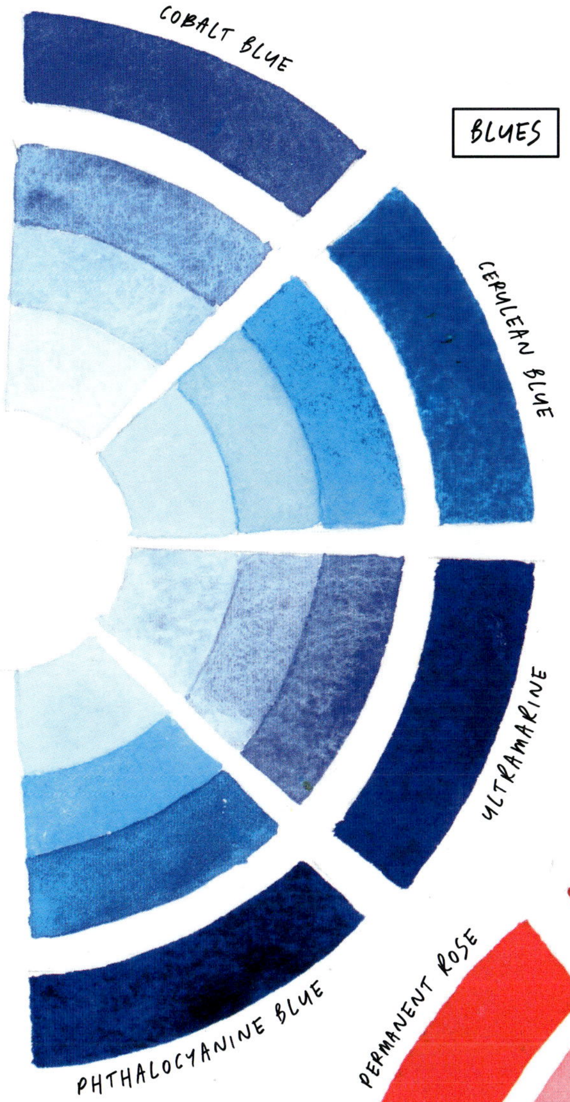
BLUES
COBALT BLUE
CERULEAN BLUE
ULTRAMARINE
PHTHALOCYANINE BLUE

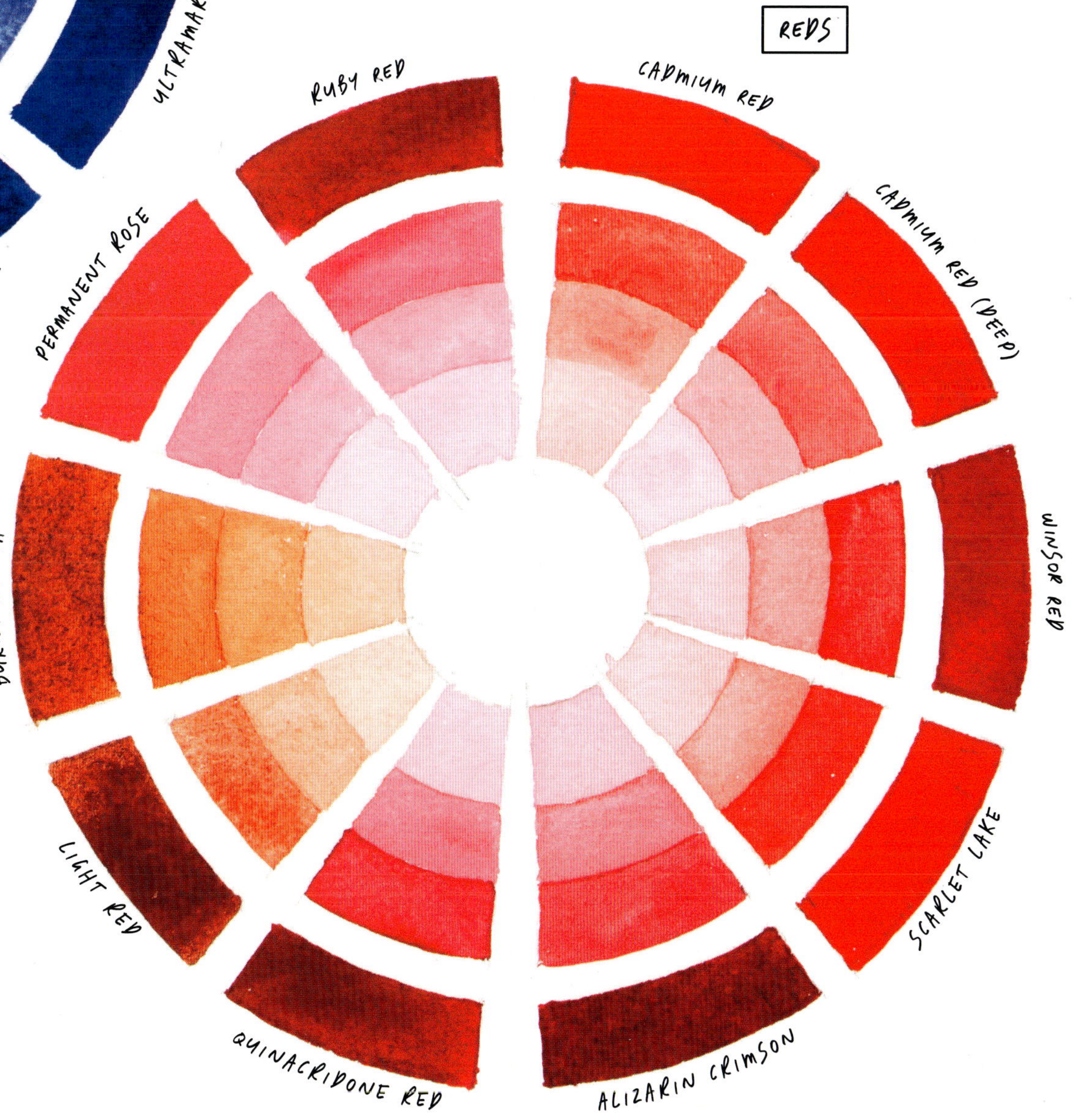
REDS
CADMIUM RED
CADMIUM RED (DEEP)
WINSOR RED
SCARLET LAKE
ALIZARIN CRIMSON
QUINACRIDONE RED
LIGHT RED
BURNT SIENNA
PERMANENT ROSE
RUBY RED

***This color wheel shows the primary and secondary color families. A primary color will always sit opposite a secondary color, creating pairs of complementaries.***

1. Blue gradually added
2. Medium range purple
3. Red gradually added
4. Blue gradually added
5. Medium range green
6. Yellow gradually added
7. Yellow gradually added
8. Medium range orange
9. Red gradually added

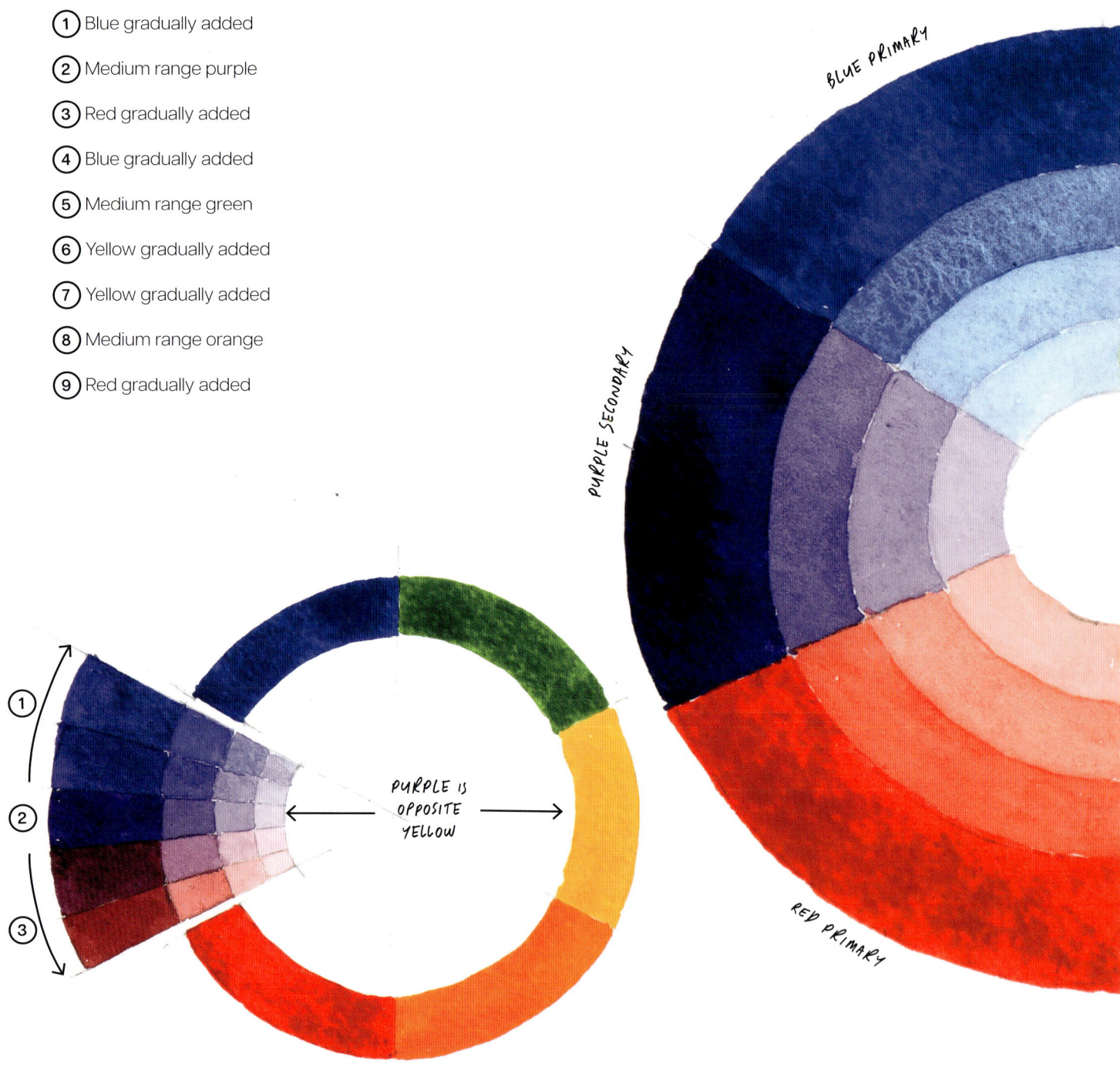

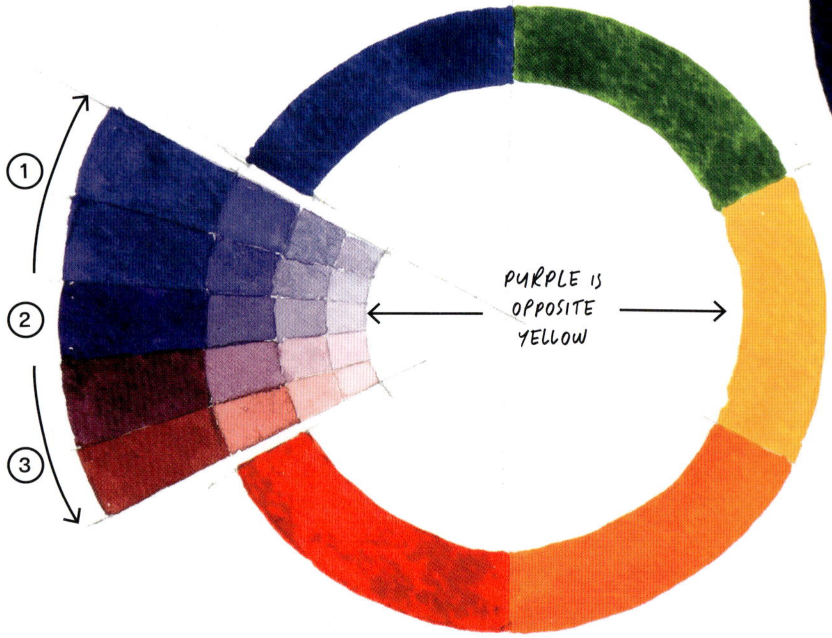
1
2
3
PURPLE IS OPPOSITE YELLOW

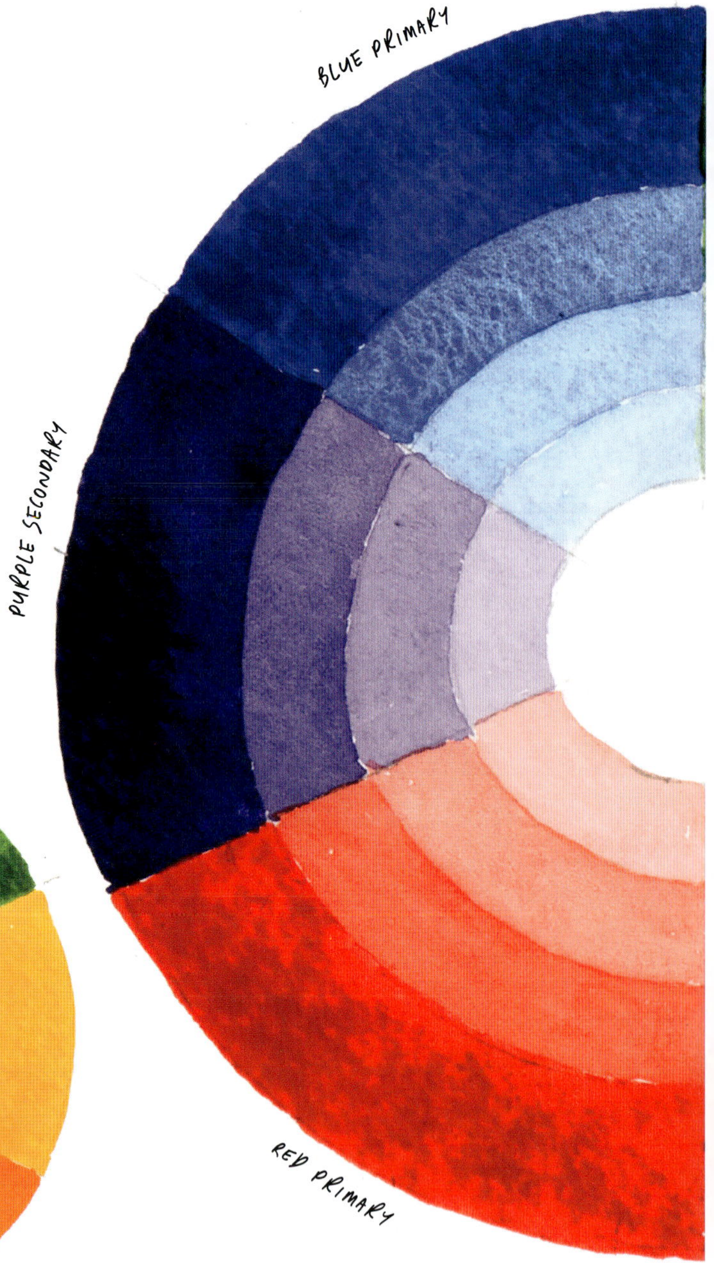
BLUE PRIMARY
PURPLE SECONDARY
RED PRIMARY

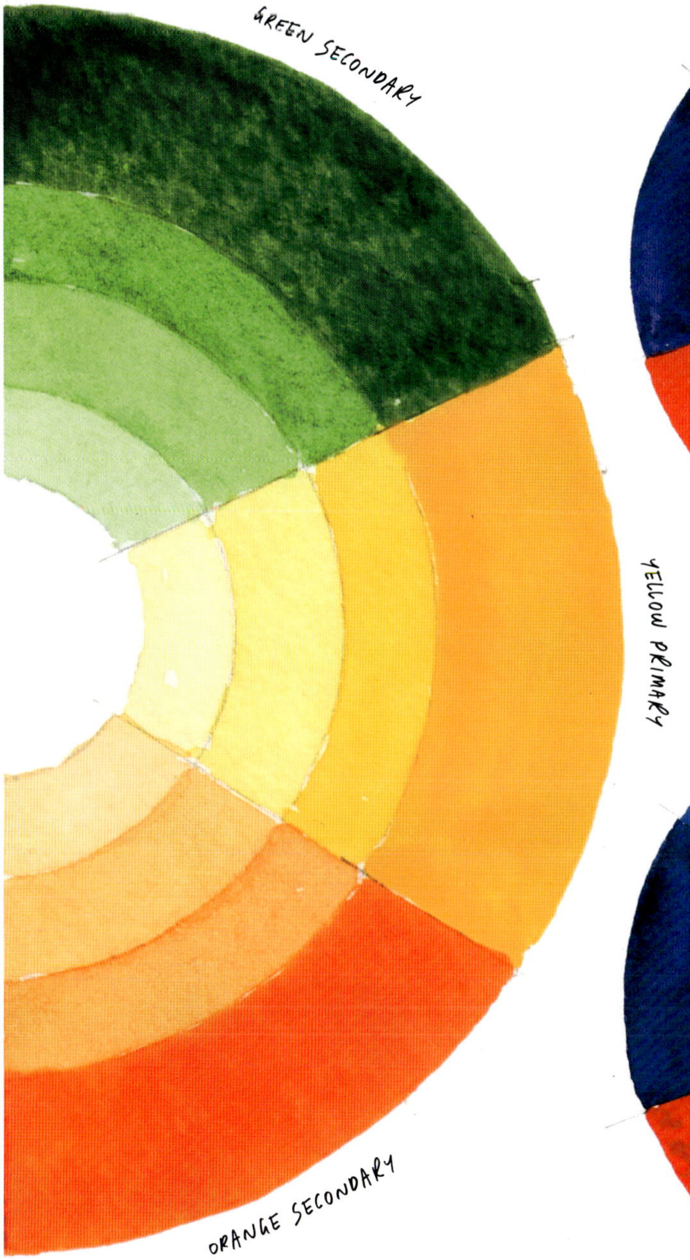
GREEN SECONDARY
YELLOW PRIMARY
ORANGE SECONDARY

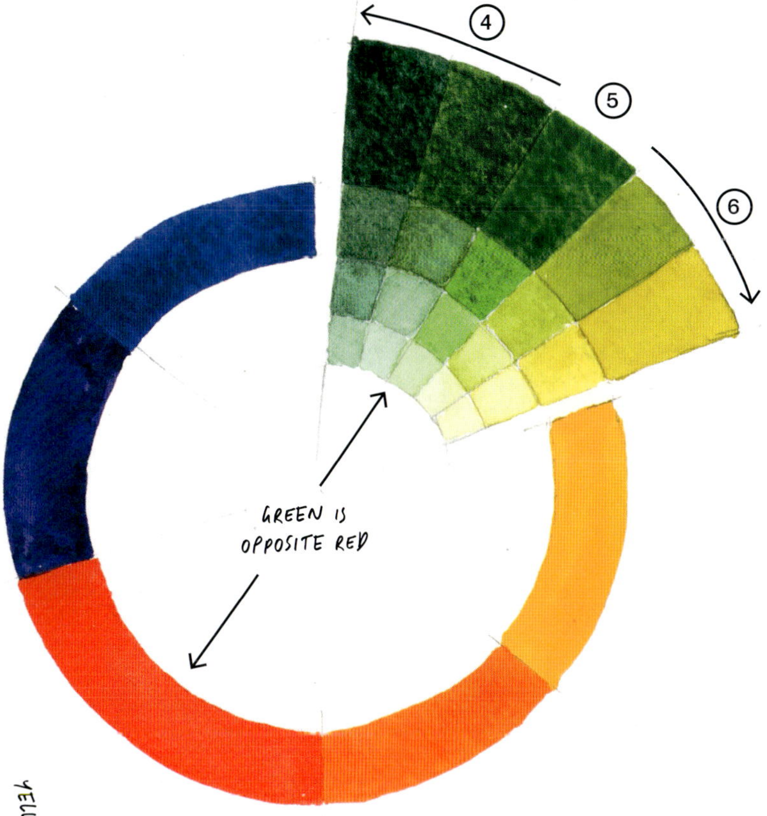
4
5
6
GREEN IS OPPOSITE RED

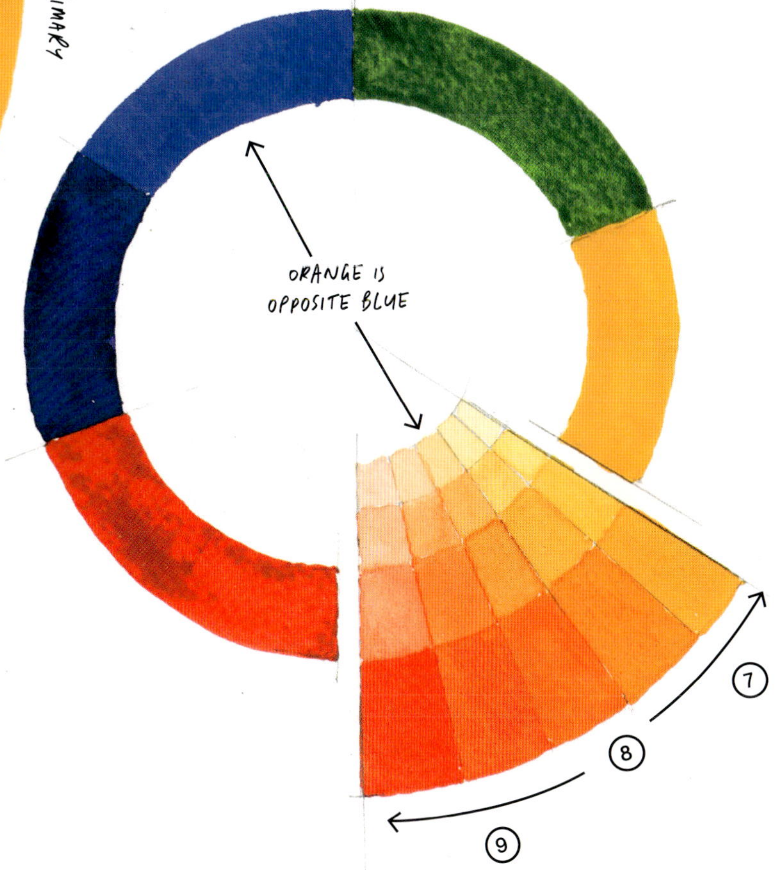
ORANGE IS OPPOSITE BLUE
7
8
9

*Color Families:*

# YELLOWS

This section looks at a selection of yellow paints that you are likely to come across initially in their raw form – straight out of the tube or pan. We will explore how yellow paints can be used to mix oranges, and then ways in which the oranges themselves can be darkened.

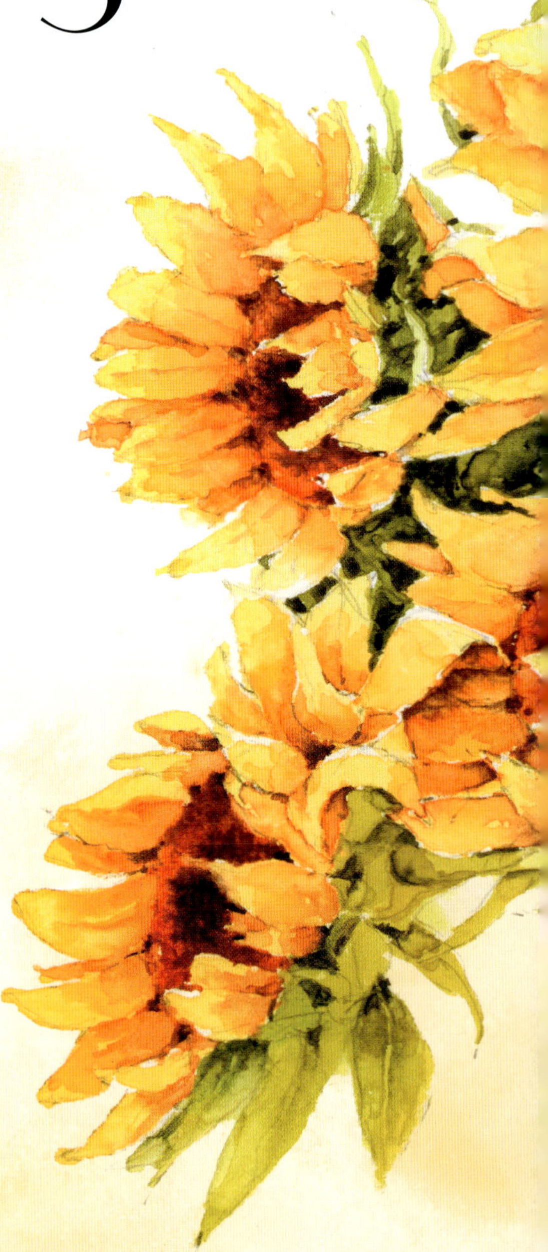

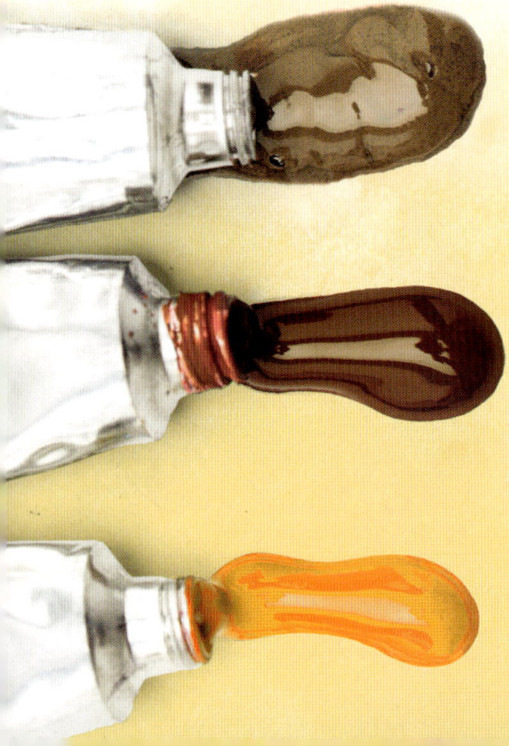

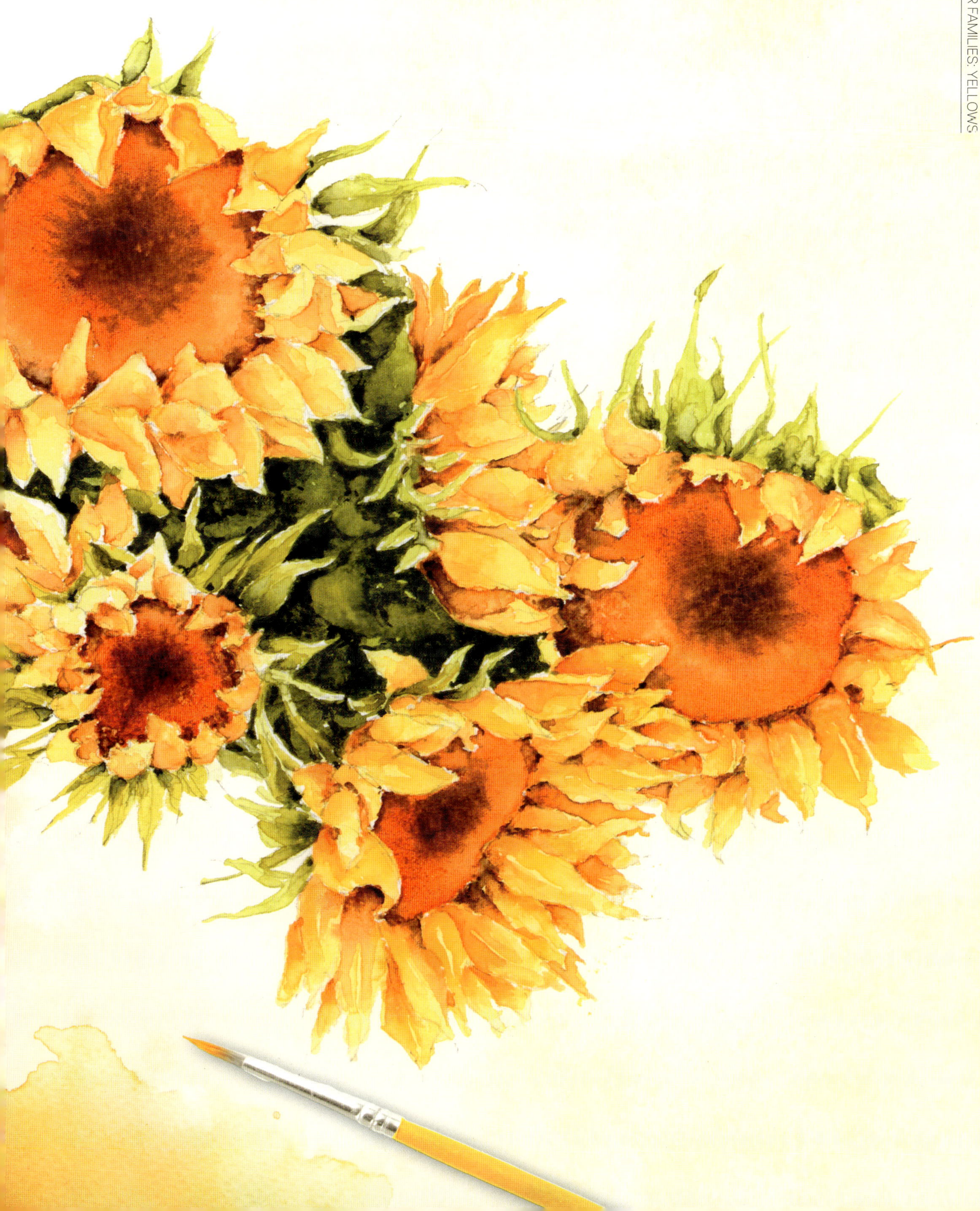

# Yellow paints

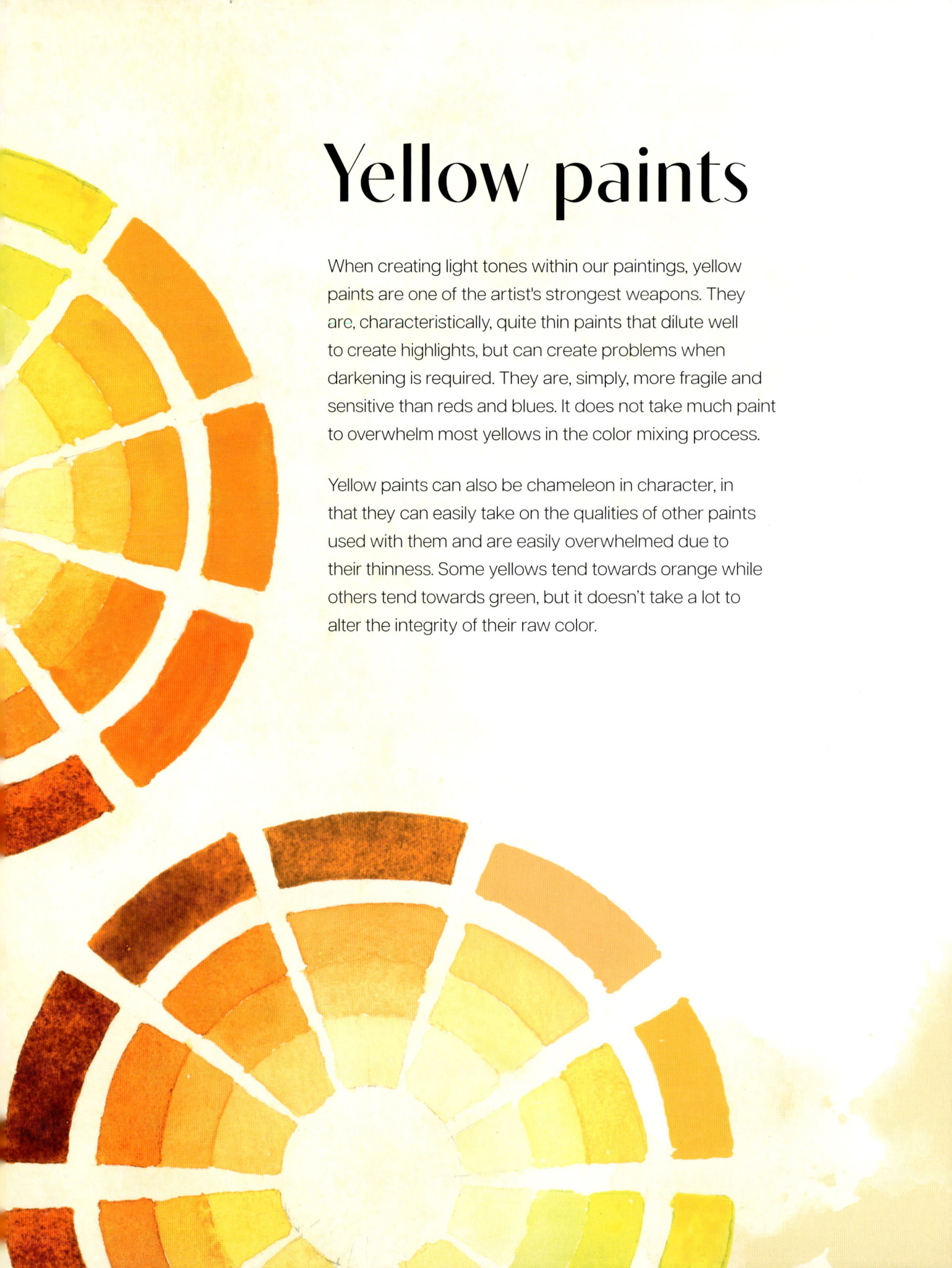

When creating light tones within our paintings, yellow paints are one of the artist's strongest weapons. They are, characteristically, quite thin paints that dilute well to create highlights, but can create problems when darkening is required. They are, simply, more fragile and sensitive than reds and blues. It does not take much paint to overwhelm most yellows in the color mixing process.

Yellow paints can also be chameleon in character, in that they can easily take on the qualities of other paints used with them and are easily overwhelmed due to their thinness. Some yellows tend towards orange while others tend towards green, but it doesn't take a lot to alter the integrity of their raw color.

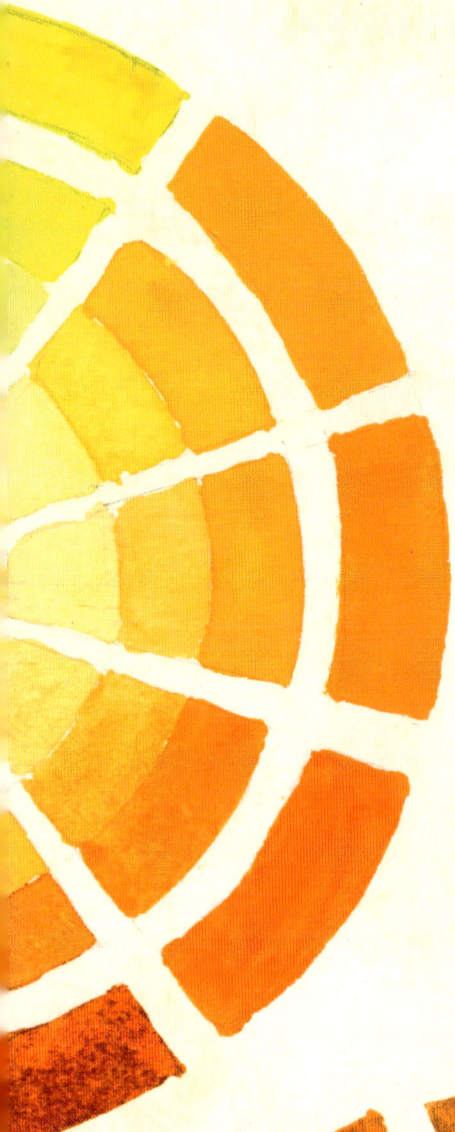

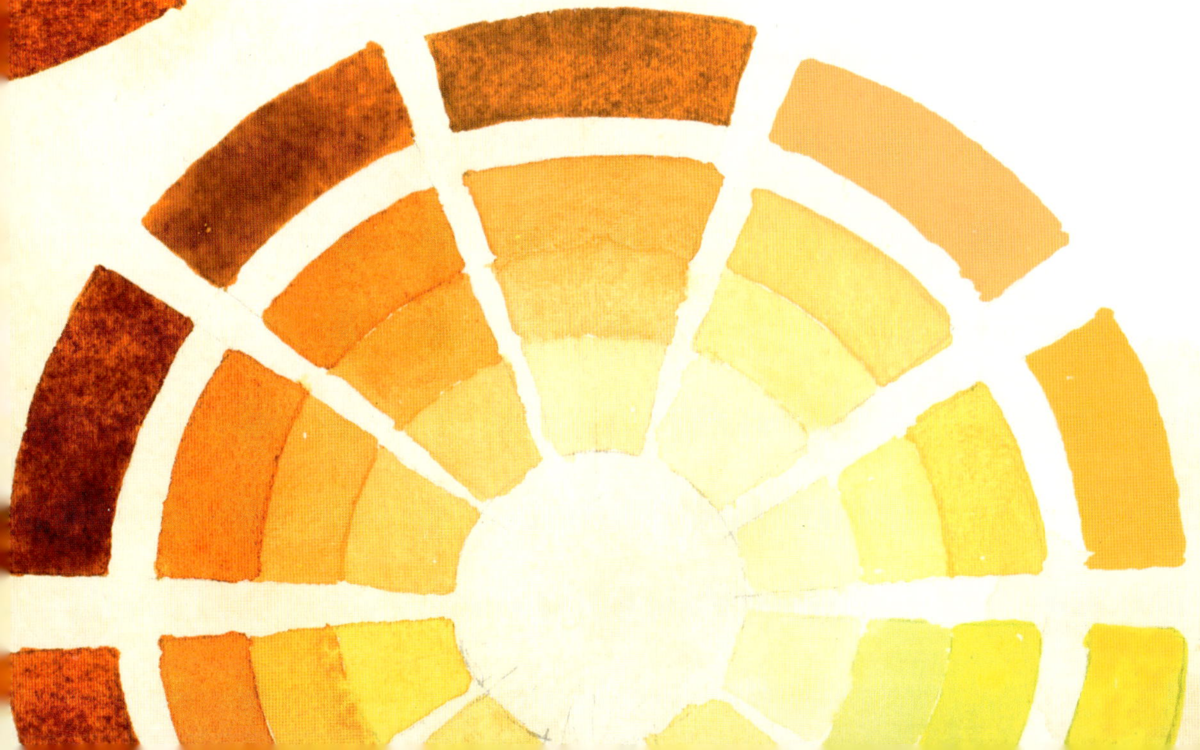

***Now to explore some of the natural characteristics of yellow paints. Here, I am using a selection commonly found in art stores and probably the first yellows artists come upon when they start buying paints.***

**LEMON YELLOW** is a thin, acidic paint that tends easily towards green. This paint can change tone very easily and needs careful handling in the mixing process.

**TURNER'S YELLOW** is a rich color initially created by mixing lead and sea salt. It is a good, free-flowing paint and mixes well with other paints from different color families.

**GAMBOGE** is a thick, glutinous paint, originally made from the gum resin of the Garcinia tree. It is a difficult paint to work with due to its thickness and requires much dilution to achieve a lighter tone. It is, however, a rich, warm color and is particularly useful in autumnal scenes.

**NAPLES YELLOW** is known to have been used by the ancient Egyptians and was created from lead. It has a slightly creamy texture and is not too translucent, but can dry to a rather flat tone.

**WINSOR + CADMIUM YELLOWS** are probably best considered side by side as there is little difference in the ways in which they dilute and mix. Winsor Yellow is the slightly stronger paint and a little goes a long way. Cadmium Yellow produces only slightly thinner tones but is a good choice for any subjects that you might wish to paint.

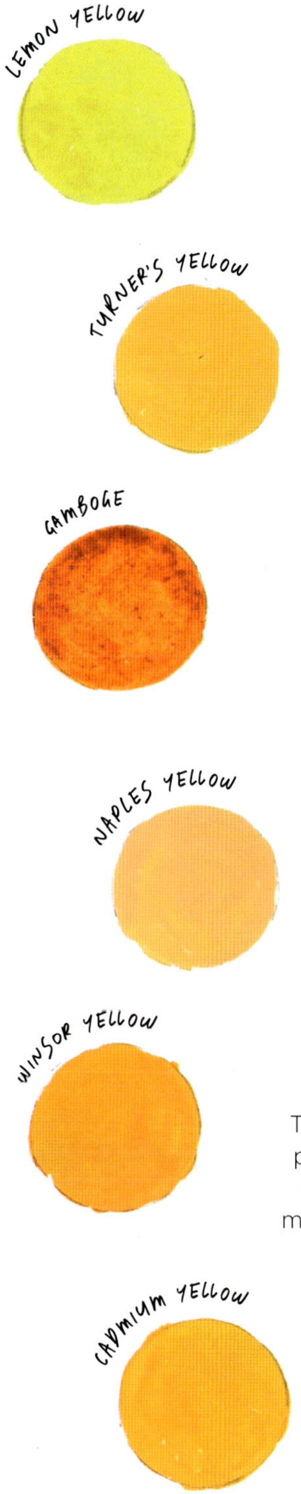
LEMON YELLOW
TURNER'S YELLOW
GAMBOGE
NAPLES YELLOW
WINSOR YELLOW
CADMIUM YELLOW

These six yellows provide you with many different mixing possibilities.

*"Yellow paints can also be chameleon in character, in that they can easily take on the qualities of other paints used with them..."*

***This chart illustrates ways in which you can test your yellow paints to see how they perform when diluted or darkened.***

## LIGHT AND DARK

The six yellow raw paints are shown around the inner ring. In the middle ring, they have been broken down into light, medium and dark. This gives you a clear view of how each particular yellow works when adding water to make it lighter, or a touch of its complementary color to make it darker. The outer ring is further divided into six light and dark variations, demonstrating how far you might be able to push the tonal qualities. You are unlikely to use more than six variations of any one color in a single painting.

Add a very small, highly controlled amount of purple as it is a powerful color to add to an already fragile one. I have used Dioxazine Purple, a strong, multi-purpose paint. It dilutes well and gives an even covering, allowing the full range of yellow tones to be pushed.

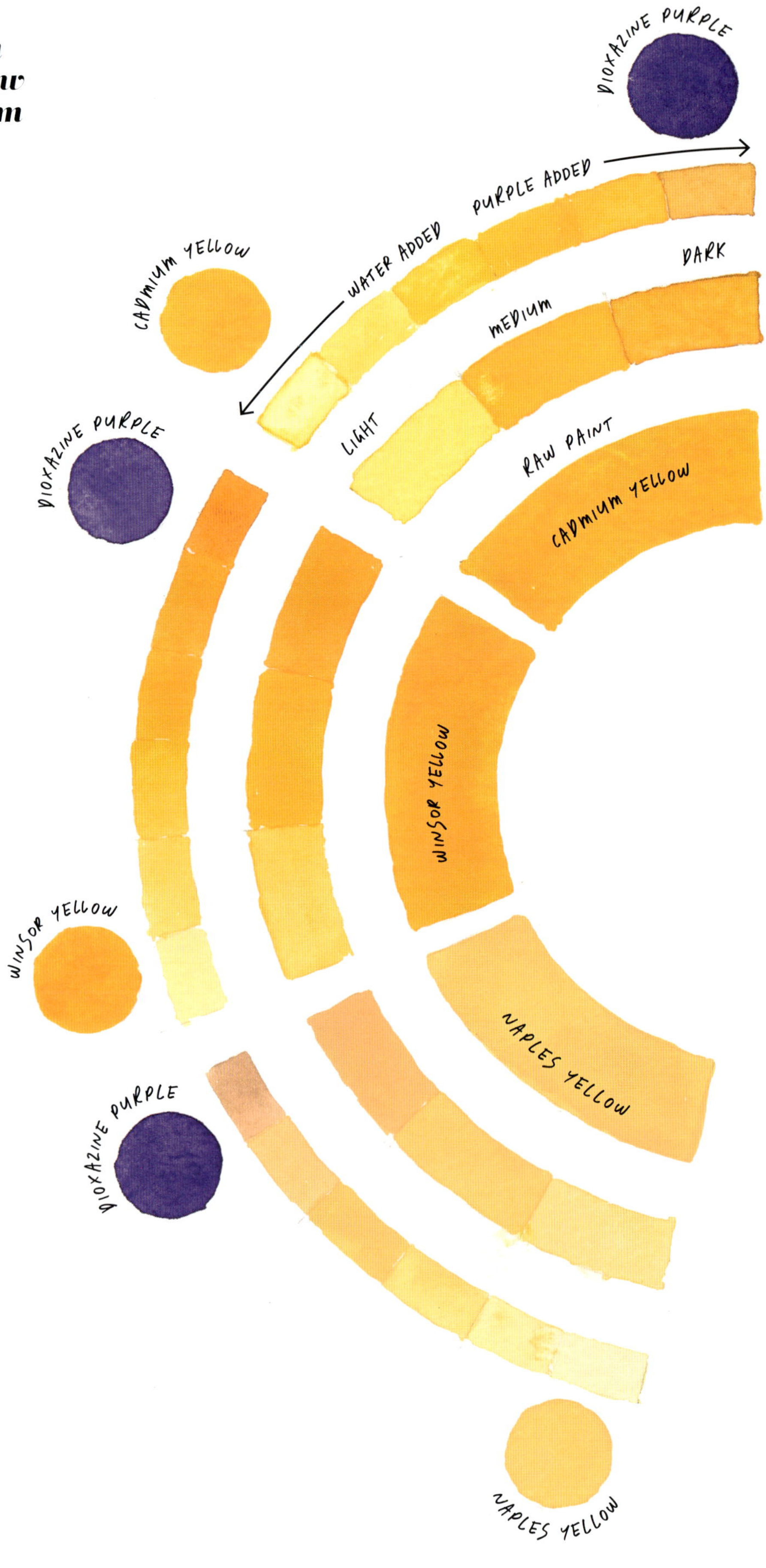
DIOXAZINE PURPLE
PURPLE ADDED
WATER ADDED
CADMIUM YELLOW
DARK
MEDIUM
LIGHT
RAW PAINT
CADMIUM YELLOW
DIOXAZINE PURPLE
WINSOR YELLOW
WINSOR YELLOW
NAPLES YELLOW
DIOXAZINE PURPLE
NAPLES YELLOW

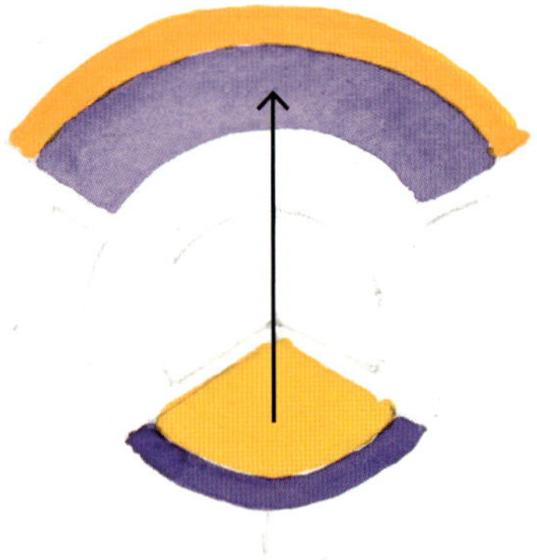

As complementary colors, the secondary color purple will always be opposite yellow on the color wheel.

**NOTE:** The various swatches of Dioxazine Purple aren't consistent – even here, the imprecise beauty of watercolor painting is at work.

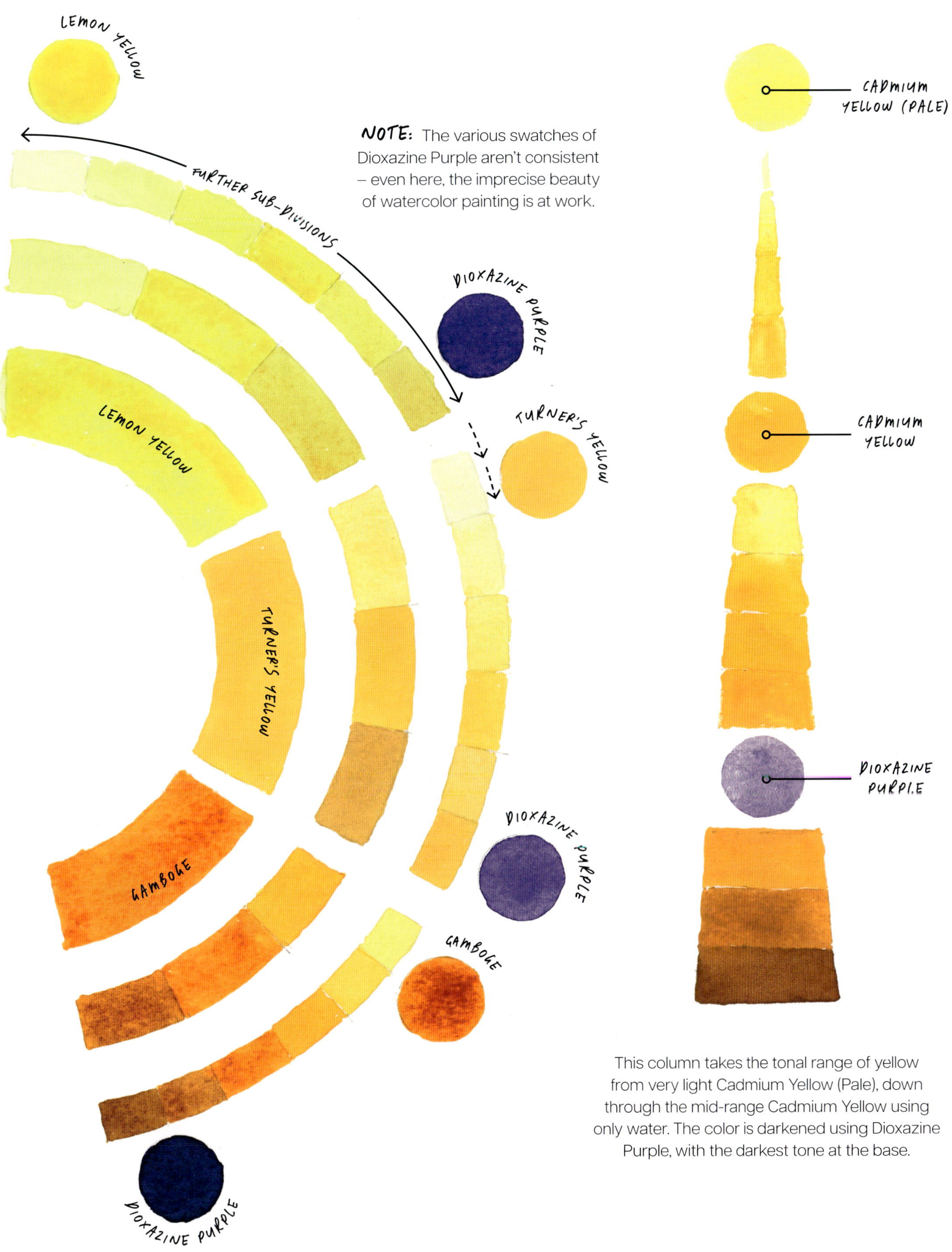
LEMON YELLOW
FURTHER SUB-DIVISIONS
DIOXAZINE PURPLE
LEMON YELLOW
TURNER'S YELLOW
TURNER'S YELLOW
GAMBOGE
DIOXAZINE PURPLE
GAMBOGE
DIOXAZINE PURPLE
CADMIUM YELLOW (PALE)
CADMIUM YELLOW
DIOXAZINE PURPLE

This column takes the tonal range of yellow from very light Cadmium Yellow (Pale), down through the mid-range Cadmium Yellow using only water. The color is darkened using Dioxazine Purple, with the darkest tone at the base.

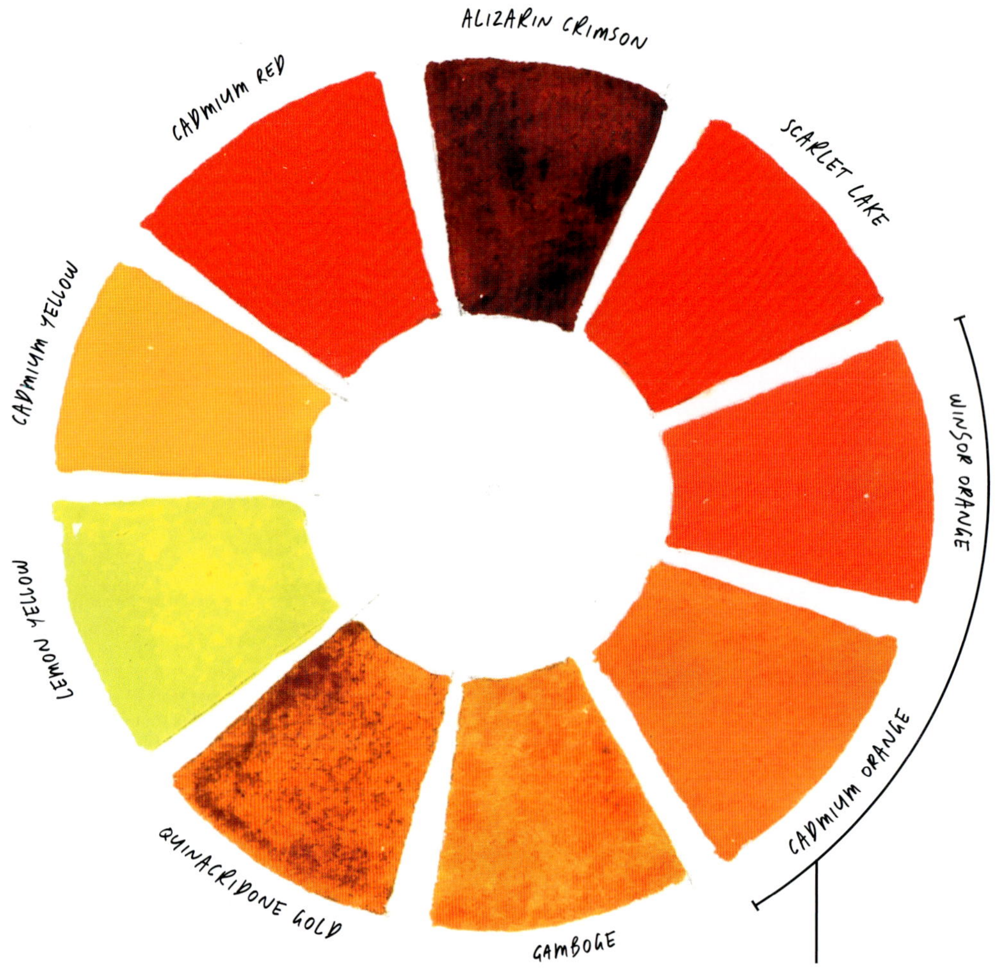
ALIZARIN CRIMSON
SCARLET LAKE
WINSOR ORANGE
CADMIUM ORANGE
GAMBOGE
QUINACRIDONE GOLD
LEMON YELLOW
CADMIUM YELLOW
CADMIUM RED

These are the two pre-mixed orange paints I will be using.

***The next four pages explore the differences between mixing your own oranges using red and yellow, and the colors or tones that you can create by adding red or yellow to pre-mixed oranges.***

## COLORS FOR MIXING ORANGE

This wheel is composed of the colors that I personally like to use in mixing oranges. I have also included two pre-mixed oranges, to be used later. The only paint shown here that I've not used in the examples that follow is Quinacridone Gold. A very powerful paint, it will quickly overwhelm any color into which it is added, so is not really valuable for testing the potential for tonal mixing.

# MIXING YELLOW AND RED

Mixing two primary colors together will, as we explored in Color Families: Basic Theories, create a secondary color. But the notion of a primary color, as we know now, was a scientific concept. Artists will always ask "Which type of primary color do you mean? Lemon Yellow? Naples Yellow?..."

The pages on mixing oranges explore what can happen when you take some of the yellows featured here and mix them with a small selection of reds.

(1) Cadmium Yellow gradually added to Cadmium Red

(2) Cadmium Yellow gradually added to Alizarin Crimson

(3) Gamboge gradually added to Cadmium Red

(4) Gamboge gradually added to Alizarin Crimson

(1)

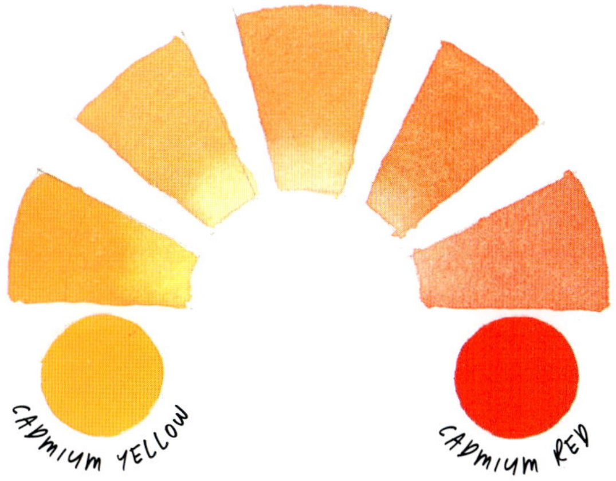
CADMIUM YELLOW
CADMIUM RED

(2)

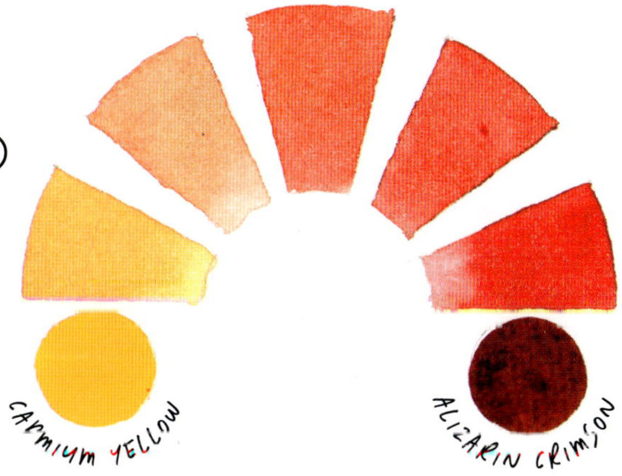
CADMIUM YELLOW
ALIZARIN CRIMSON

**NOTE:** Cadmium colors are very "stable", making them automatic choices for color mixing – they don't overpower, yet they are never weak.

(3)

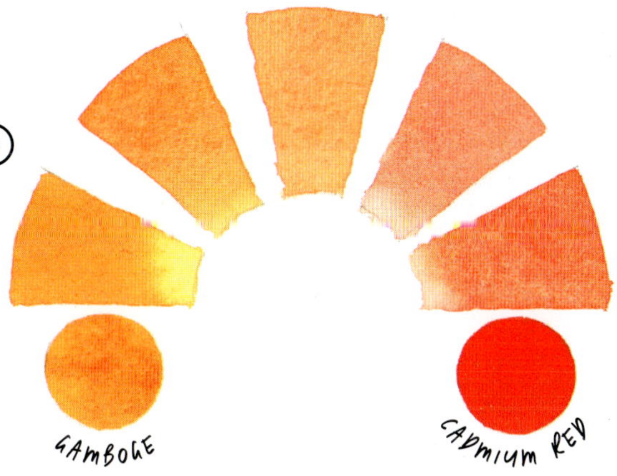
GAMBOGE
CADMIUM RED

(4)

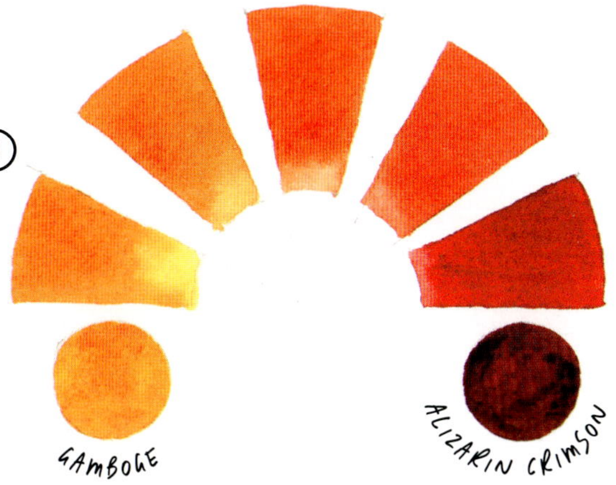
GAMBOGE
ALIZARIN CRIMSON

***Now it's time to expand the choice of oranges available to us by introducing a couple of pre-mixed oranges – Winsor Orange and Cadmium Orange.***

## MIXING THE RIGHT COLOR

Next, we will need to look carefully at our subjects and consider exactly what type of orange we need to mix. The answer, of course, will depend entirely on your personal requirements. A still life group with a mixture of fruits may require an orange with some yellow added, while an autumnal snapshot with pumpkins and fallen leaves may demand an orange with some red added.

It is interesting to compare the range of orange tones created by mixing assorted yellows and reds, and then looking at the "straight out of the tube" pre-mixed oranges. The yellow and red mixes can often appear dull and sometimes a little muddy compared to the vibrancy of the pre-mixed oranges.

My personal preference for creating either lighter or stronger oranges is to start with a pre-mixed orange and add new colors to this. The strength of the pre-mixed colors allows them to be used on their own, although you would be unusually fortunate to find the exact color you need straight out of the tube or pan. By adding other colors within the same color family, you will be able to alter, extend, mute or increase the vibrancy of the pre-mixed oranges. In fact, I would go so far as to say that the possibilities for mixing new colors have no limits. For that reason, these colors are always sitting in my painting kit.

*"...you would be unusually fortunate to find the exact color you need straight out of the tube or pan."*

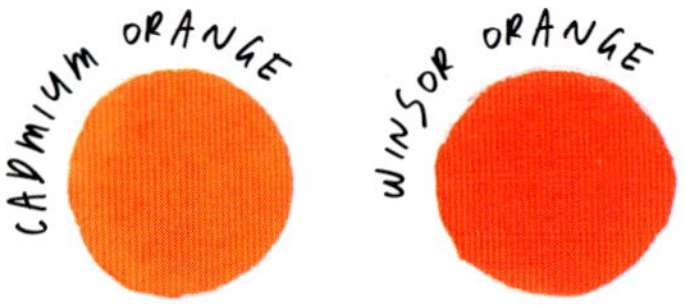
CADMIUM ORANGE
WINSOR ORANGE

Both Cadmium Orange and Winsor Orange are readily available. Each has slightly different qualities and tones which helps to create more subtle extensions of tonal ranges.

**ORANGE MIXING:** The top and bottom bars demonstrate the range of nine colors from yellow to red, via Cadmium Orange and Winsor Orange.

1. Cadmium Yellow gradually added to Cadmium Orange
2. Cadmium Red gradually added to Cadmium Orange
3. Cadmium Yellow gradually added to Winsor Orange
4. Cadmium Red gradually added to Winsor Orange

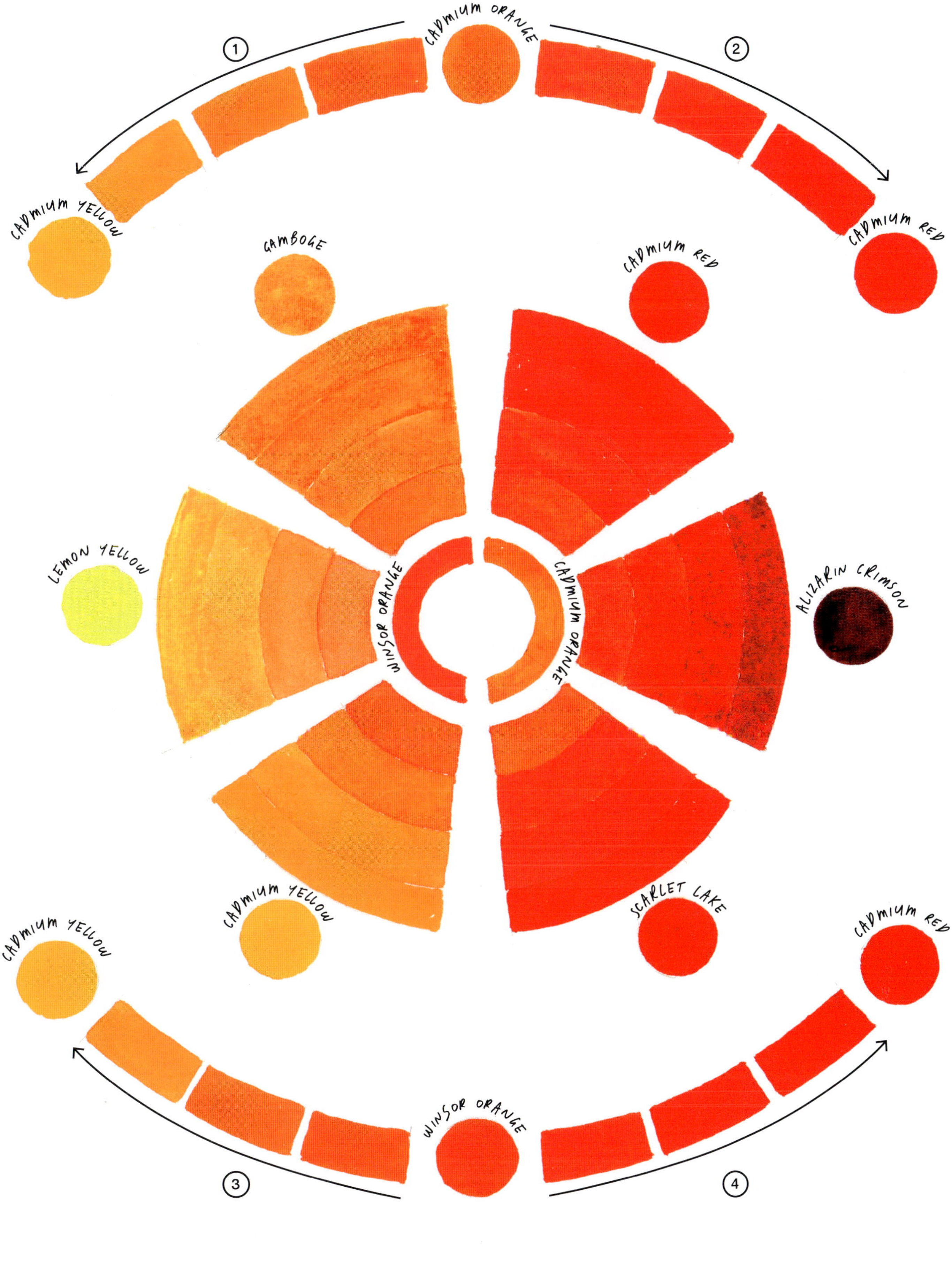
CADMIUM ORANGE
1
2
CADMIUM YELLOW
CADMIUM RED
GAMBOGE
CADMIUM RED
LEMON YELLOW
WINSOR ORANGE
CADMIUM ORANGE
ALIZARIN CRIMSON
CADMIUM YELLOW
SCARLET LAKE
CADMIUM YELLOW
CADMIUM RED
WINSOR ORANGE
3
4

***Having created the best oranges, we will now consider how to darken them. I have taken my two pre-mixed oranges – Winsor and Cadmium – and pushed the tonal limits as far as I could.***

## DARKENING THE TONE

The pre-mixed oranges half-way along the columns are the starting points here.

(1) In the middle of the column is a mixture of Winsor Orange and Winsor Yellow, lightened towards the inner circle by adding increasingly diluted Winsor Yellow (more water added for each section). Moving outwards from the center mixture, pure Winsor Orange is added to the mix, darkening the color in stages. Ultramarine is added at the very last stages.

(2) In the middle of the column is a mixture of Winsor Orange and Winsor Red. Increasing quantities of diluted Winsor Orange are added in stages towards the center of the circle. Moving outwards from the middle mix, pure Winsor Red is added in stages with Ultramarine being added at the final stages.

(3) In the middle of the column is a mixture of Winsor Orange and Alizarin Crimson. Increasing quantities of diluted Winsor Orange are added towards the centre, lightening the tone. Moving outwards, increasing quantities of Alizarin Crimson are added, darkening the tone. Ultramarine is added at the final stages, darkening the orange without tuning it brown.

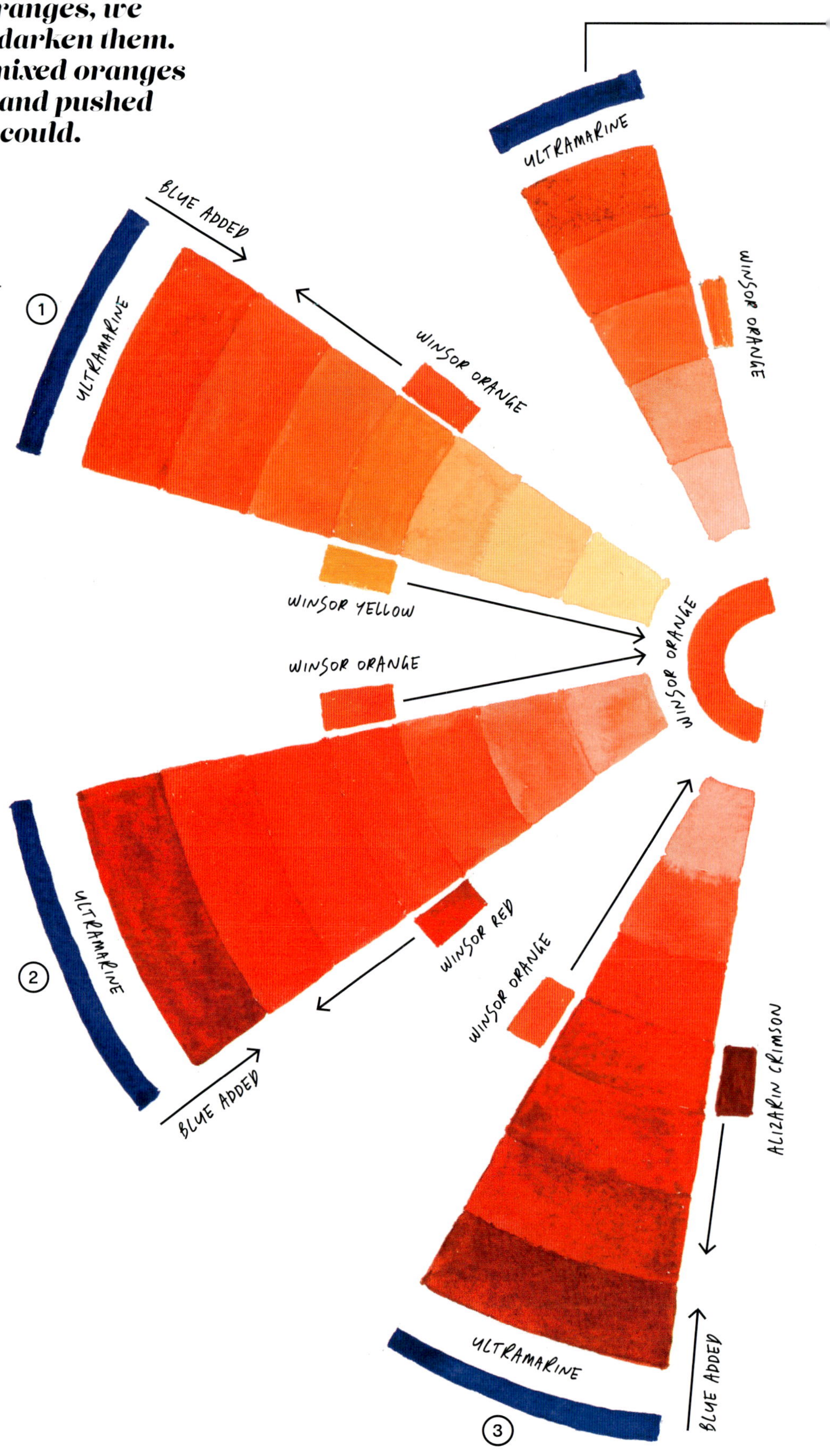

ULTRAMARINE
WINSOR ORANGE
BLUE ADDED
1
ULTRAMARINE
WINSOR ORANGE
WINSOR YELLOW
WINSOR ORANGE
WINSOR ORANGE
ULTRAMARINE
2
WINSOR RED
WINSOR ORANGE
BLUE ADDED
ALIZARIN CRIMSON
ULTRAMARINE
3
BLUE ADDED

## COMPLEMENTARY COLORS AND WATER

The top two columns explore just how far I could take raw Cadmium Orange and Winsor Orange by adding our chosen blue (the complementary color to orange) in one direction, and diluting with water in the other.

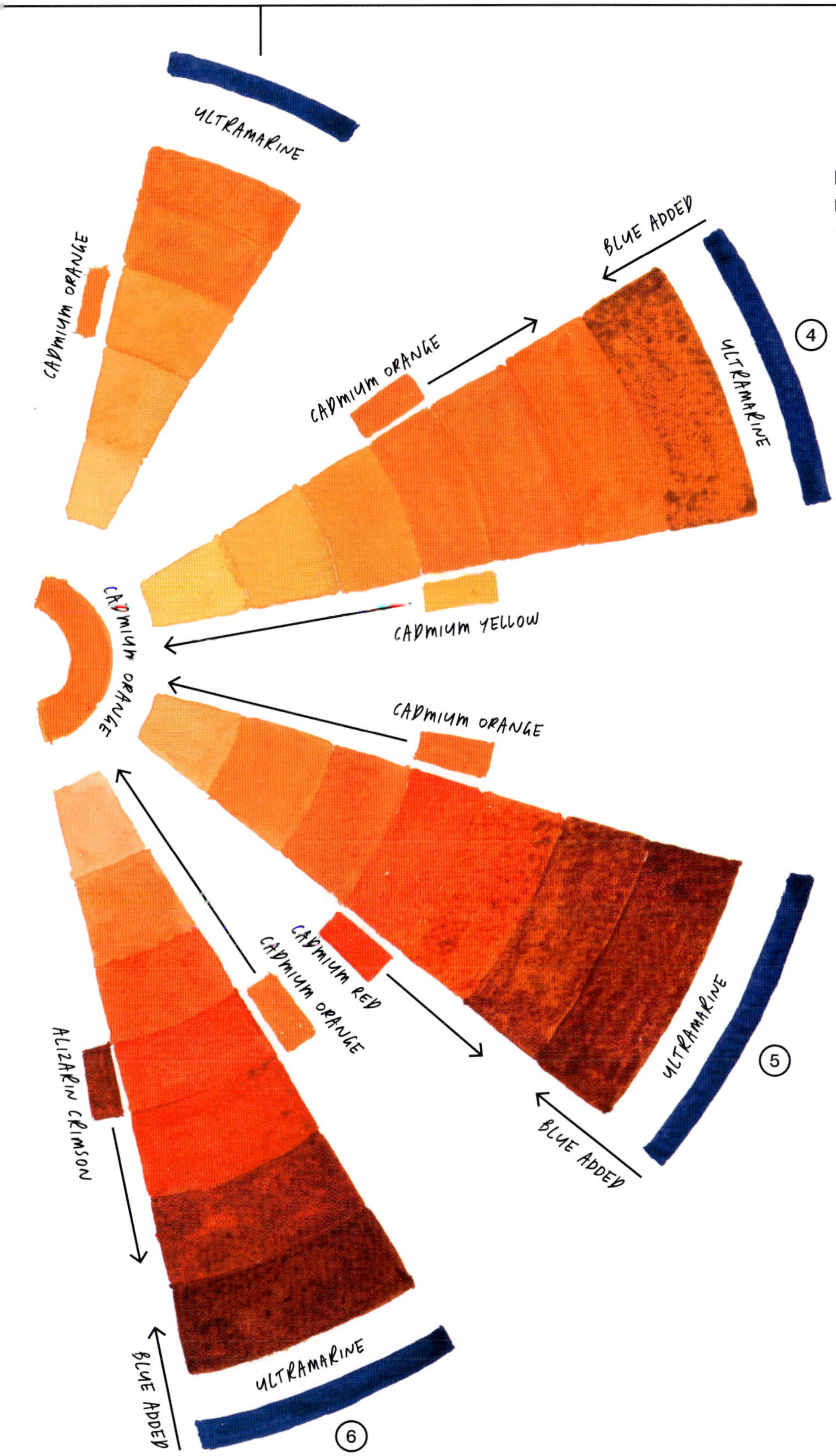

ULTRAMARINE
CADMIUM ORANGE
BLUE ADDED
CADMIUM ORANGE
ULTRAMARINE
4
CADMIUM YELLOW
CADMIUM ORANGE
CADMIUM ORANGE
CADMIUM RED
CADMIUM ORANGE
ALIZARIN CRIMSON
ULTRAMARINE
5
BLUE ADDED
ULTRAMARINE
BLUE ADDED
6


(4) In the middle of the column is a mixture of Cadmium Orange and Cadmium Yellow, lightened towards the center by adding increasingly diluted Cadmium Yellow. Moving outwards from the middle mixture, pure Cadmium Orange is added to the mix, darkening the color in stages. Ultramarine is added at the very last stages.

(5) In the middle of the column is a mixture of Cadmium Orange and Cadmium Red. Increasing amounts of diluted Cadmium Orange are added in stages towards the center of the circle. Moving outwards from the middle mix, pure Cadmium Red is added to the mix in stages with Ultramarine being added at the final stages.

(6) In the middle of the column is a mixture of Cadmium Orange and Alizarin Crimson. Increasing quantities of diluted Cadmium Orange are added towards the center, lightening the tone. Moving outwards, increasing quantities of Alizarin Crimson are added, darkening the tone. Ultramarine is added at the final stages, darkening the orange without altering the integrity of the orange.

***This example shows yellows and oranges used in a composition. For the peppers on an orange tablecloth, I have mixed as many tones as possible using colors already featured.***

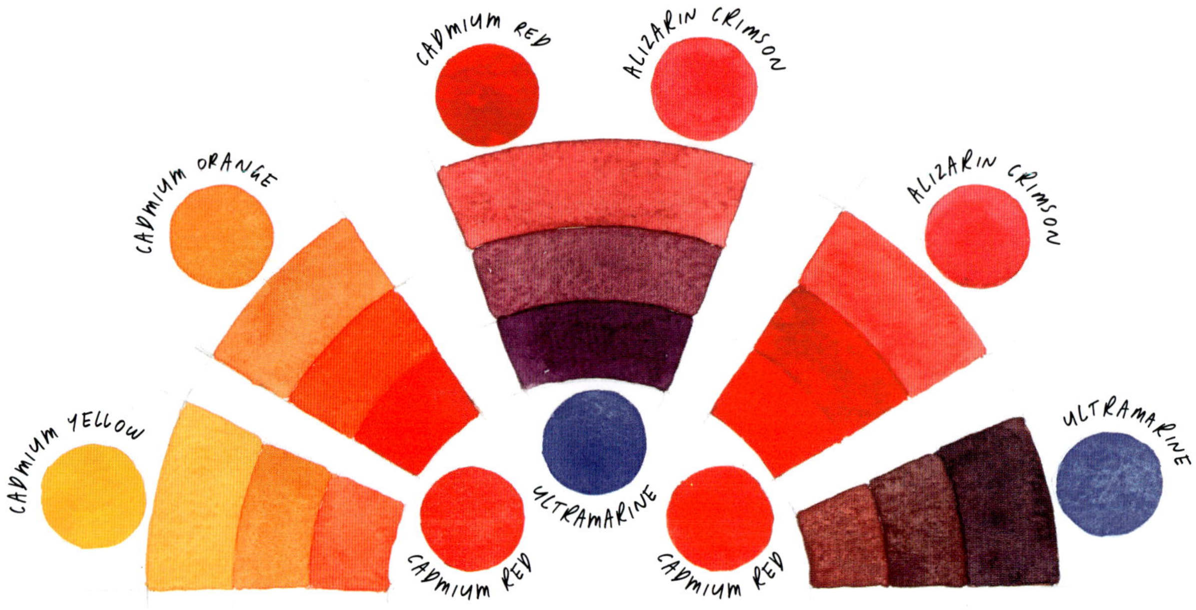
CADMIUM RED
ALIZARIN CRIMSON
CADMIUM ORANGE
ALIZARIN CRIMSON
CADMIUM YELLOW
ULTRAMARINE
ULTRAMARINE
CADMIUM RED
CADMIUM RED

This chart illustrates the color mixes I used to create the whole range of yellow, orange, red and purple tones in this still life painting.

**STAGE 1**

In this stage, the lightest colors were washed onto the paper. These form the highlights once dried.

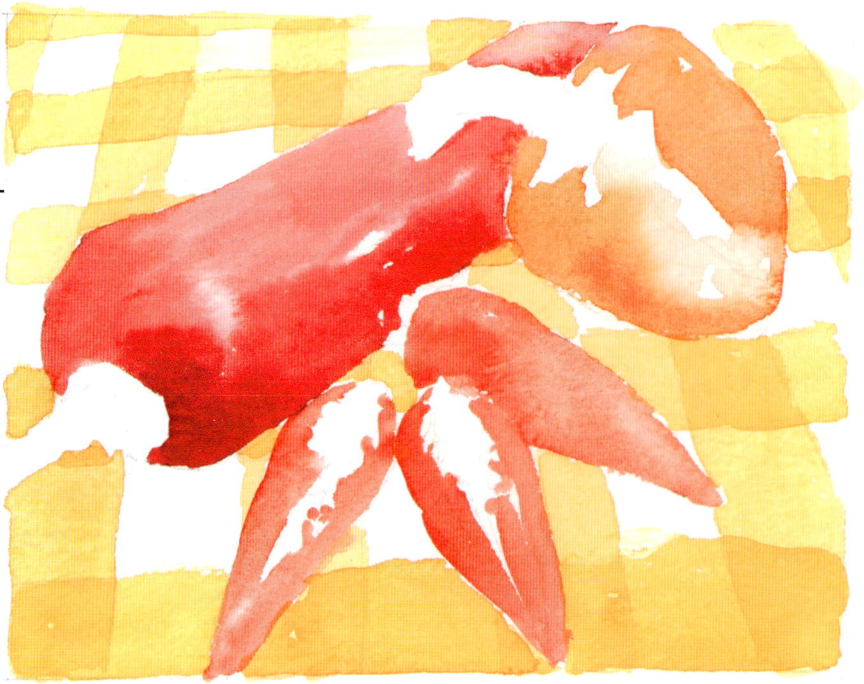

STAGE 2

The reds and blues were mixed with the oranges to create the mid-tones and begin to create a sense of form.

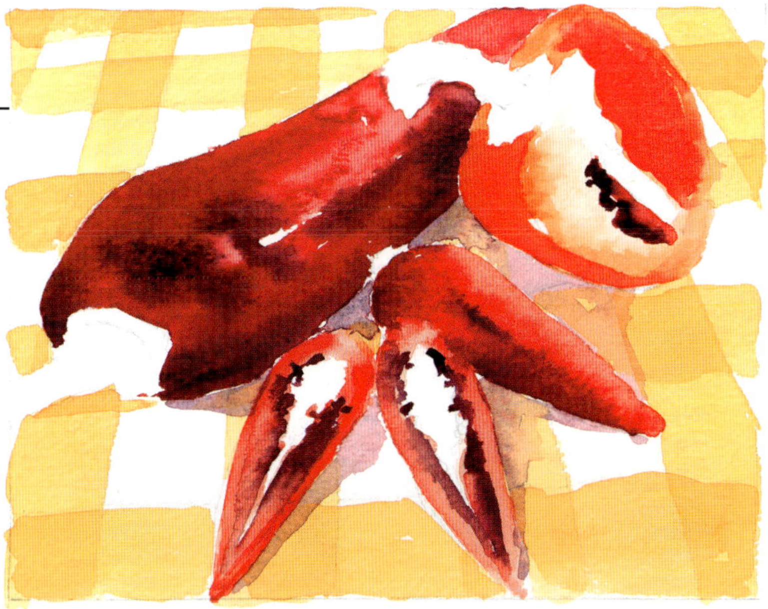

FINAL PAINTING

Crimson was added to the reds and oranges to create the colors for the shaded areas. Blue was added to these colors to establish the shadows cast on the tablecloth.

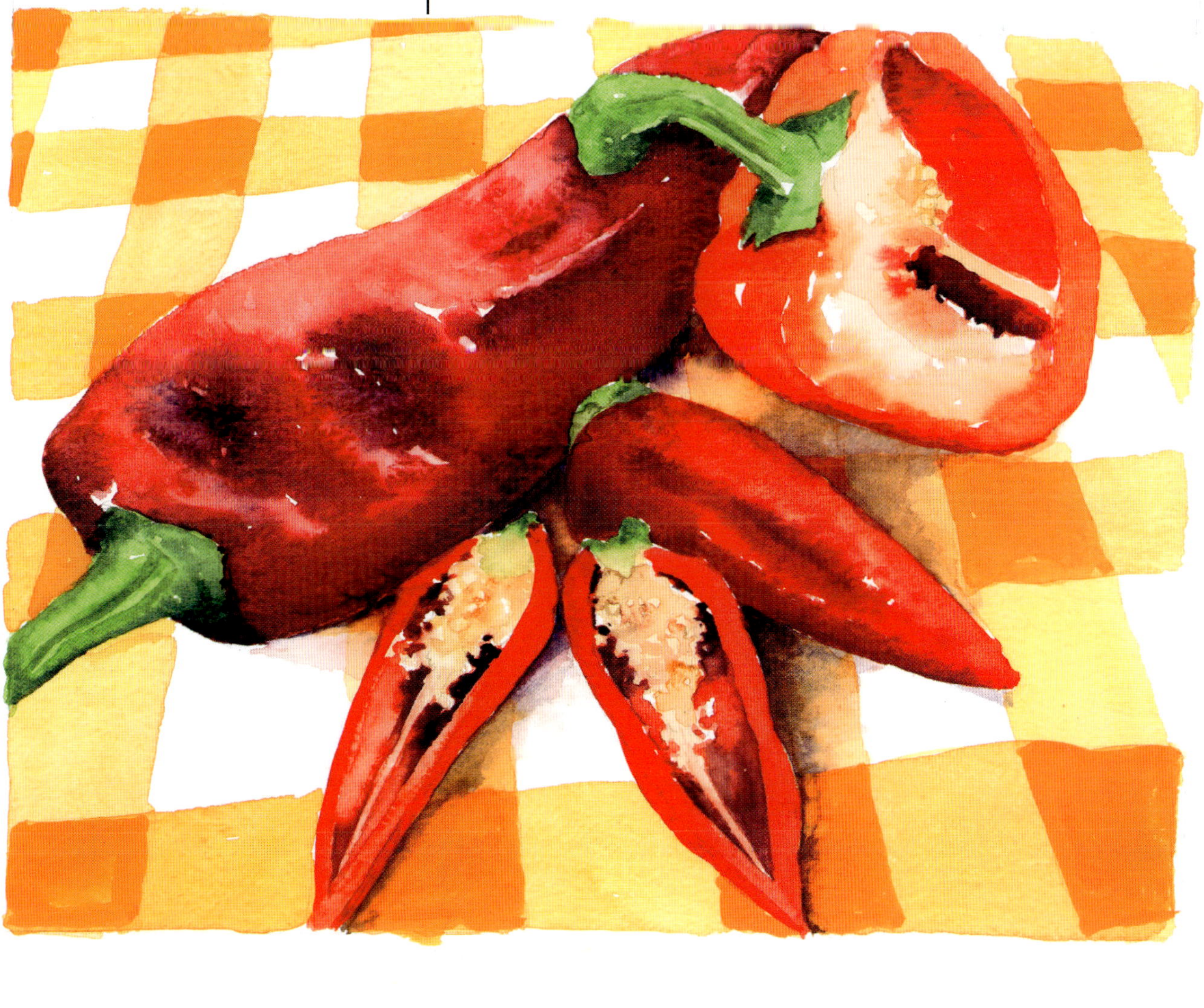

*Color Families:*

# REDS

Next we will look at a selection of red paints that you are most likely to encounter in art stores. We will move on to explore the effectiveness of creating purples by mixing reds with blues, then how to make purples darker.

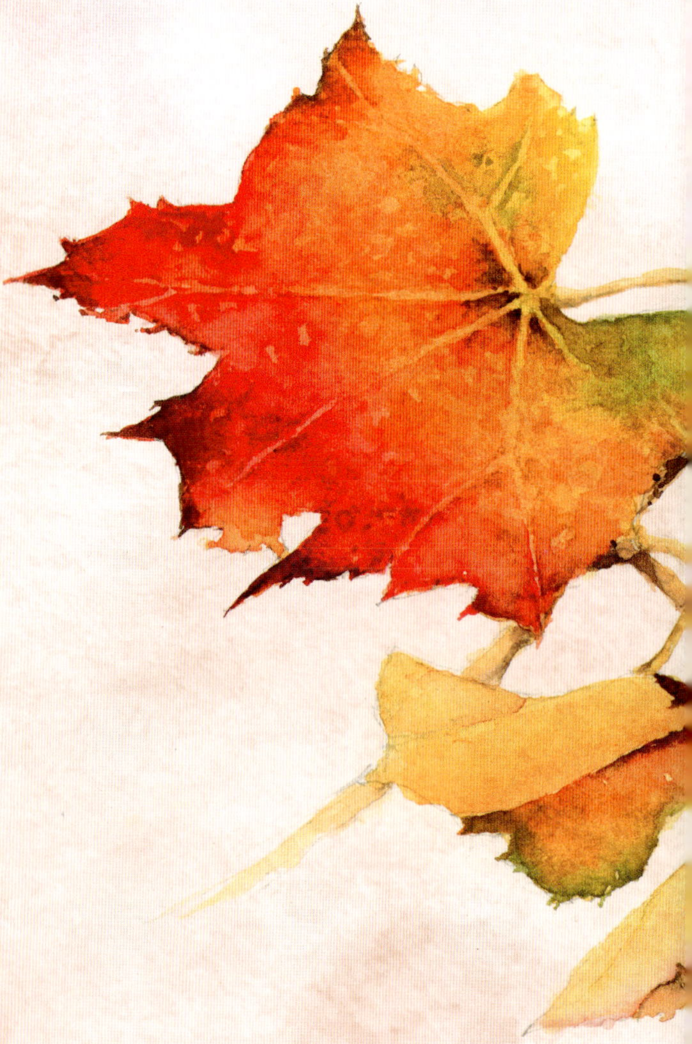

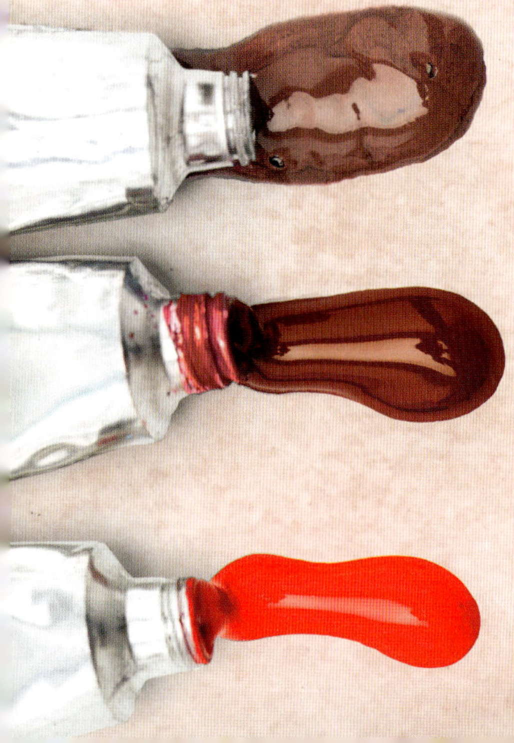

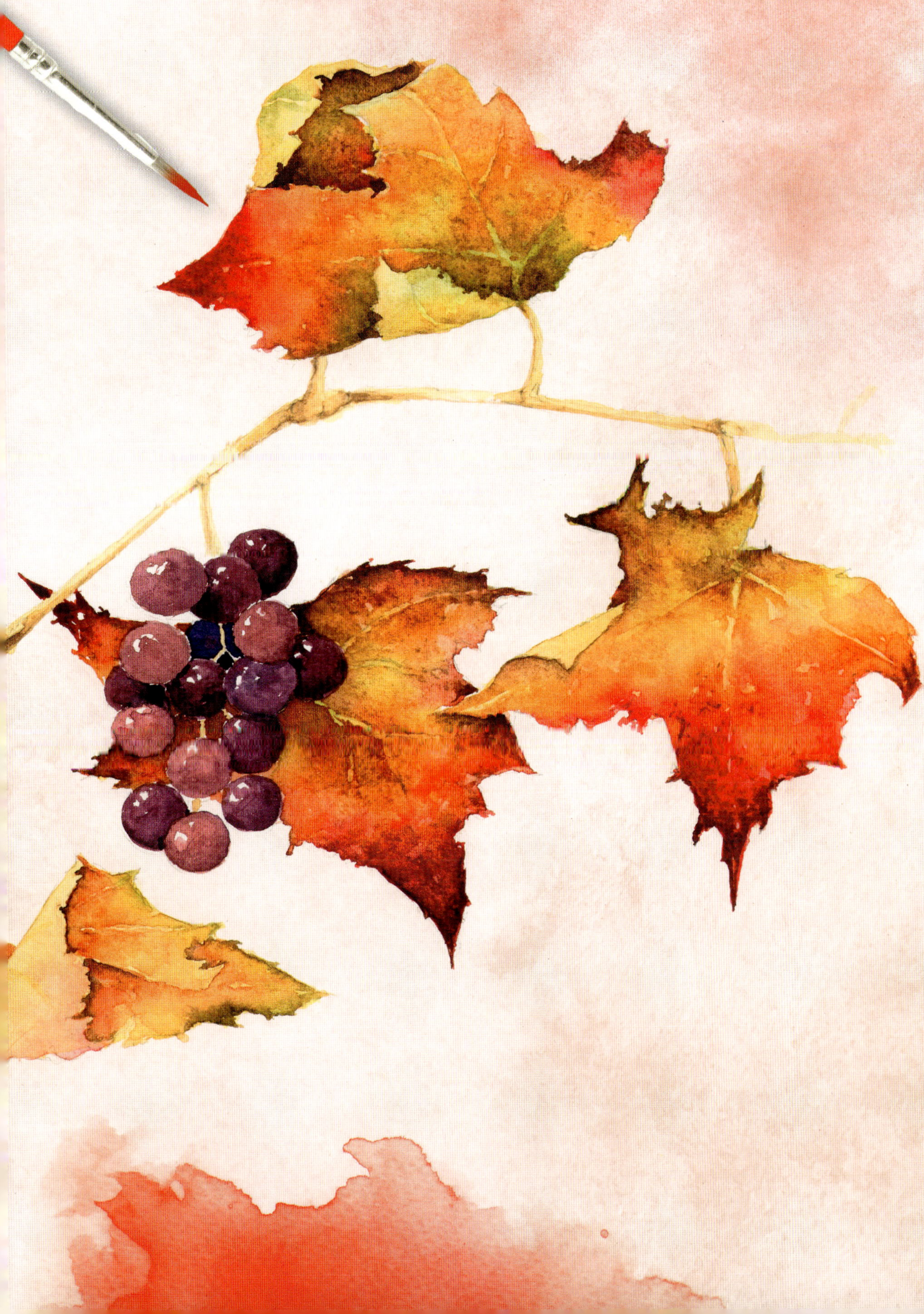

# Red paints

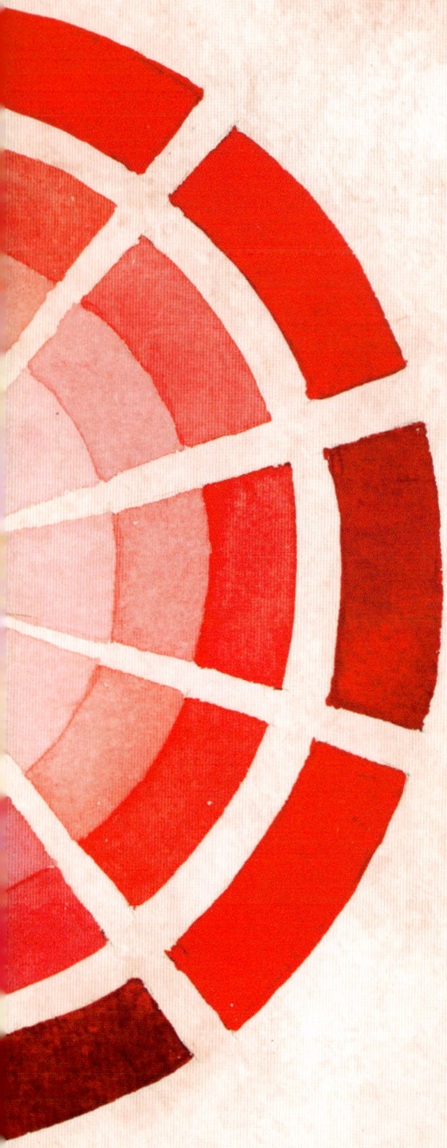

It can be difficult to gauge red paints in their raw, undiluted state, as they all look very similar. Only the darker paints that tend towards purple seem to stand out. Once diluted, however, many differences become evident. Generally, they are complex, vibrant and powerful paints and are, therefore, perhaps one of the most difficult color families to paint with. As some are essentially dyes, use with care and a light touch. A little will go a long way and their influence on surrounding colors is extensive.

One of the most glaring aspects of the red Light and Dark color mixing chart is just how "cold" many of the red paints appear when not used in conjunction with yellows and oranges.

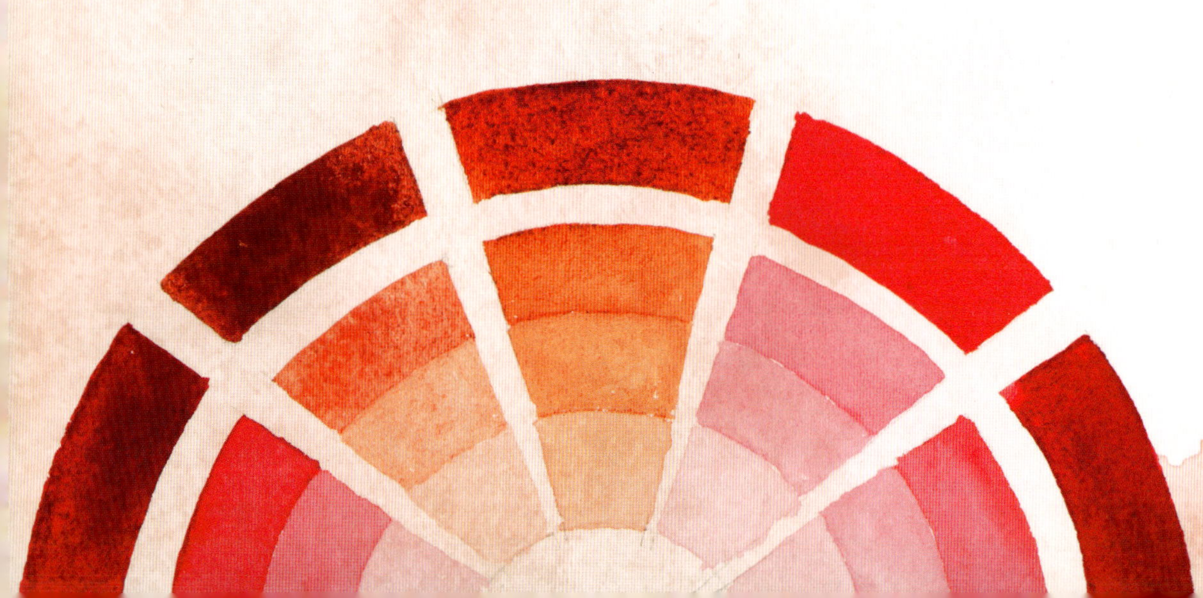

***Now to explore some of the natural characteristics and key features of red paints. I am using a selection commonly found in art stores.***

**QUINACRIDONE RED** is a strong dye, originally developed for the automobile industry. Like Alizarin Crimson, it tends towards blue, but noticeably more so when diluted. It dilutes well however and is a good, although potentially overpowering, mixer.

**CADMIUM RED** is very similar in appearance to Winsor Red, but possibly a little warmer, and is closer in its raw state to Scarlet Lake. It mixes very well and has good diluting qualities.

**PERMANENT ROSE**, as the name suggests, is a thin, luminous pink with a cool blue undertone, yet it holds sufficient "redness" to be included in this category. Its value in creating color in flower borders is undeniable, but otherwise it does have its limitations.

**WINSOR RED** has a very wide tonal range when diluted. This can change from a very light pink to the deepest, impenetrable red at the other end of the scale. It is a medium range, strong and solid red.

**ALIZARIN CRIMSON** has a slight tendency towards blue and is an ideal companion to Ultramarine (blue) which I personally use for creating shadows in hot climates. It has very good covering power.

**SCARLET LAKE** is a bit of a "people pleaser." It has a tendency towards blue and is usually classified as a "cold" color but can be used for creating warm shadows when mixed with Ultramarine. It has good covering power.

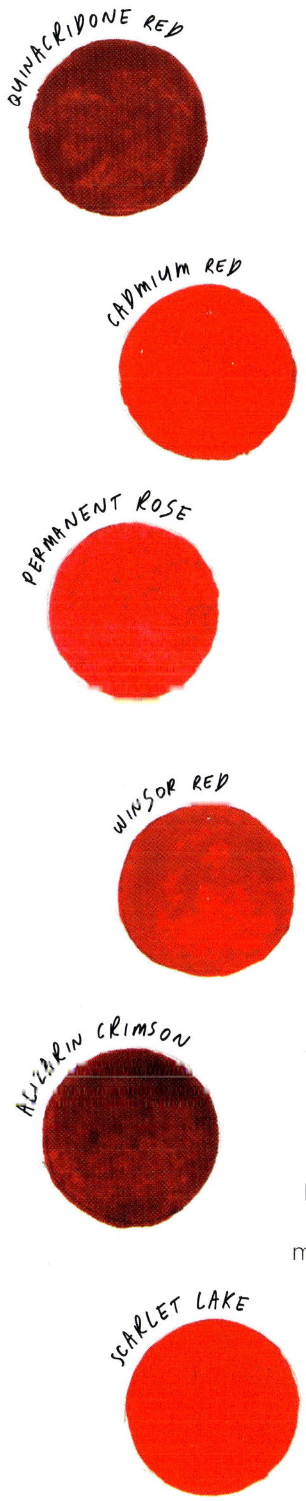
QUINACRIDONE RED
CADMIUM RED
PERMANENT ROSE
WINSOR RED
ALIZARIN CRIMSON
SCARLET LAKE

These six reds provide you with many different mixing possibilities.

***This chart illustrates ways in which you can test your red paints to see how they perform when diluted or darkened.***

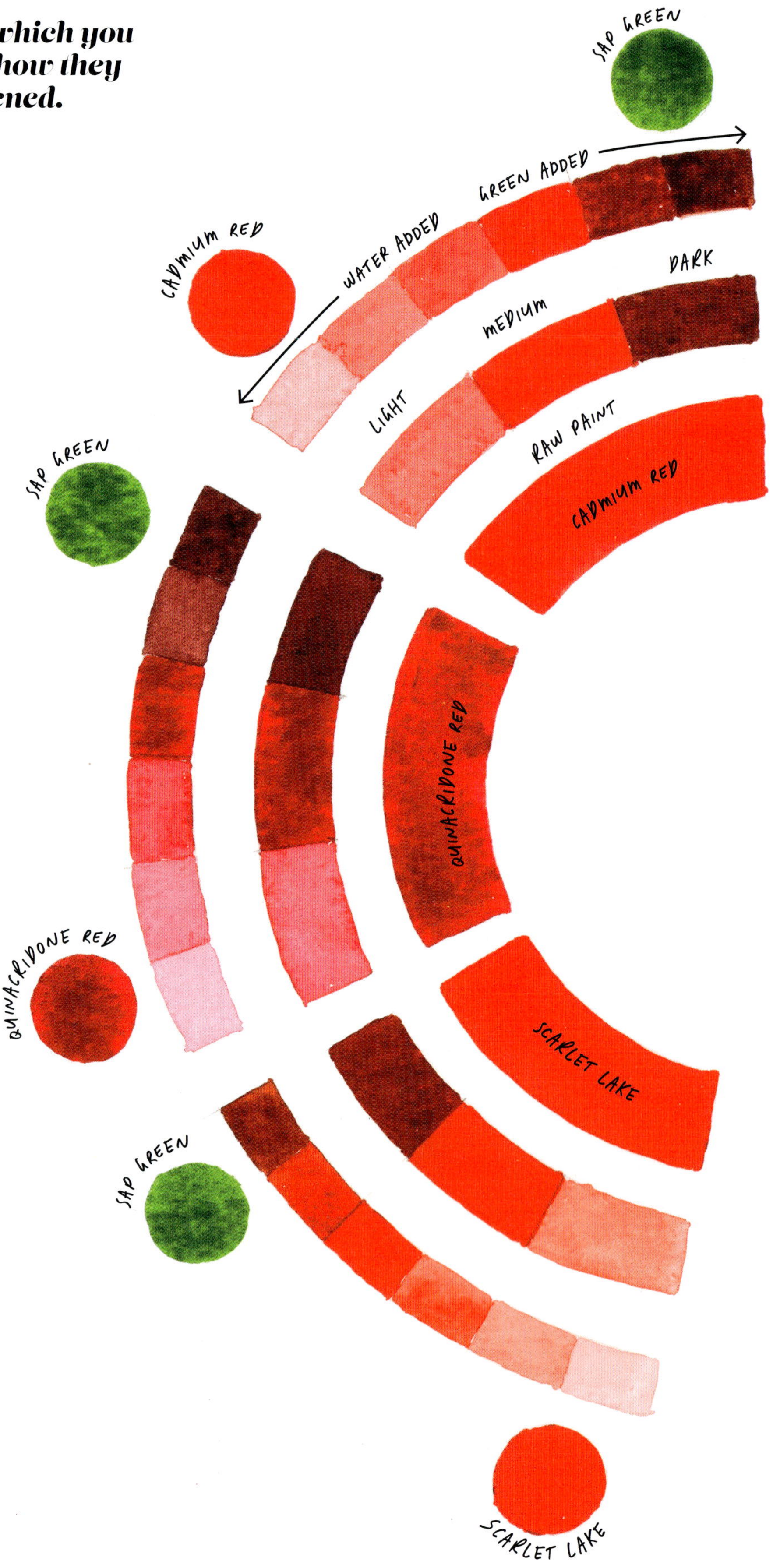
SAP GREEN
GREEN ADDED
CADMIUM RED
WATER ADDED
DARK
MEDIUM
LIGHT
RAW PAINT
CADMIUM RED
SAP GREEN
QUINACRIDONE RED
QUINACRIDONE RED
SCARLET LAKE
SAP GREEN
SCARLET LAKE

## LIGHT AND DARK

This chart explores how far you may take the tonal range of red paints, as well as how they respond to being lightened and darkened. The three divisions – light, medium and dark tones – are your starting point. Next, subdivide these further. This offers a clear view of how each particular red works when adding water to lighten it, or a touch of its complementary color to make it darker. The outer ring is further divided into six light and dark variations, illustrating how far you might be able to push the tonal qualities. You are unlikely to use more than six variations of any one color in a single painting.

For the complementary color I have used Sap Green. This is my default green – an uncomplicated, mid-tone, warmish green which is easy to use and control.

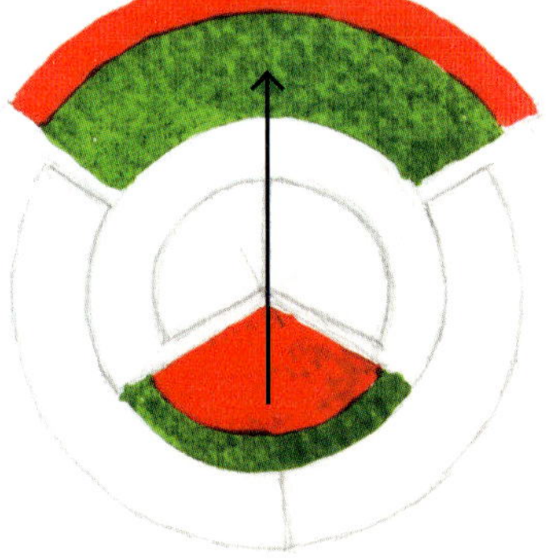

As complementary colors, the secondary color green will always be opposite red on the color wheel.

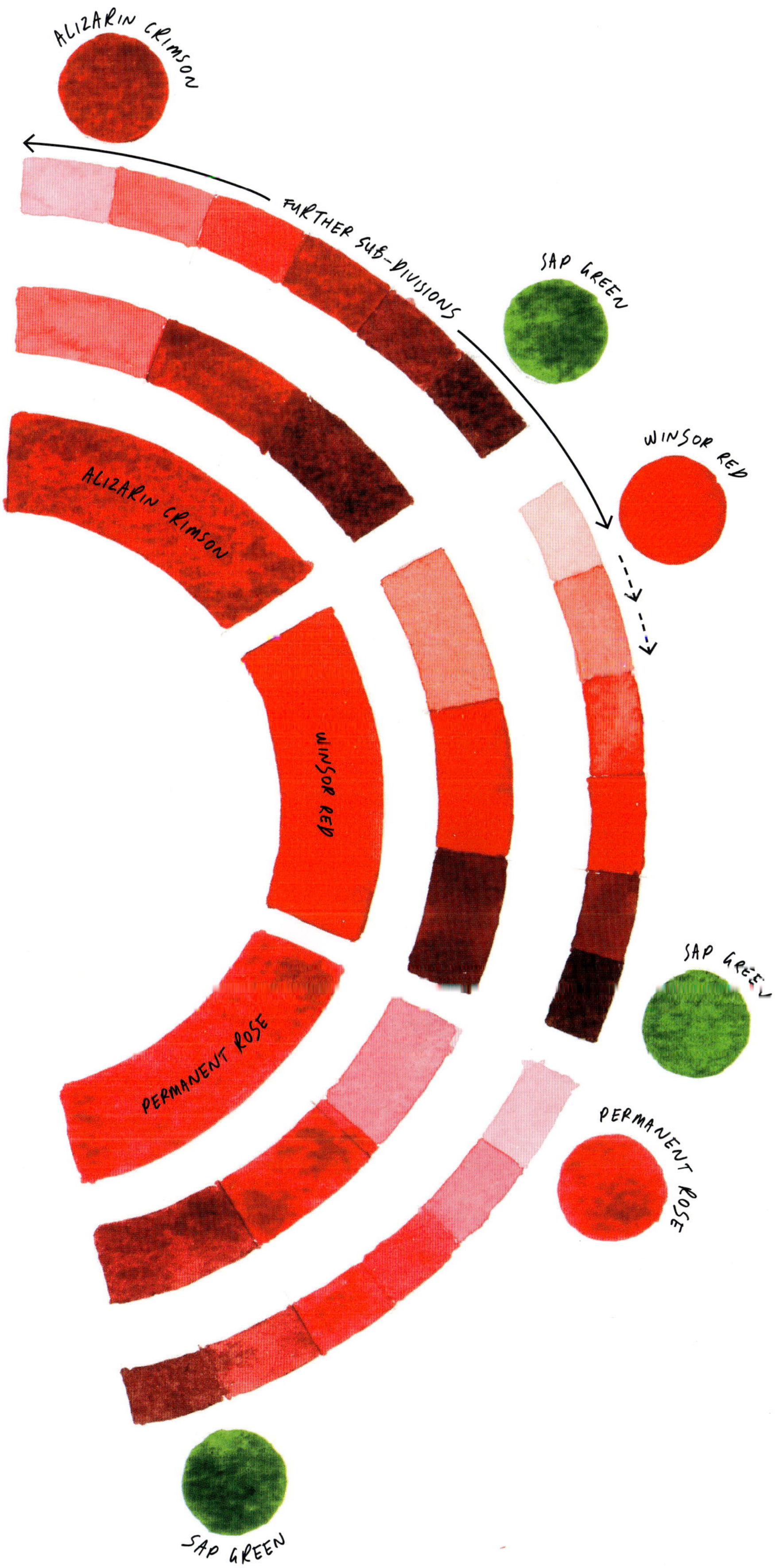
ALIZARIN CRIMSON
FURTHER SUB-DIVISIONS
SAP GREEN
WINSOR RED
ALIZARIN CRIMSON
WINSOR RED
SAP GREEN
PERMANENT ROSE
PERMANENT ROSE
SAP GREEN

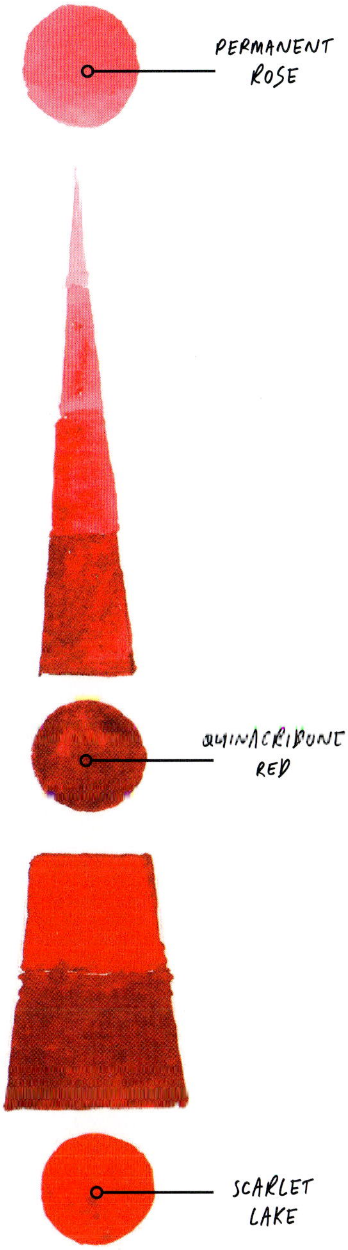
PERMANENT ROSE
QUINACRIDONE RED
SCARLET LAKE

This column explores the tonal range created using three different reds and no green. From very light Permanent Rose, down through the mid-range Quinacridone Red using only water, the color is then darkened using Scarlet Lake.

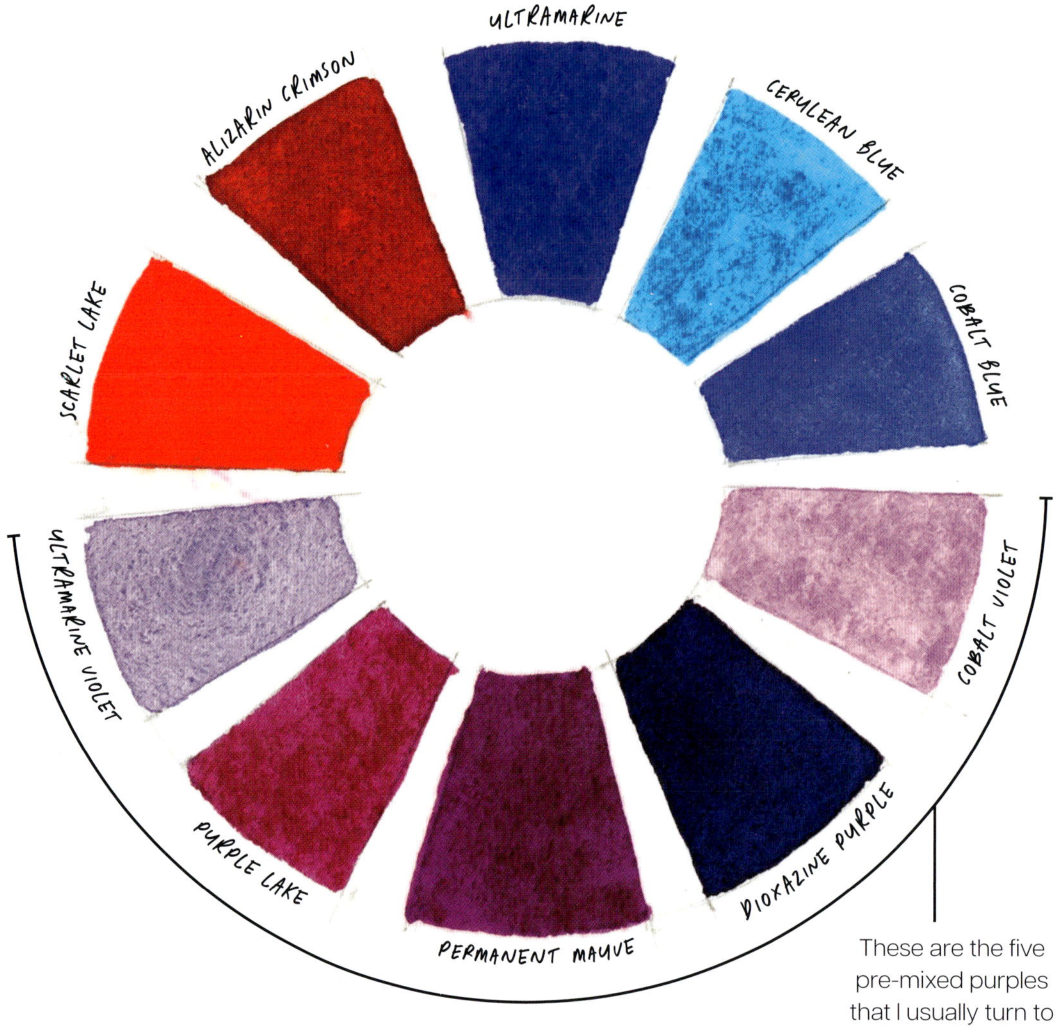
ULTRAMARINE
CERULEAN BLUE
COBALT BLUE
COBALT VIOLET
DIOXAZINE PURPLE
PERMANENT MAUVE
PURPLE LAKE
ULTRAMARINE VIOLET
SCARLET LAKE
ALIZARIN CRIMSON

These are the five pre-mixed purples that I usually turn to for their reliablility.

***The next four pages explore the differences between mixing your own purples using red and blue, and using pre-mixed purples as a "stepping off" point.***

## COLORS FOR MIXING PURPLE

This wheel is composed of the colors that I personally like to use in mixing purples. In these charts, again, I have used ready-mixed, shop-bought purples as my central starting point. Purple Lake makes its first appearance alongside the frequently used Dioxazine Purple. Purple Lake tends towards red in its raw state, while Dioxazine Purple leans towards the blue end of the color spectrum.

## MIXING RED AND BLUE

Purple is a color that does not often appear in its raw state in nature. You will find a few fruits and animal feathers, but little else of substance. For this reason, we will often use purple as a mixer or a color to add to others to influence their overall appearance.

So, it is important to "get the feel" for which purples need more red in their composition, and which need more blue. As always, mixing your own paints is more likely to help you find the color you require, allowing you to judge how warm, cold, gentle or intense your purples will be.

1. Scarlet Lake gradually added to Ultramarine
2. Alizarin Crimson gradually added to Cerulean Blue
3. Purple Lake gradually added to Ultramarine
4. Alizarin Crimson gradually added to Dioxazine Purple

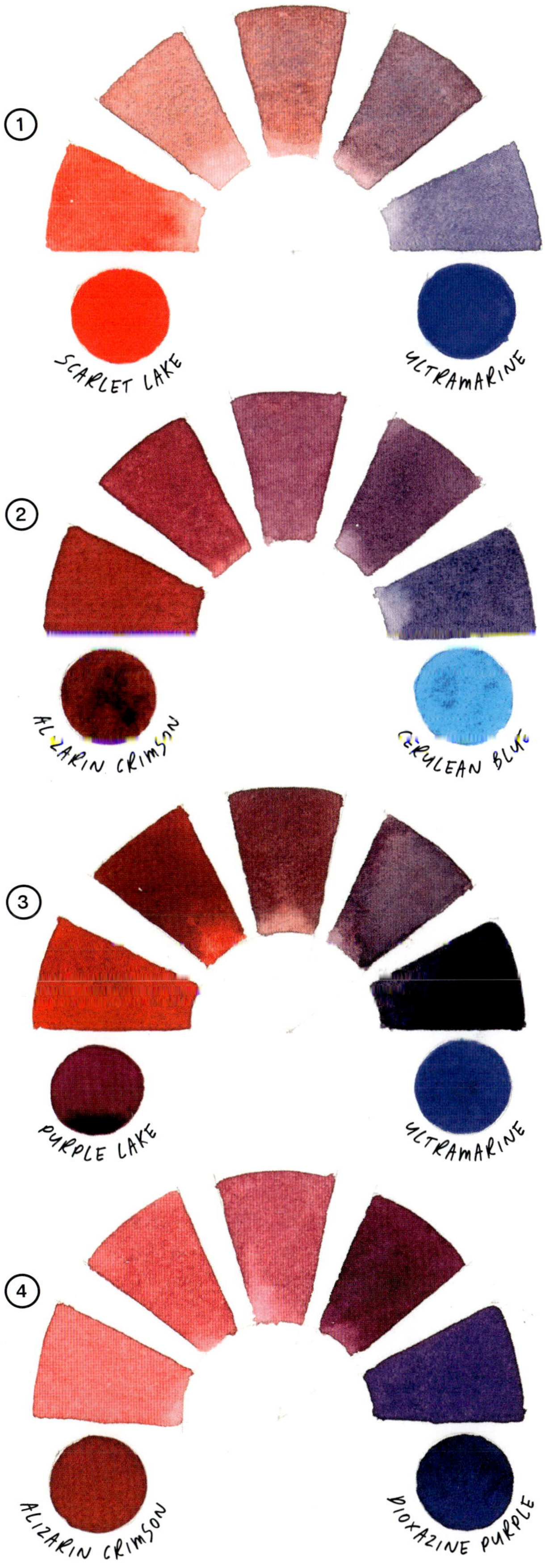
1
SCARLET LAKE
ULTRAMARINE
2
ALIZARIN CRIMSON
CERULEAN BLUE
3
PURPLE LAKE
ULTRAMARINE
4
ALIZARIN CRIMSON
DIOXAZINE PURPLE

**_Now it's time to expand the choice of purples available to us by using a couple of pre-mixed purples – Purple Lake and Dioxazine Purple._**

## MIXING THE RIGHT COLOR

Here I have used reds and blues to modify the different types of purple that can be created when mixed with either of the two shop-bought colors. Again, the contrast between the variations in tones created by mixing with these two paints, and the purples mixed using assorted reds and blues is notable. The pre-mixed paints assist in the creation of some strong and vibrant colors while the red and blue mixes appear dull in comparison, with some almost tending towards gray.

The central column looks at how two of the lesser used purples work when mixed with members of their own families of origin. Cobalt Violet is a thin, light paint that appears to have a chalky appearance when mixed with its relative, Cobalt Blue. Ultramarine Violet is so blue that it doesn't change dramatically when mixed with its relative, Ultramarine (blue). This doesn't mean that it has no practical application – it is best used when subtlety of tone is required.

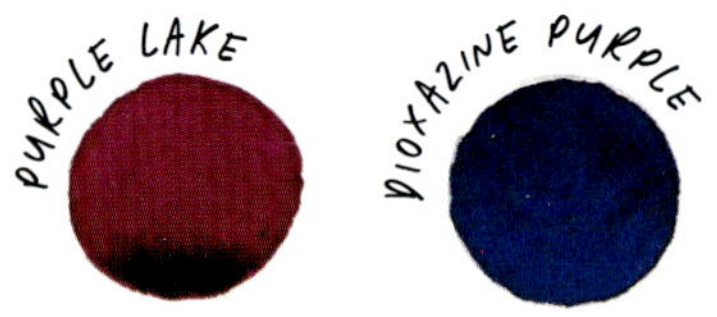
PURPLE LAKE
DIOXAZINE PURPLE

These two paints were chosen as mixers precisely for their different qualities. Purple Lake has a sharp, near acidic feel to it while Dioxazine Purple has a much warmer appearance.

**PUSHING THE LIMITS:** The wide variety of qualities held in the red and blue paints I have chosen here will allow you to really push the limits of your color mixing practice.

1. Reds added to Purple Lake
2. Blues added to Purple Lake
3. Reds added to Dioxazine Purple
4. Blues added to Dioxazine Purple

*"Again, the contrast between the variations in tones created by mixing with these two paints, and the purples mixed using assorted reds and blues, is notable."*

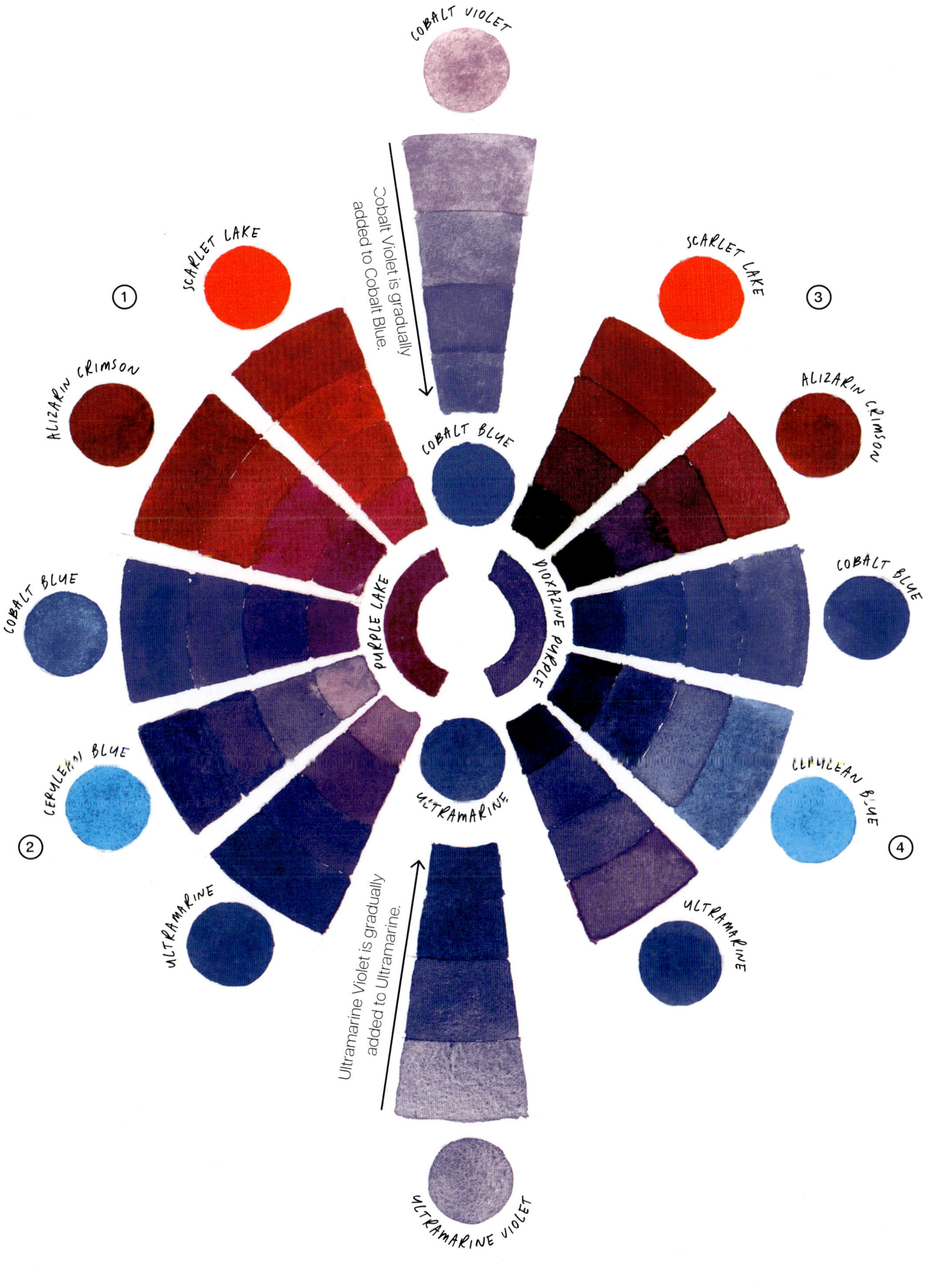
COBALT VIOLET
Cobalt Violet is gradually added to Cobalt Blue.
SCARLET LAKE
1
ALIZARIN CRIMSON
SCARLET LAKE
3
ALIZARIN CRIMSON
COBALT BLUE
PURPLE LAKE
DIOXAZINE PURPLE
COBALT BLUE
COBALT BLUE
BLUE
2
ULTRAMARINE
ULTRAMARINE
4
ULTRAMARINE
Ultramarine Violet is gradually added to Ultramarine.
ULTRAMARINE VIOLET

***Having explored how some of the best purples can be created, we now need to explore ways in which these purples might be made darker.***

## DARKENING THE TONE

The pre-mixed purples half-way along the columns are the starting points here.

(1) In the middle of the column is a mixture of Purple Lake and Cerulean Blue, lightened towards the inner circle by adding increasingly diluted Cerulean Blue (more water added for each section). Moving outwards from the center mixture, pure Purple Lake is added to the mix, darkening the color in stages. Cadmium Yellow is added at the very last stages.

(2) In the middle of the column is a mixture of Purple Lake and Ultramarine. Increasing quantities of diluted Ultramarine are added in stages towards the center of the circle. Moving outwards from the middle mix, pure Purple Lake is added to the mix in stages with Cadmium Yellow being added at the final stages.

(3) In the middle of the column is a mixture of Purple Lake and Phthalocyanine Blue. Increasing quantities of diluted blue are added towards the center, lightening the tone. Moving outwards, increasing quantities of Purple Lake are added, darkening the tone. Cadmium Yellow is added at the final stages darkening the purple as much as I dared.

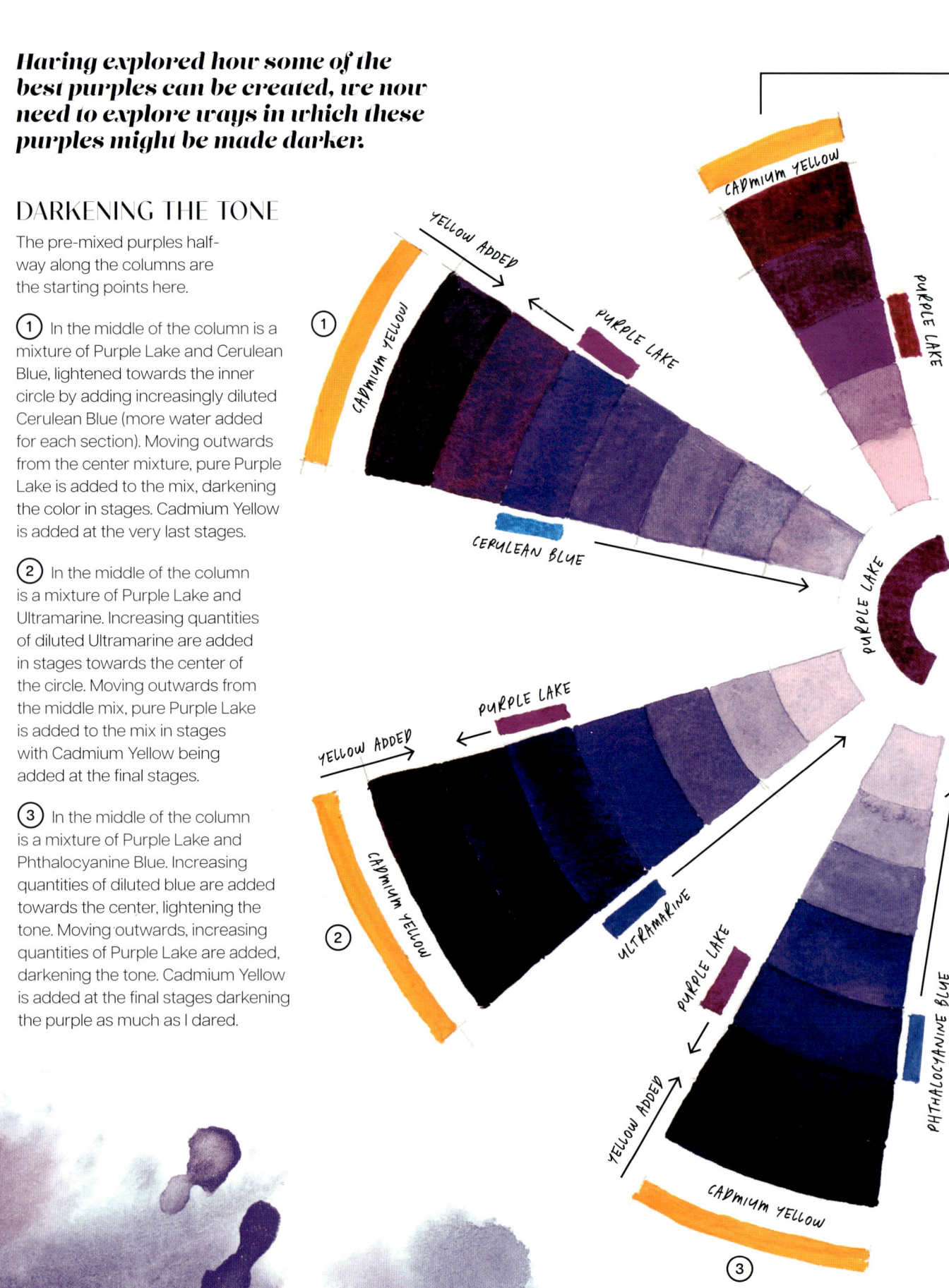

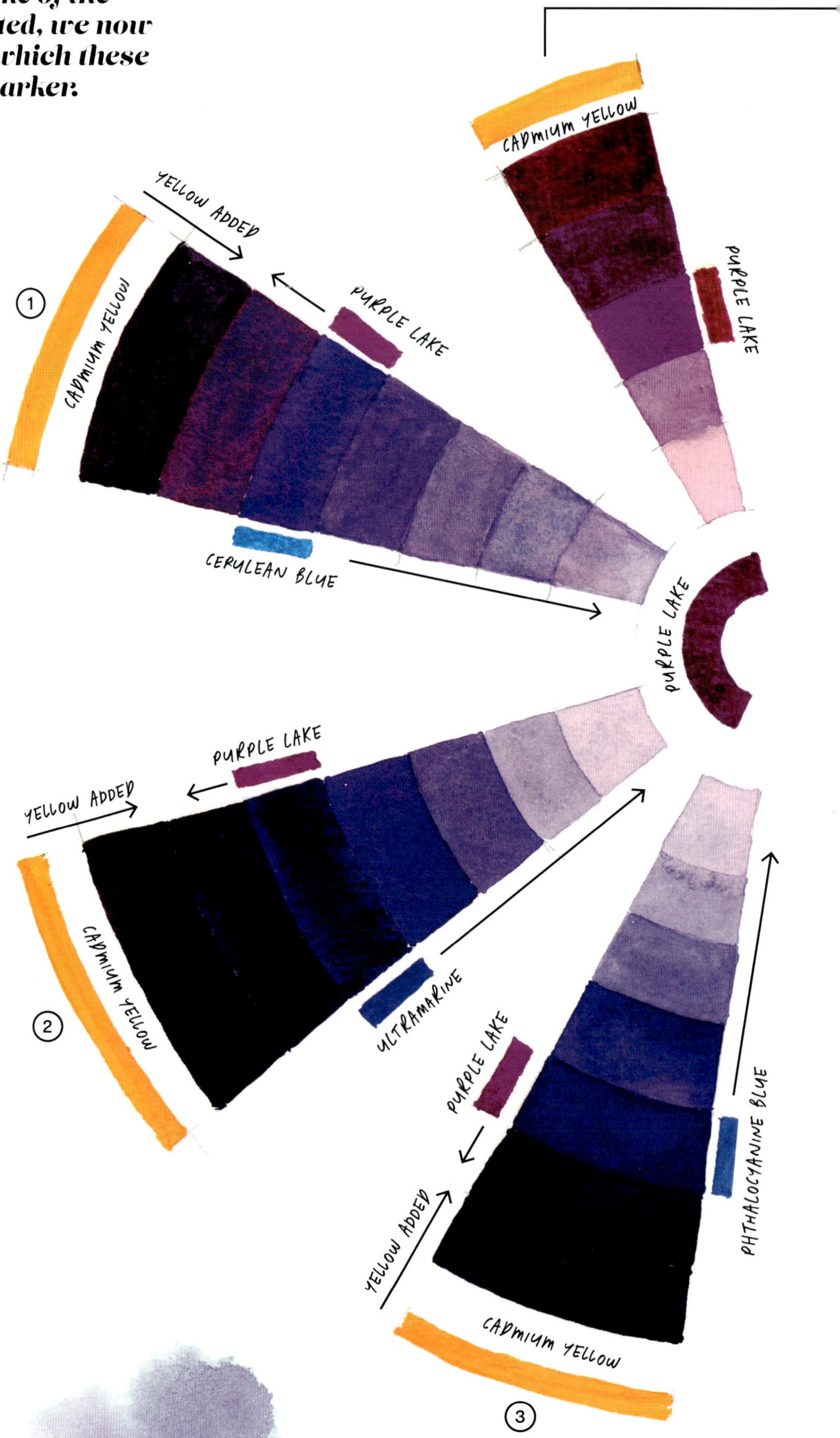

CADMIUM YELLOW
PURPLE LAKE
YELLOW ADDED
1
CADMIUM YELLOW
PURPLE LAKE
CERULEAN BLUE
PURPLE LAKE
PURPLE LAKE
YELLOW ADDED
CADMIUM YELLOW
2
ULTRAMARINE
PURPLE LAKE
PHTHALOCYANINE BLUE
YELLOW ADDED
CADMIUM YELLOW
3

## COMPLEMENTARY COLORS AND WATER

These columns explore just how far I could take raw Purple Lake and Dioxazine Purple by adding our chosen yellow (the complementary color to purple) in one direction, and diluting with water in the other.

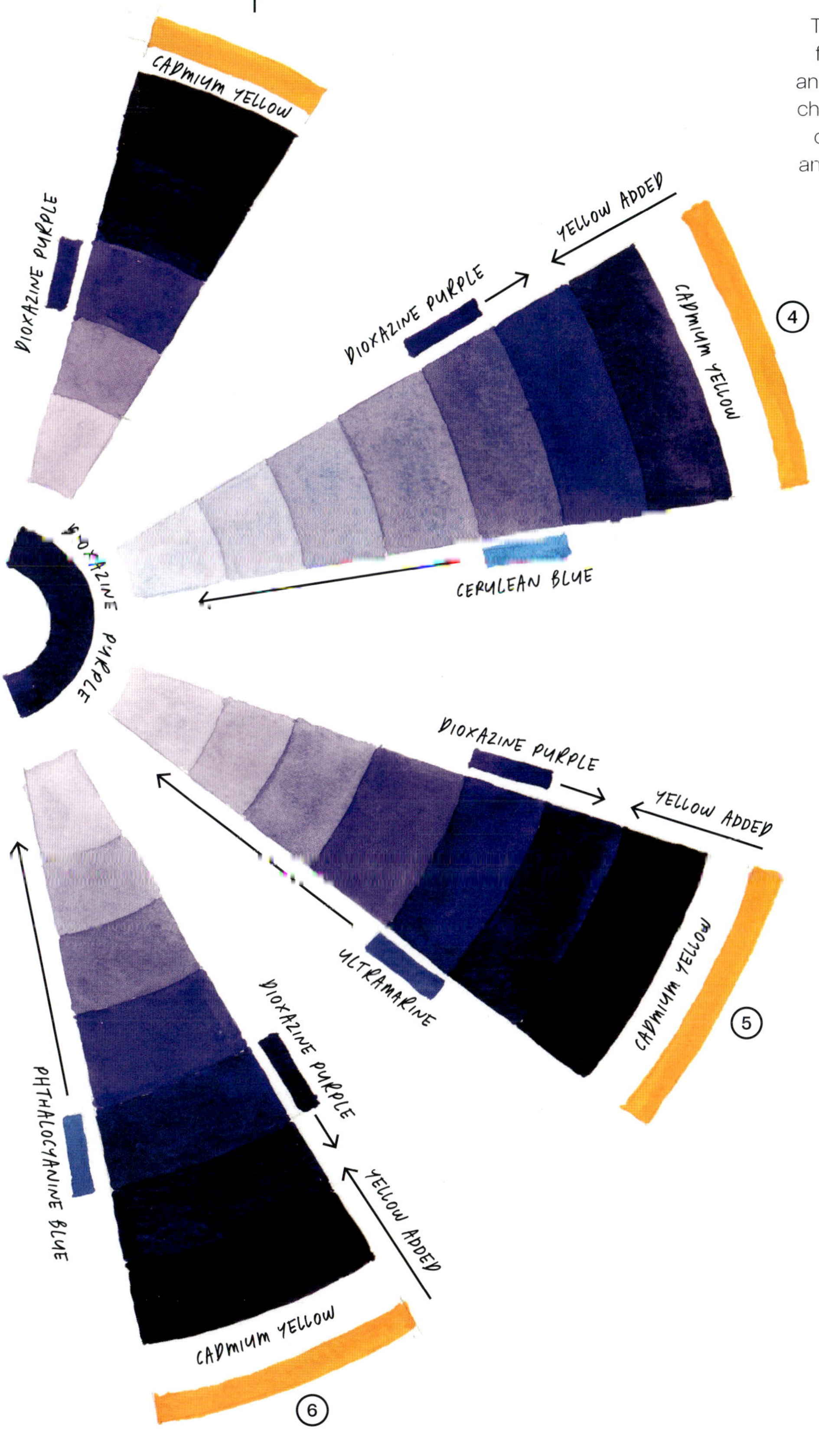
CADMIUM YELLOW
DIOXAZINE PURPLE
YELLOW ADDED
DIOXAZINE PURPLE
CADMIUM YELLOW
4
CERULEAN BLUE
DIOXAZINE PURPLE
DIOXAZINE PURPLE
YELLOW ADDED
ULTRAMARINE
CADMIUM YELLOW
5
DIOXAZINE PURPLE
PHTHALOCYANINE BLUE
YELLOW ADDED
CADMIUM YELLOW
6

(4) In the middle of the column is a mixture of Dioxazine Purple and Cerulean Blue, lightened towards the inner circle by adding increasingly diluted Cerulean Blue. Moving outwards from the middle mixture, pure Dioxazine Purple is added to the mix, darkening the color in stages. Cadmium Yellow is added at the very last stages.

(5) In the middle of the column is a mixture of Dioxazine Purple and Ultramarine. Increasing amounts of diluted Ultramarine are added in stages towards the center of the circle. Moving outwards from the middle mix, pure Dioxazine Purple is added to the mix in stages with Cadmium Yellow being added at the final stages.

(6) In the middle of the column is a mixture of Dioxazine Purple and Phthalocyanine Blue. Increasing quantities of diluted blue are added towards the center, lightening the tone. Moving outwards, increasing quantities of Dioxazine Purple are added, darkening the tone. Cadmium Yellow is added at the final stages, darkening the purple without altering its integrity too much.

***This still life uses reds and purples, the fruits casting colored shadows onto the white bowl and tablecloth, a great way to practice the process of creating colored shadows.***

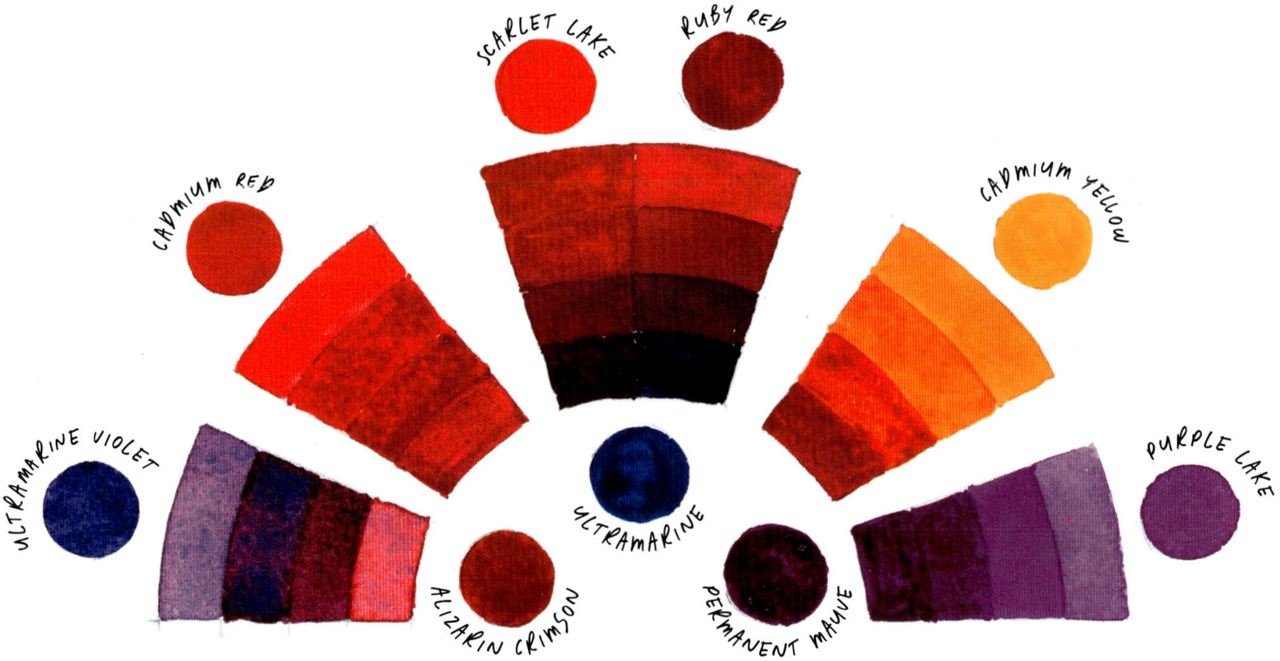
SCARLET LAKE
RUBY RED
CADMIUM RED
CADMIUM YELLOW
ULTRAMARINE VIOLET
ULTRAMARINE
PURPLE LAKE
ALIZARIN CRIMSON
PERMANENT MAUVE

This chart illustrates the range of colors and tones in the still life painting and the colors I used to mix them.

STAGE 1

In this stage the basic shapes and lightest tones of the fruits were created. The white bowl is already starting to take care of itself.

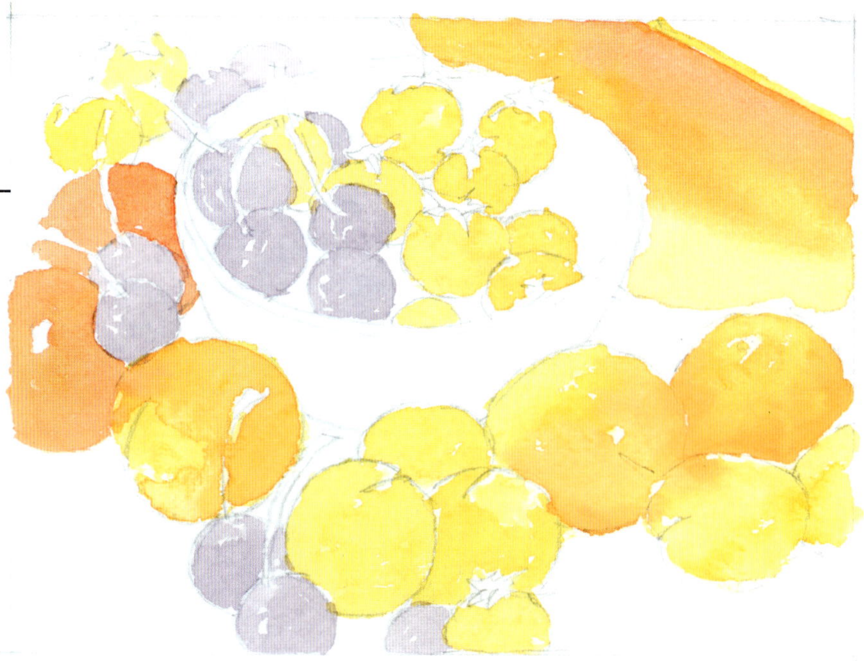

STAGE 2

Here the essential colors were established, and some of the paints allowed to run and bleed into the bowl and white surface.

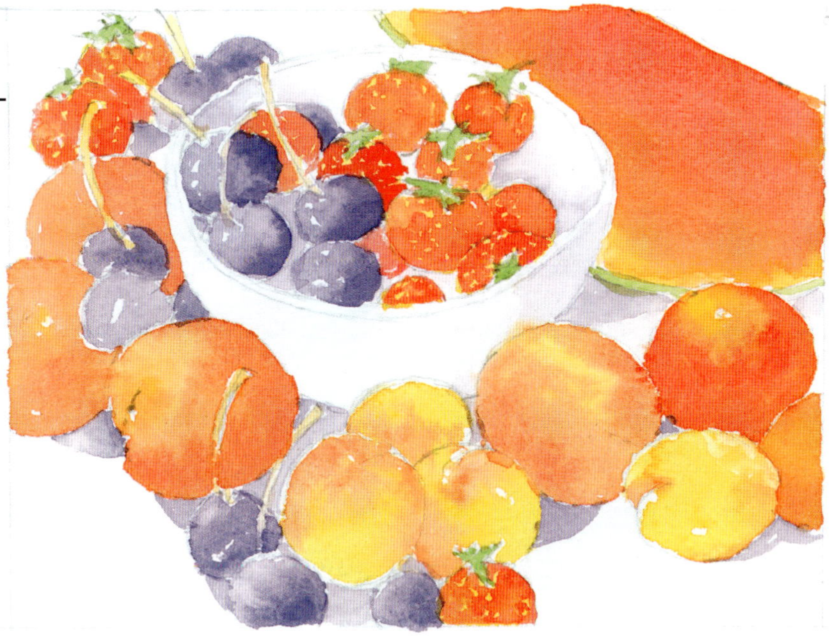

FINAL PAINTING

The shaded sections and shadows were painted in this final stage creating color in the darkest recesses.

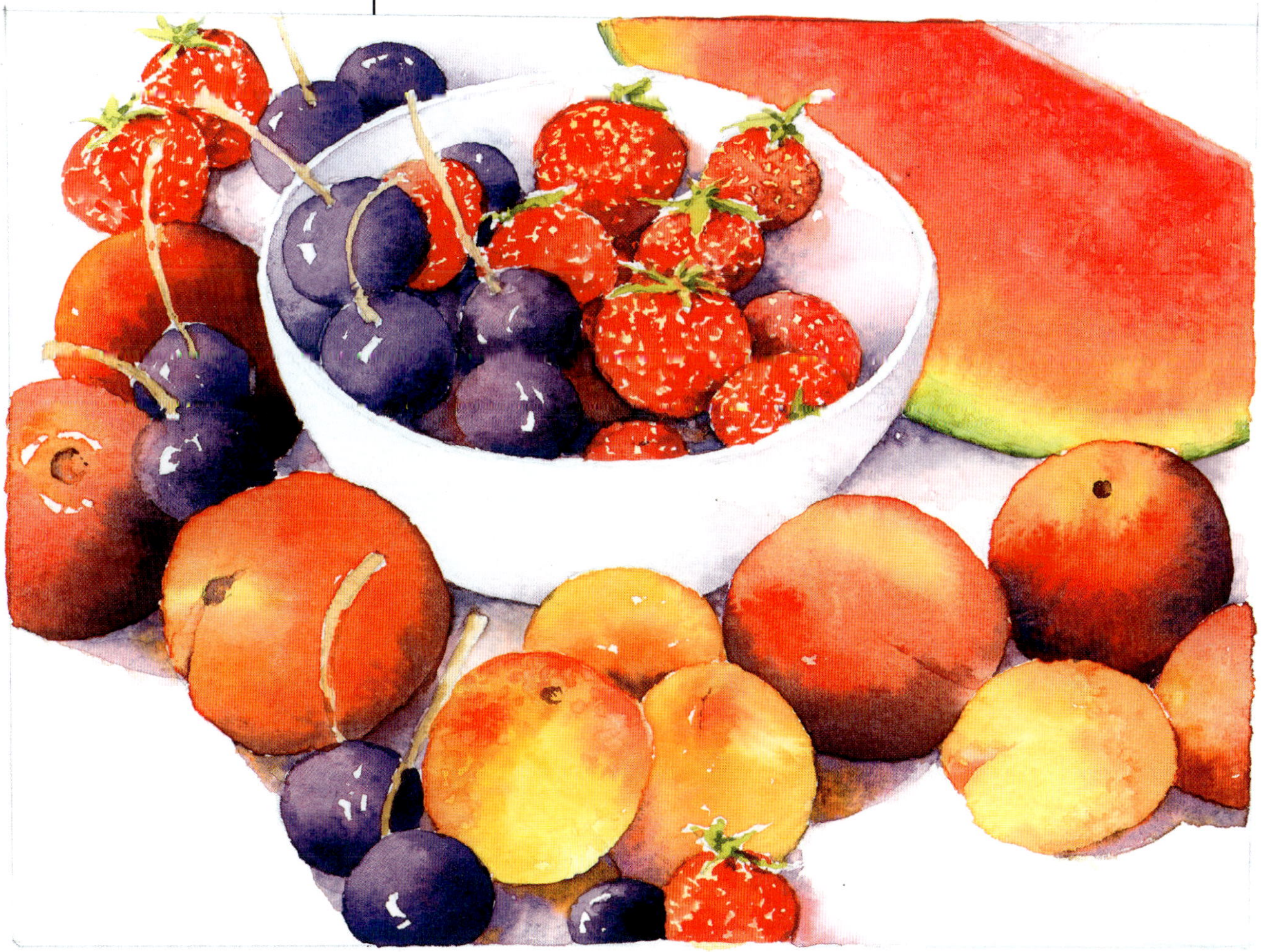

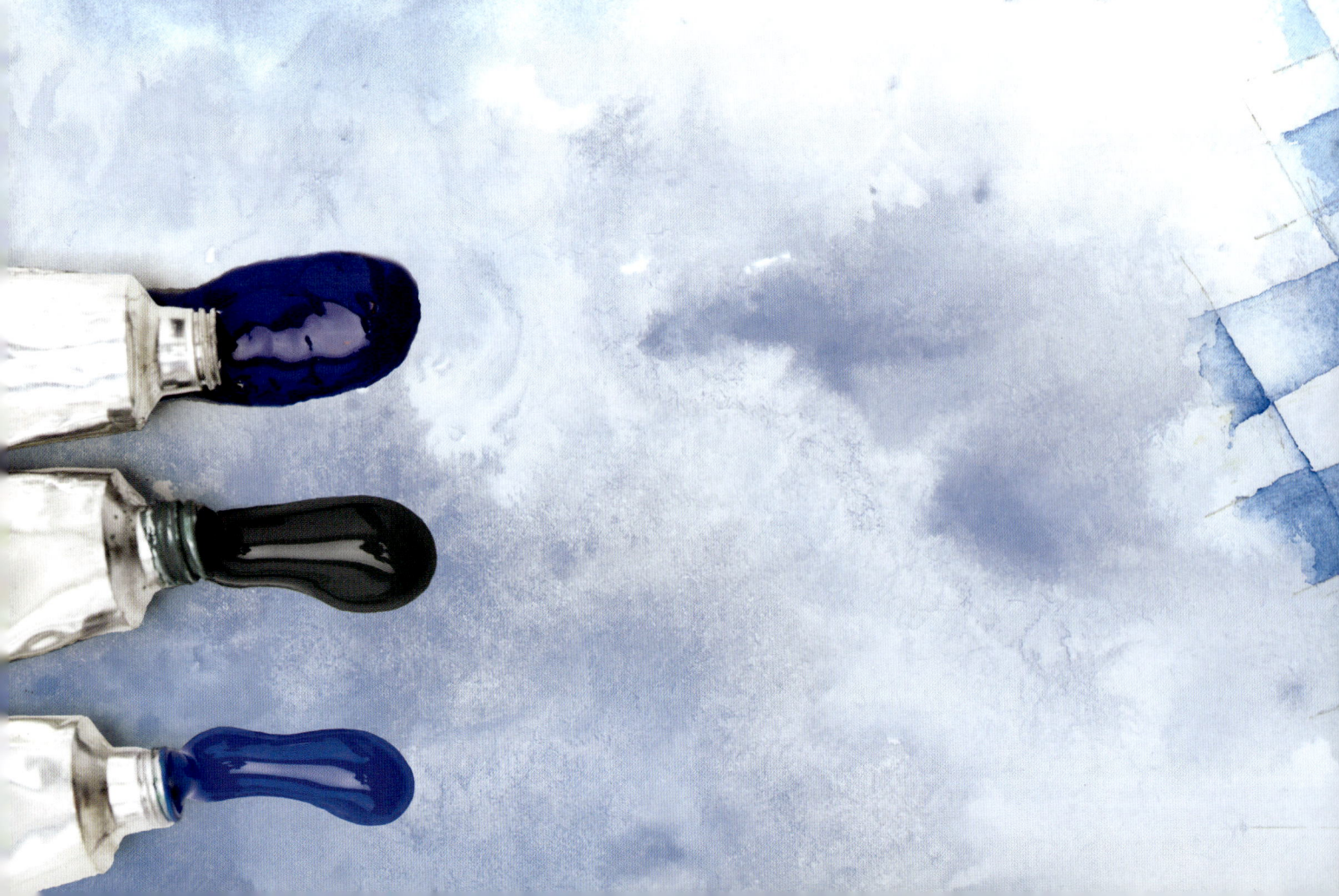

*Color Families:*

# BLUES

Finally in this chapter we will examine a selection of paints that you will find useful for mixing and influencing the feel of other colors. We will move on to explain the role that blues have in mixing greens and the wide variety of these that can be found in nature.

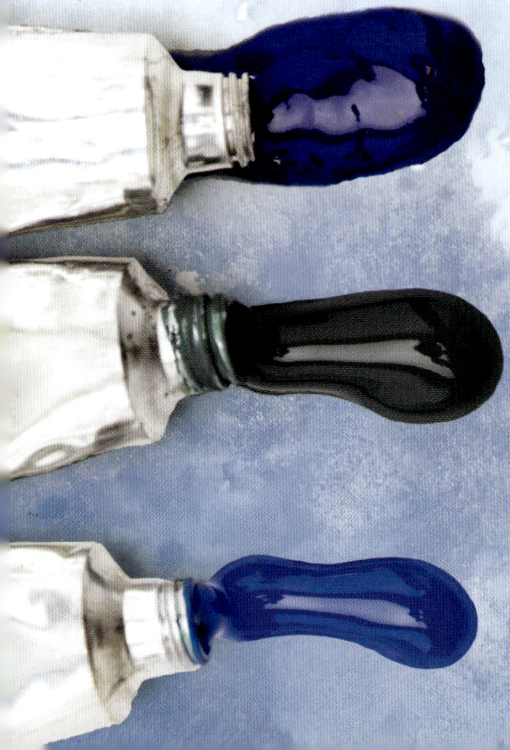

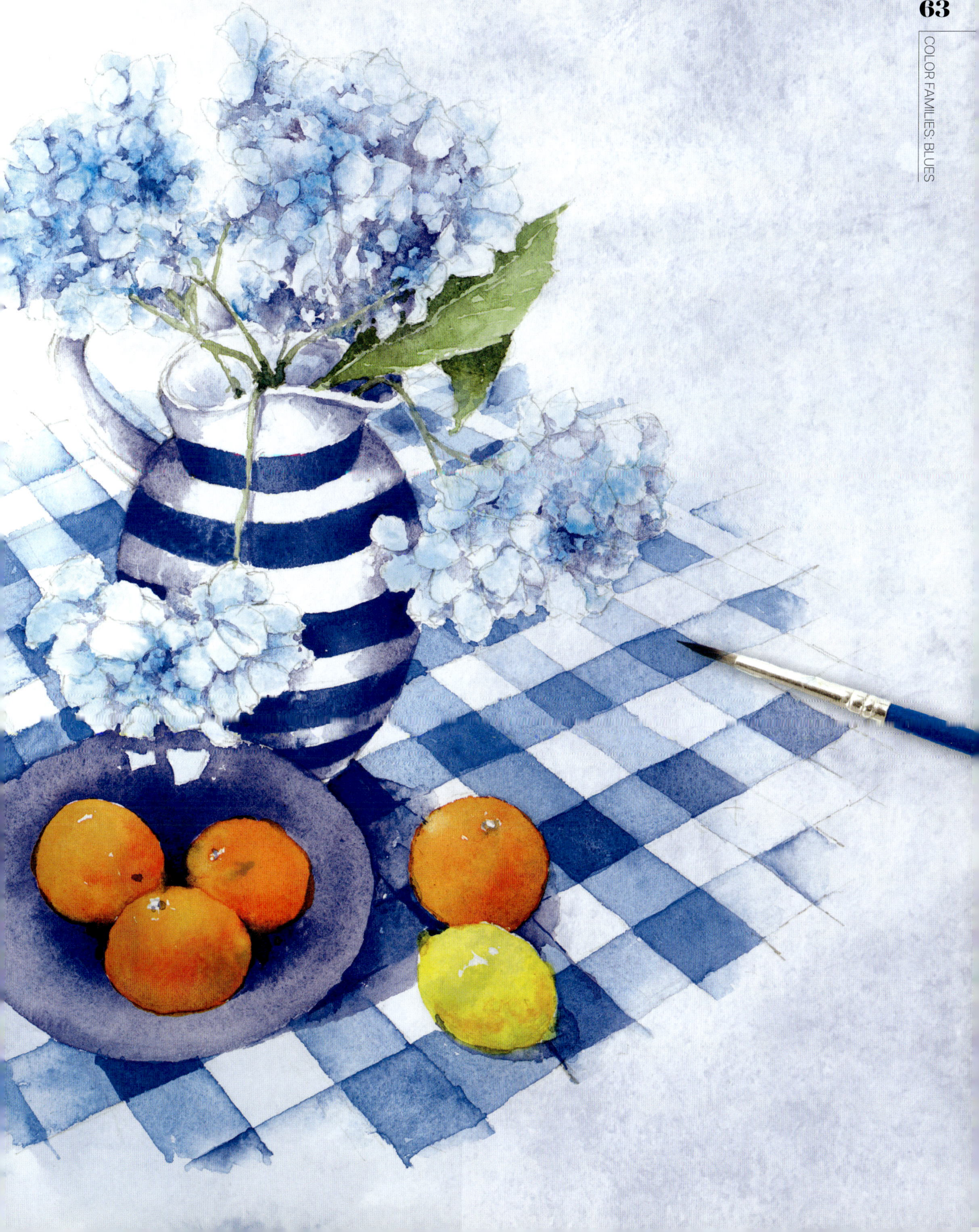

# Blue paints

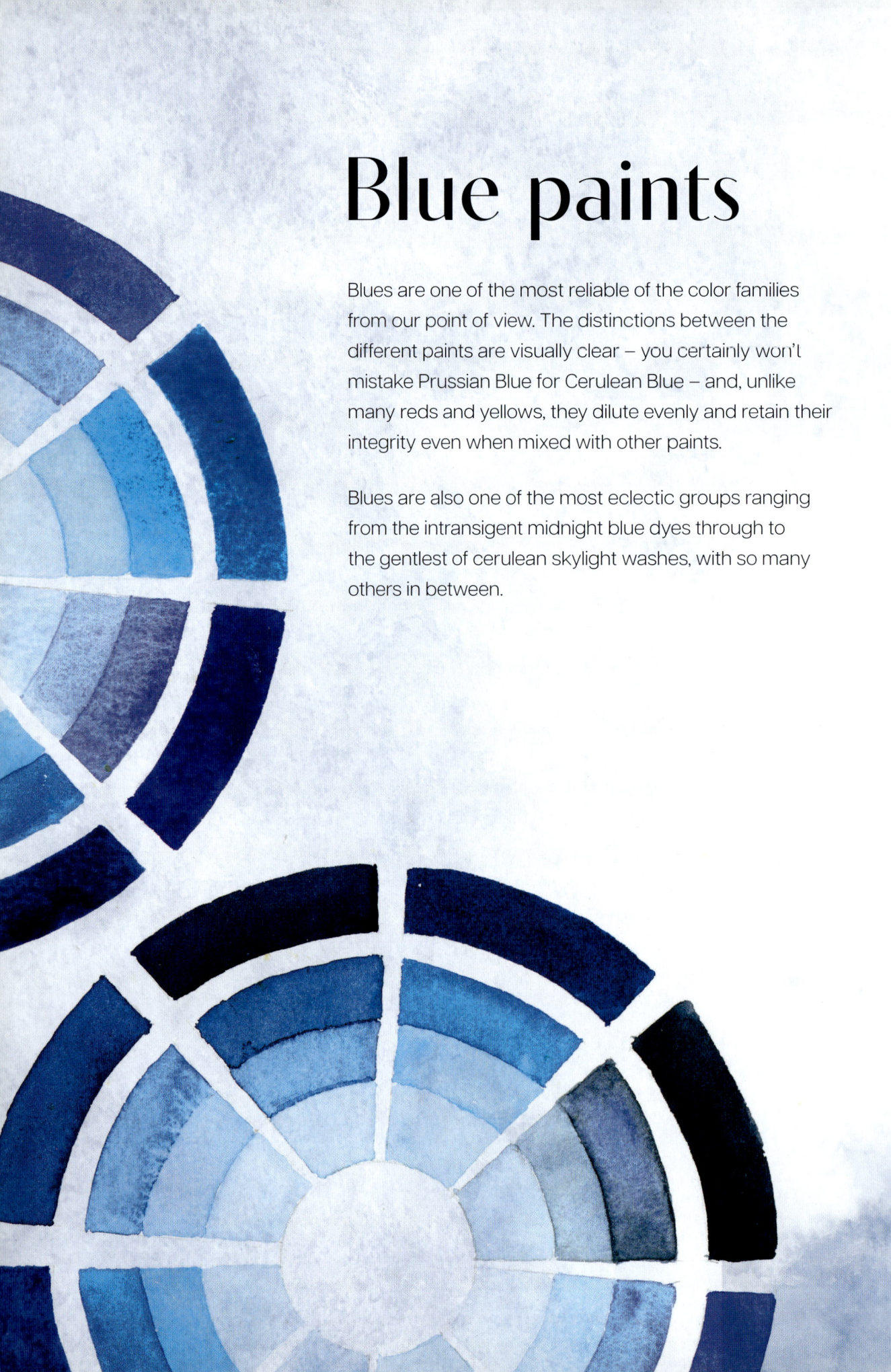

Blues are one of the most reliable of the color families from our point of view. The distinctions between the different paints are visually clear – you certainly won't mistake Prussian Blue for Cerulean Blue – and, unlike many reds and yellows, they dilute evenly and retain their integrity even when mixed with other paints.

Blues are also one of the most eclectic groups ranging from the intransigent midnight blue dyes through to the gentlest of cerulean skylight washes, with so many others in between.

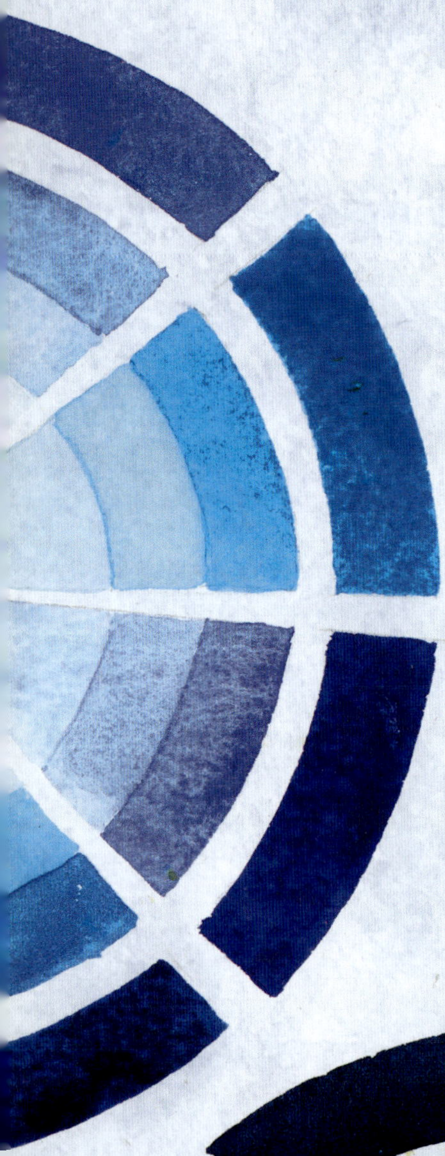

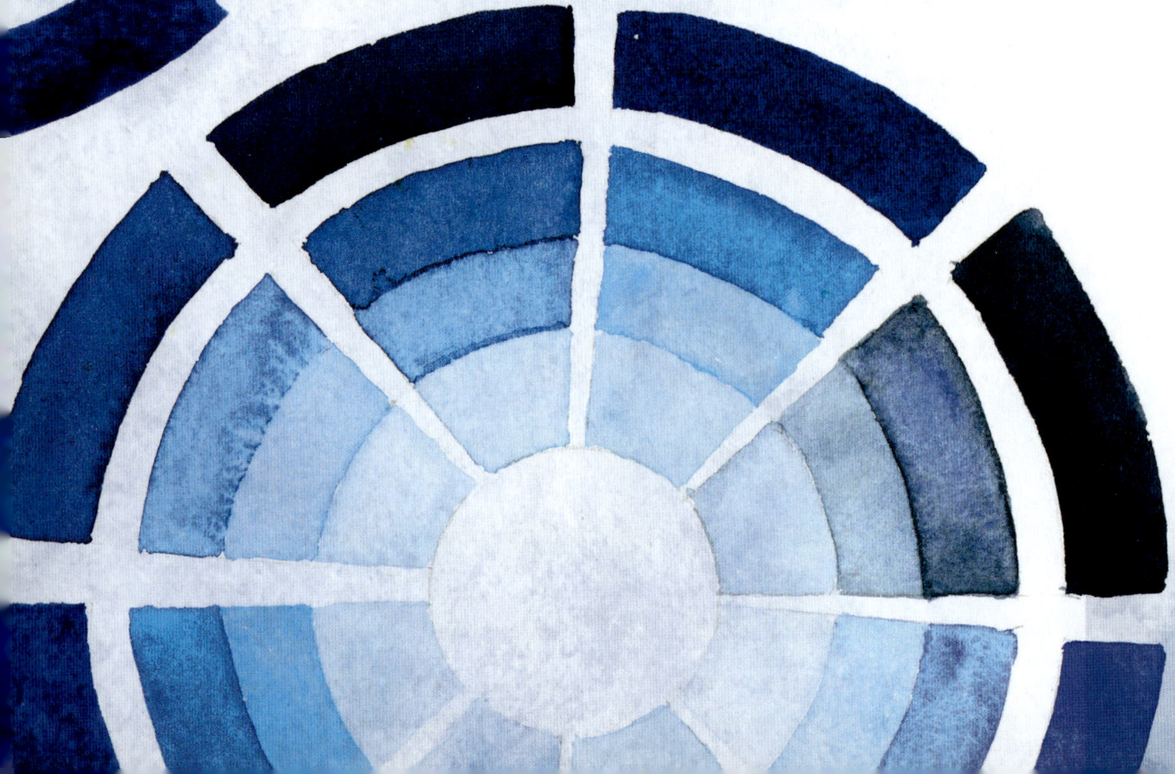

## *Here is the palette of six blues I have chosen for these mixing experiments.*

**PRUSSIAN BLUE** was initially a dye and so requires handling with care. Its cold, dark intensity makes it particularly useful when painting storm-laden skies. It is difficult to control, but a drop of very wet paint onto paper can produce some highly atmospheric results.

**ULTRAMARINE** has been chosen for its warmth, strength and all-round flexibility. A universal performer, it can be relied upon to warm up most situations. It both darkens and lightens well, performing with equilibrium at both ends of the scale. Having its origins in rock (lapis lazuli) it does granulate. This can be an advantage for many subjects, but is not always so good for skies.

**PHTHALOCYANINE BLUE** is quite a cold, clinical blue that tends towards green very quickly, picking up the yellow element of orange, its complementary color. It can be disappointing at the other end of the scale. When diluted, it disappears to almost nothing.

**COBALT BLUE** is included for its medium range qualities and its versatile coverage. It darkens fairly well when mixed with orange, but falls a little flat at the other end of the scale when diluted.

**WINSOR BLUE** is a strong and powerful blue which darkens very easily and quickly. It is hard to imagine a darker tone on the far tonal edges that can still be classified as blue as can be achieved with this paint. This strong, intense blue shares some qualities with Ultramarine but is not as warm.

**CERULEAN BLUE** tends towards green when darkened and, again, appears a little thin when water is added. It is invaluable for sky tones.

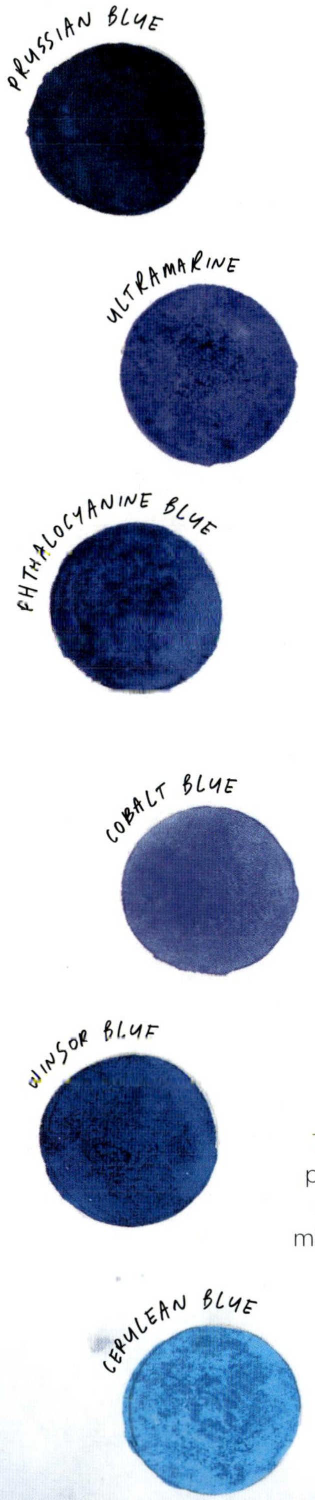
PRUSSIAN BLUE
ULTRAMARINE
PHTHALOCYANINE BLUE
COBALT BLUE
WINSOR BLUE
CERULEAN BLUE

These six blues provide you with many different mixing possibilities.

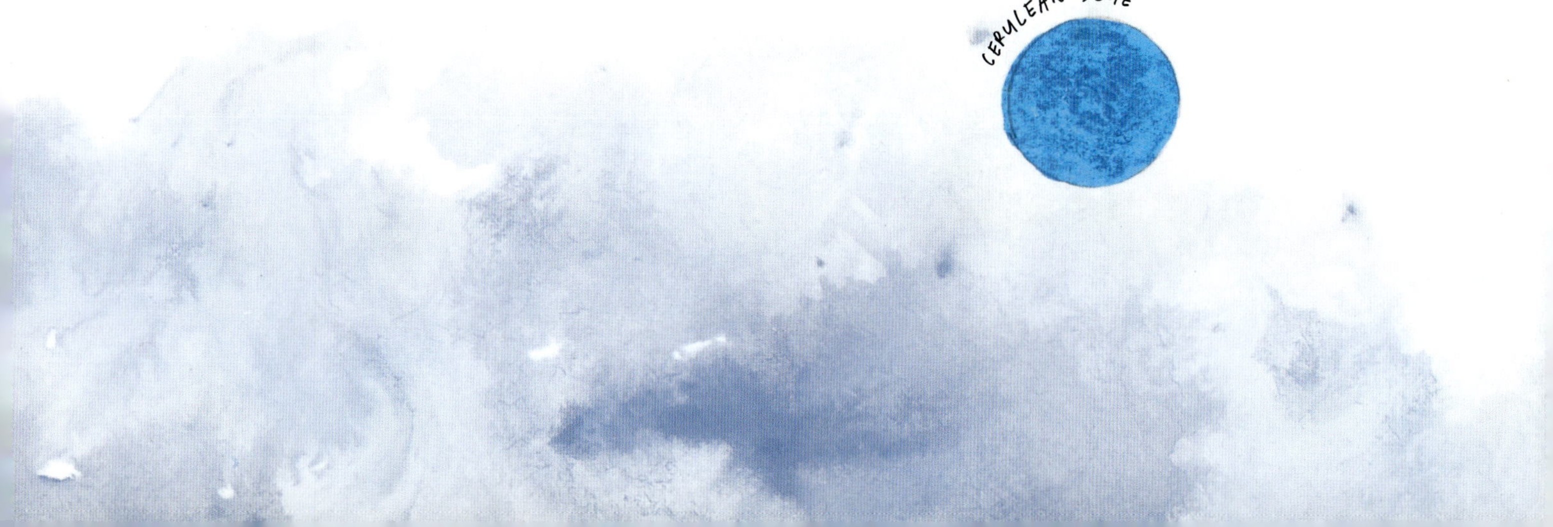

***This chart illustrates ways in which you can test your blue paints to see how they perform when diluted or darkened.***

## LIGHT AND DARK

The six blue raw (straight from the tube) paints are shown around the inner ring. In the middle ring, they have been broken down into light, medium and dark. Try these divisions first to provide a clear view of how each particular blue works when adding water to make it lighter, or a touch of its complementary color (orange) to make it darker. The outer ring is further divided into six light and dark variations, demonstrating how far you might be able to push the tonal qualities. You are unlikely to use more than six variations of any one color in a single painting.

I have chosen Cadmium Orange as the complementary color here for its "what you see is what you get" qualities. It won't overwhelm the blues and will retain its mid-range warmth when mixed.

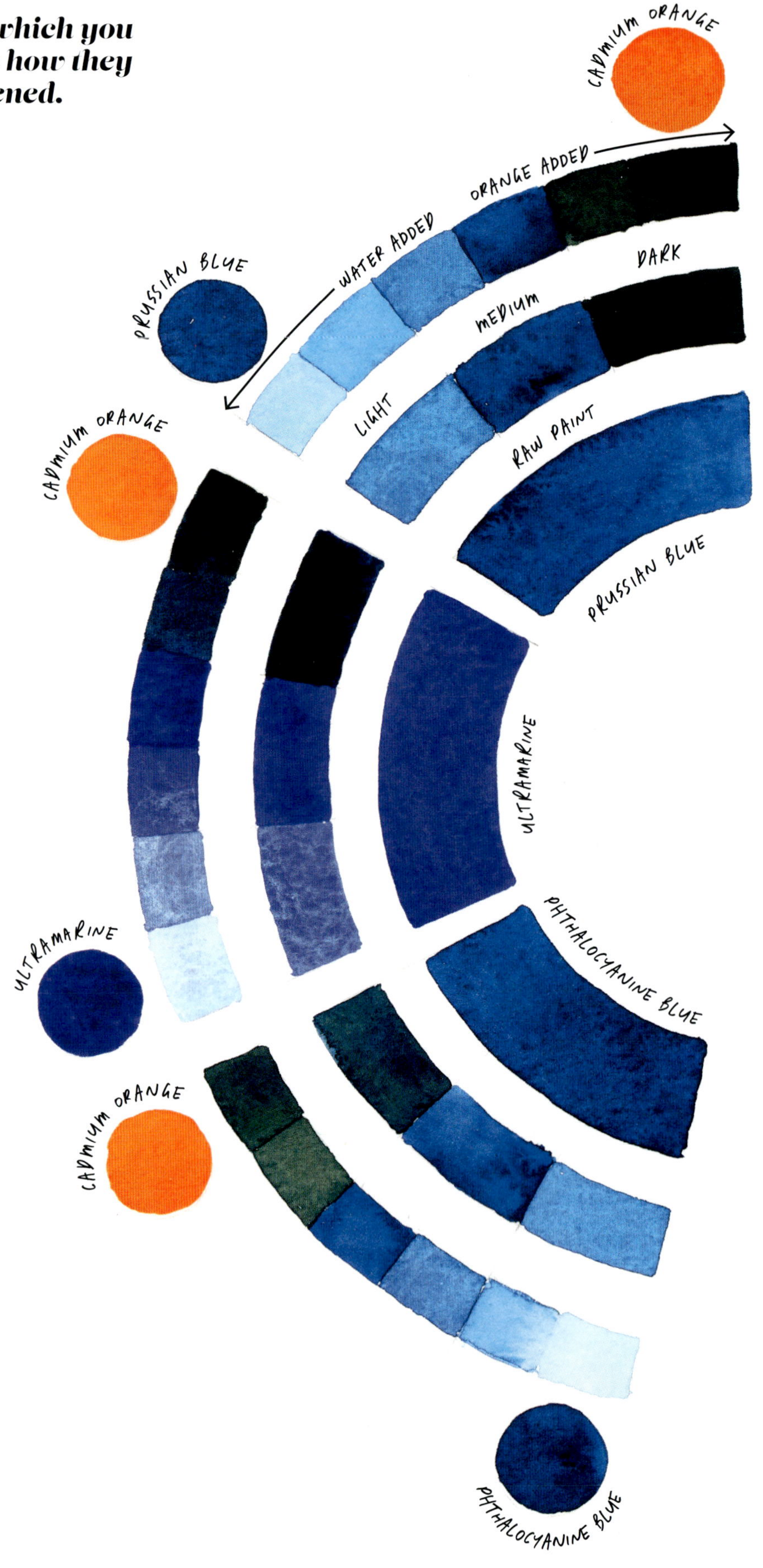

CADMIUM ORANGE
ORANGE ADDED
WATER ADDED
PRUSSIAN BLUE
DARK
MEDIUM
LIGHT
RAW PAINT
CADMIUM ORANGE
PRUSSIAN BLUE
ULTRAMARINE
PHTHALOCYANINE BLUE
ULTRAMARINE
CADMIUM ORANGE
PHTHALOCYANINE BLUE


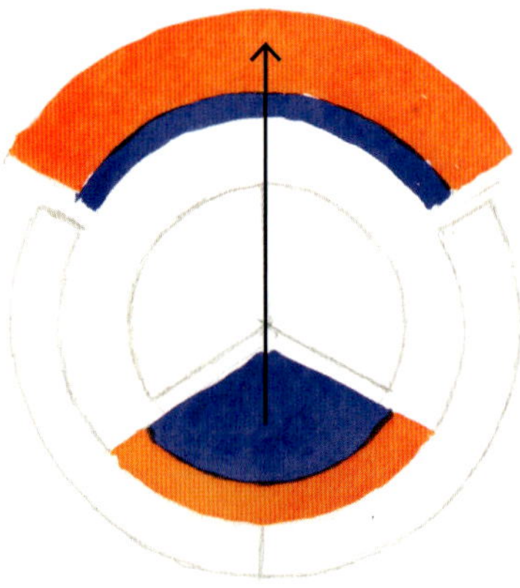

As complementary colors, the secondary color orange will always be opposite blue on the color wheel.

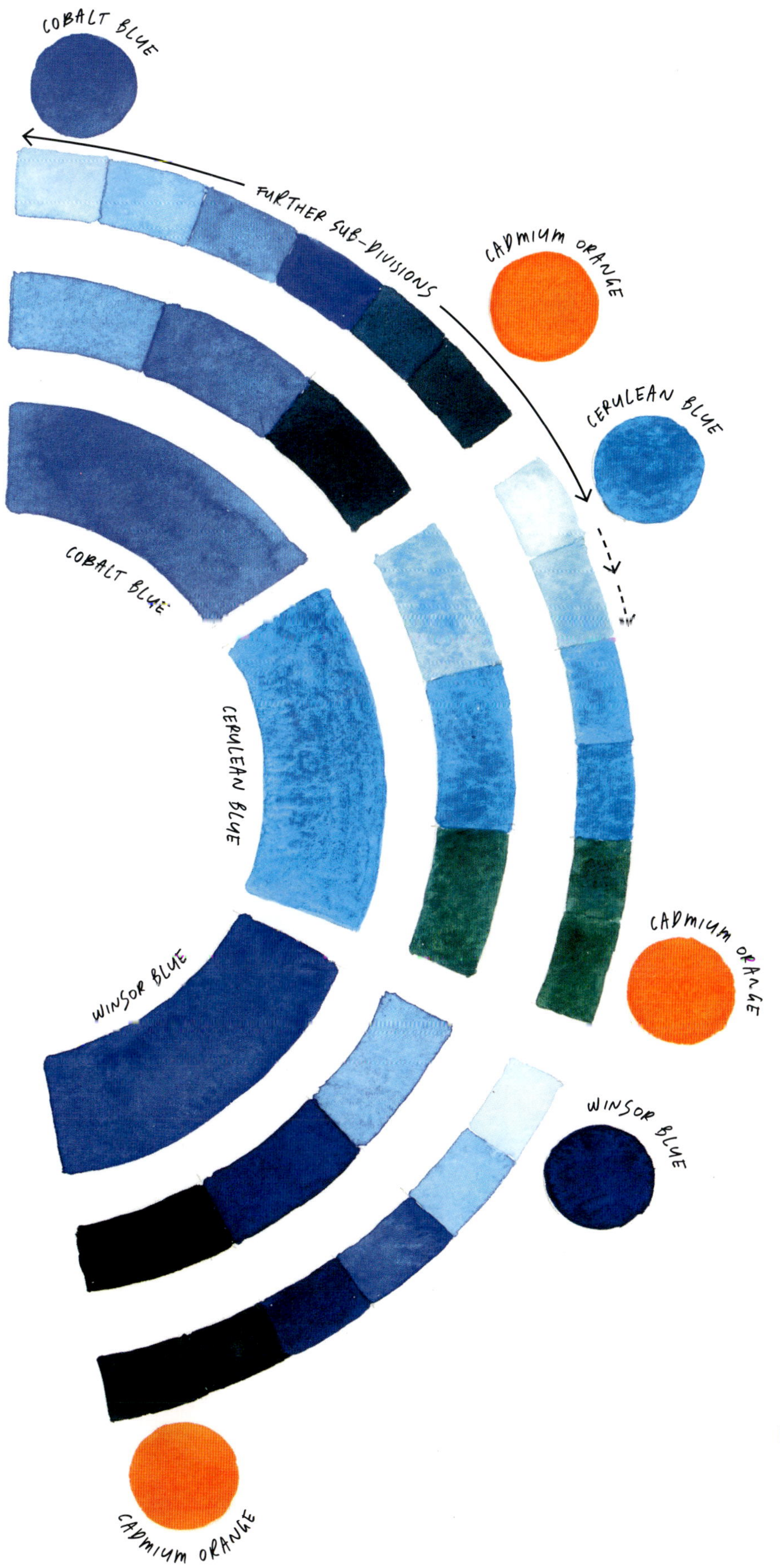
COBALT BLUE
FURTHER SUB-DIVISIONS
CADMIUM ORANGE
CERULEAN BLUE
COBALT BLUE
CERULEAN BLUE
CADMIUM ORANGE
WINSOR BLUE
WINSOR BLUE
CADMIUM ORANGE

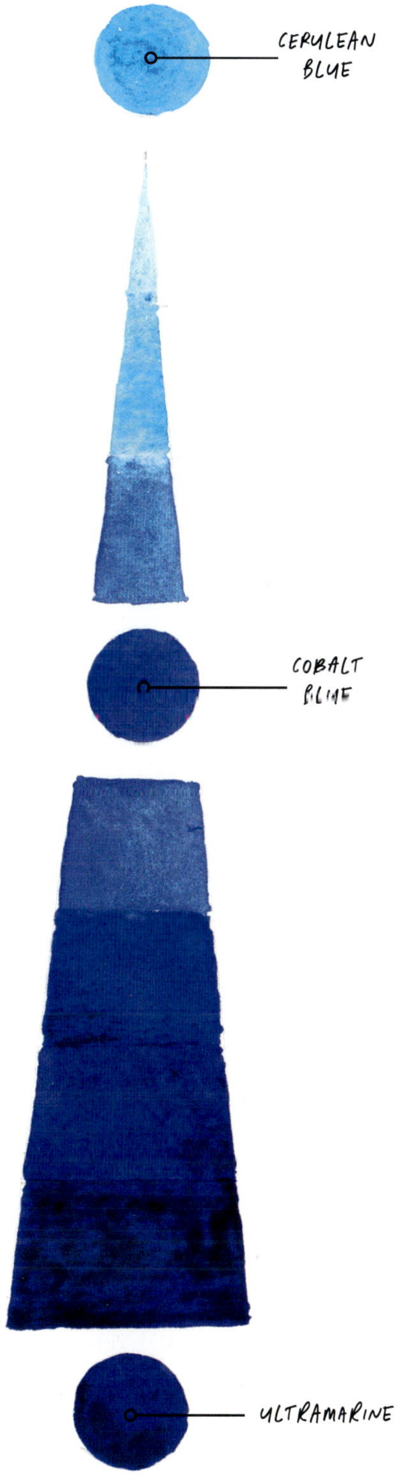
CERULEAN BLUE
COBALT BLUE
ULTRAMARINE

This column examines the tonal ranges of blues that can be created, moving from Cerulean Blue (one of the lightest blues) through the medium-ranked Cobalt Blue, to the darkest Ultramarine.

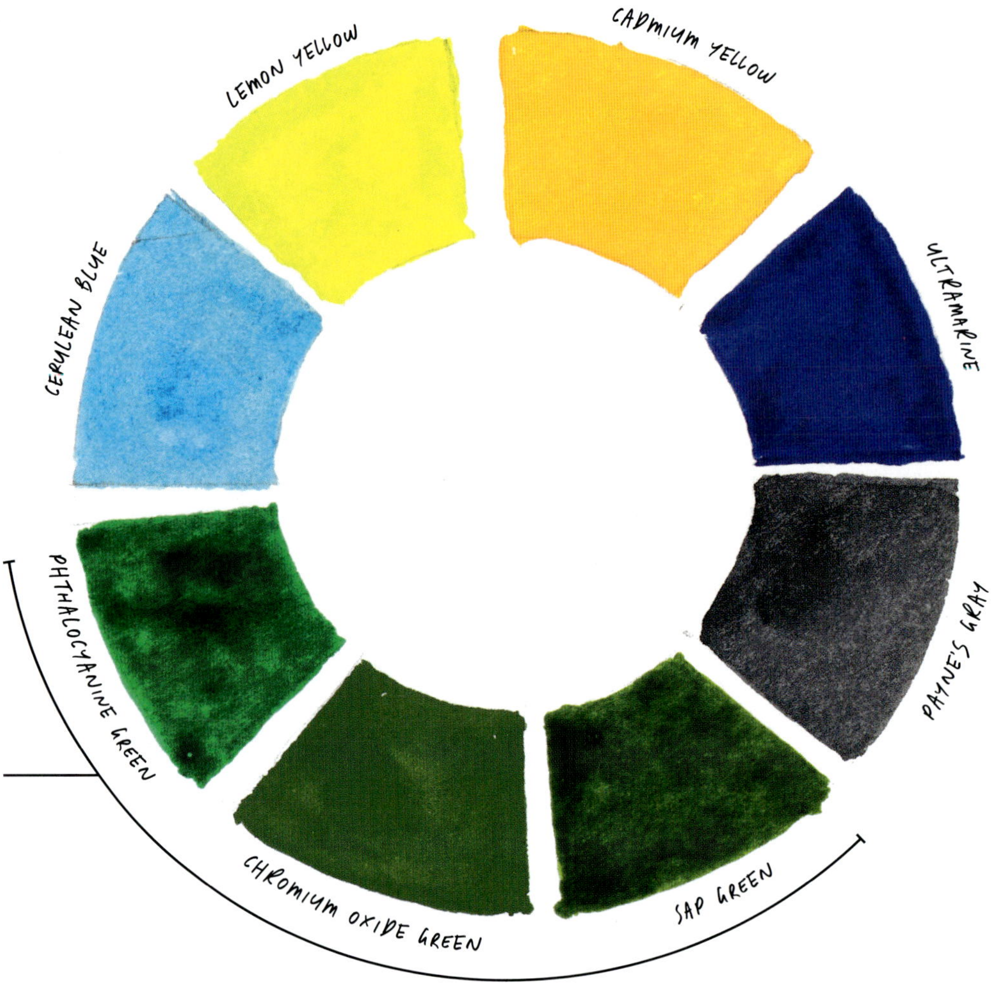

LEMON YELLOW
CADMIUM YELLOW
ULTRAMARINE
PAYNE'S GRAY
SAP GREEN
CHROMIUM OXIDE GREEN
PHTHALOCYANINE GREEN
CERULEAN BLUE


The three pre-mixed greens include Chromium Oxide Green, which can be difficult to mix with other colors, but more on that later.

***The next four pages explore the differences between mixing your own greens using blue and yellow, and the colors or tones that you can create by adding blue or yellow to pre-mixed greens.***

## COLORS FOR MIXING GREEN

This wheel is composed of the colors that I personally like to use in mixing my own variations and tones of greens. I have also included three pre-mixed greens to be used later.

## MIXING BLUE AND YELLOW

Unlike the other two families that we have considered, the transition from blue to green can be considerably more successful. The greens created when blues and yellows are combined illustrate a wealth of possibilities. They are sharp and bright, and it is not hard to see the many purposes that these mixes could be put to.

1. Lemon Yellow gradually added to Ultramarine
2. Cadmium Yellow gradually added to Ultramarine
3. Lemon Yellow gradually added to Cerulean Blue
4. Cadmium Yellow gradually added to Cerulean Blue

1

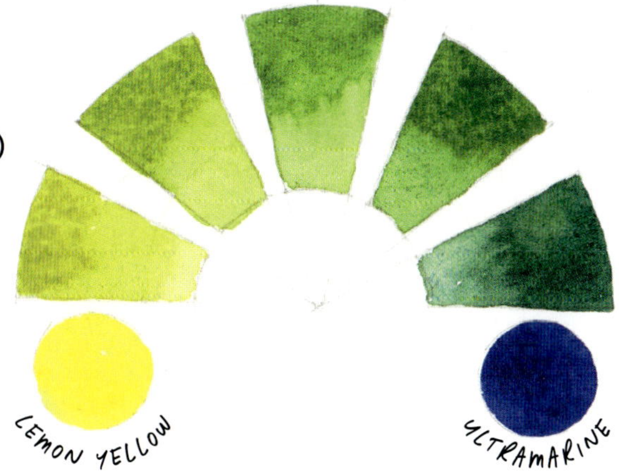
LEMON YELLOW
ULTRAMARINE

2

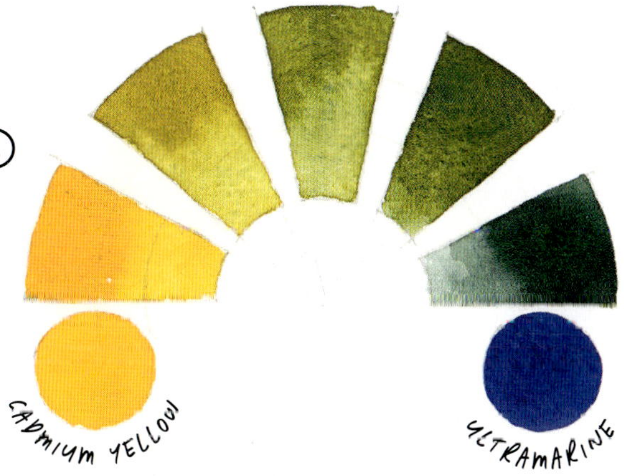
CADMIUM YELLOW
ULTRAMARINE

3

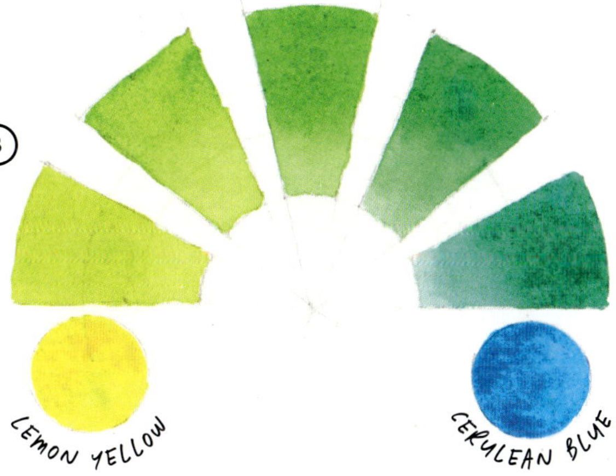
LEMON YELLOW
CERULEAN BLUE

4

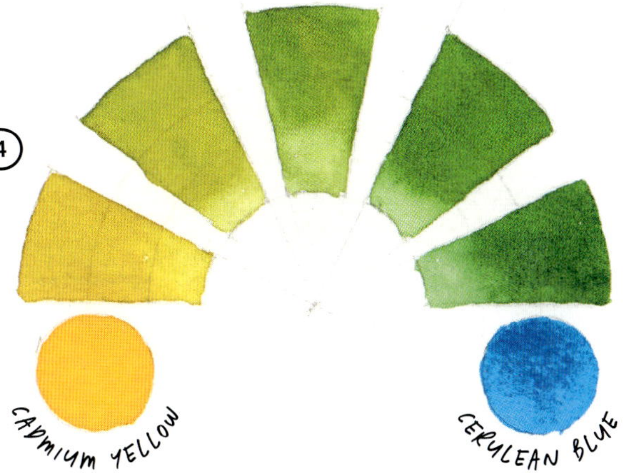
CADMIUM YELLOW
CERULEAN BLUE

***Now it's time to expand the choice of greens available to us by introducing a couple of pre-mixed greens – Chromium Oxide Green and Sap Green.***

## MIXING THE RIGHT COLOR

Again, in this chart I have devised a system to help gauge just how many, and more importantly, exactly what type of green you can create using a pre-mixed color and one other paint. The tulips painting that follows provided me with an excellent opportunity to use a full range of color mixes and tones, going a little beyond the standard light, medium and dark greens.

The ready-mixed greens have both had one other color added to them in increasing quantities as you move towards the outer circle. This process also involved adding a touch of water to enable a good flow of paint. This was particularly important when using the rather "chalky" Chromium Oxide Green paint.

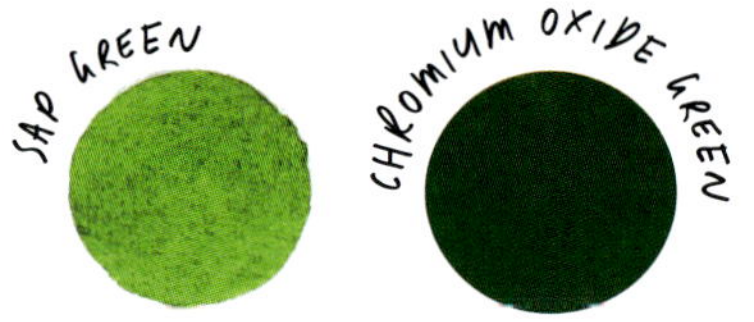

SAP GREEN
CHROMIUM OXIDE GREEN


The two pre-mixed greens that I have used to test their potential for mixing are Sap Green and Chromium Oxide Green, which makes its first appearance here. Sap Green has already been featured several times in this book and is an excellent "starter green" that can work well with most other colors. Chromium Oxide Green, however, is rather different. Sometimes known as Chrome Green, it is a thick, chalky paint that doesn't handle particularly well as it tends to flatten any color mixed into it. I have included it as it does have many uses in painting foliage.

**CHANGING TONES:** This chart explores how you can influence the appearance of a pre-mixed green by adding one other color and some water.

1. Yellows added to Sap Green
2. Blues added to Sap Green
3. Blues added to Chromium Oxide Green
4. Yellows added to Chromium Oxide Green

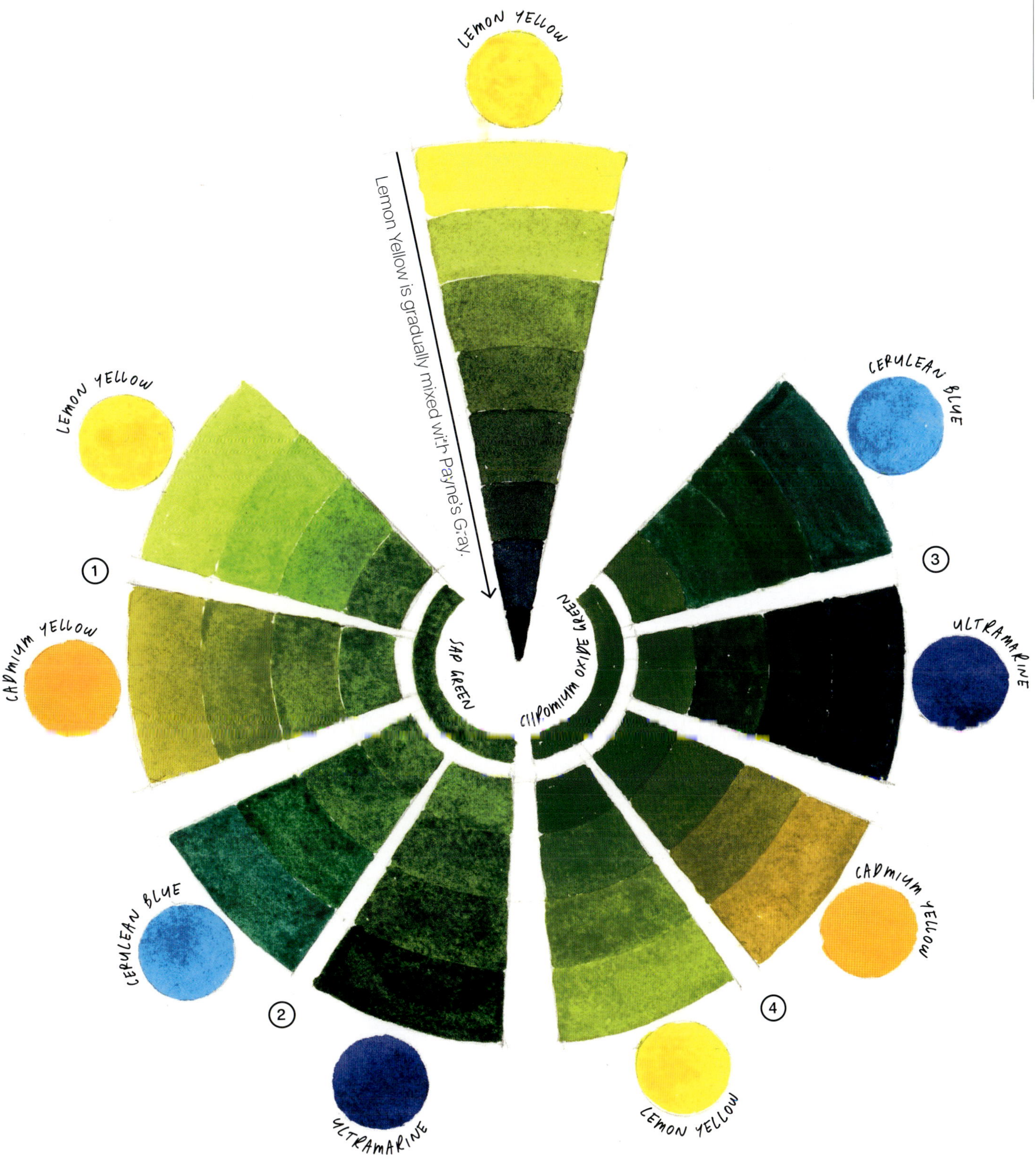
LEMON YELLOW
Lemon Yellow is gradually mixed with Payne's Gray.
LEMON YELLOW
1
CADMIUM YELLOW
SAP GREEN
CHROMIUM OXIDE GREEN
CERULEAN BLUE
3
ULTRAMARINE
CERULEAN BLUE
2
ULTRAMARINE
CADMIUM YELLOW
4
LEMON YELLOW

***Let's now explore how to darken the greens. I've changed the pre-mixed Chromium Oxide Green to Phthalocyanine Green, which is generally more conducive to creating a range of usable tones.***

## DARKENING THE TONE

The pre-mixed greens half-way along the columns are the starting points here.

(1) In the middle of the column is a mixture of Sap Green and Cadmium Yellow, lightened towards the inner circle by adding increasingly diluted Cadmium Yellow (more water added for each section). Moving outwards from the center mixture, pure Sap Green is added to the mix, darkening the color in stages. Cadmium Red is added at the very last stages.

(2) In the middle of the column is a mixture of Sap Green and Indian Yellow. Increasing quantities of diluted Indian Yellow are added in stages towards the center of the circle. Moving outwards from the middle mix, pure Sap Green is added to the mix in stages with Cadmium Red being added at the final stages.

(3) In the middle of the column is a mixture of Sap Green and Lemon Yellow. Increasing quantities of diluted Lemon Yellow are added towards the center, lightening the tone. Moving outwards, increasing quantities of Sap Green are added, darkening the tone. Cadmium Red is added at the final stages, darkening the green as much as I dared.

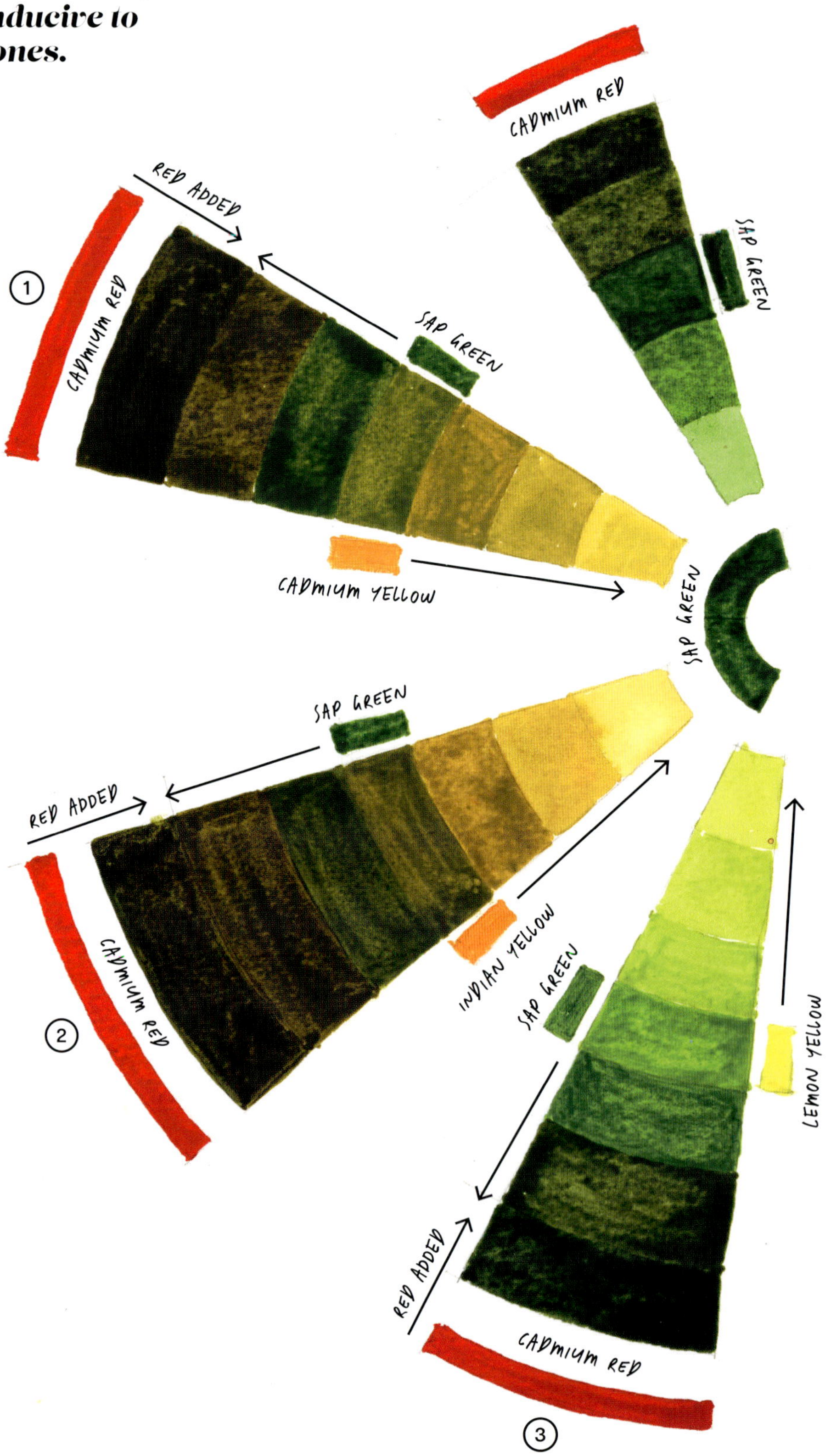
CADMIUM RED
SAP GREEN
RED ADDED
1
CADMIUM RED
SAP GREEN
CADMIUM YELLOW
SAP GREEN
SAP GREEN
RED ADDED
CADMIUM RED
2
INDIAN YELLOW
SAP GREEN
LEMON YELLOW
RED ADDED
CADMIUM RED
3

## COMPLEMENTARY COLORS AND WATER

The top two columns explore just how far I could take raw Sap Green and Phthalocyanine Green by adding our chosen red (the complementary color to green) in one direction, and diluting with water in the other.

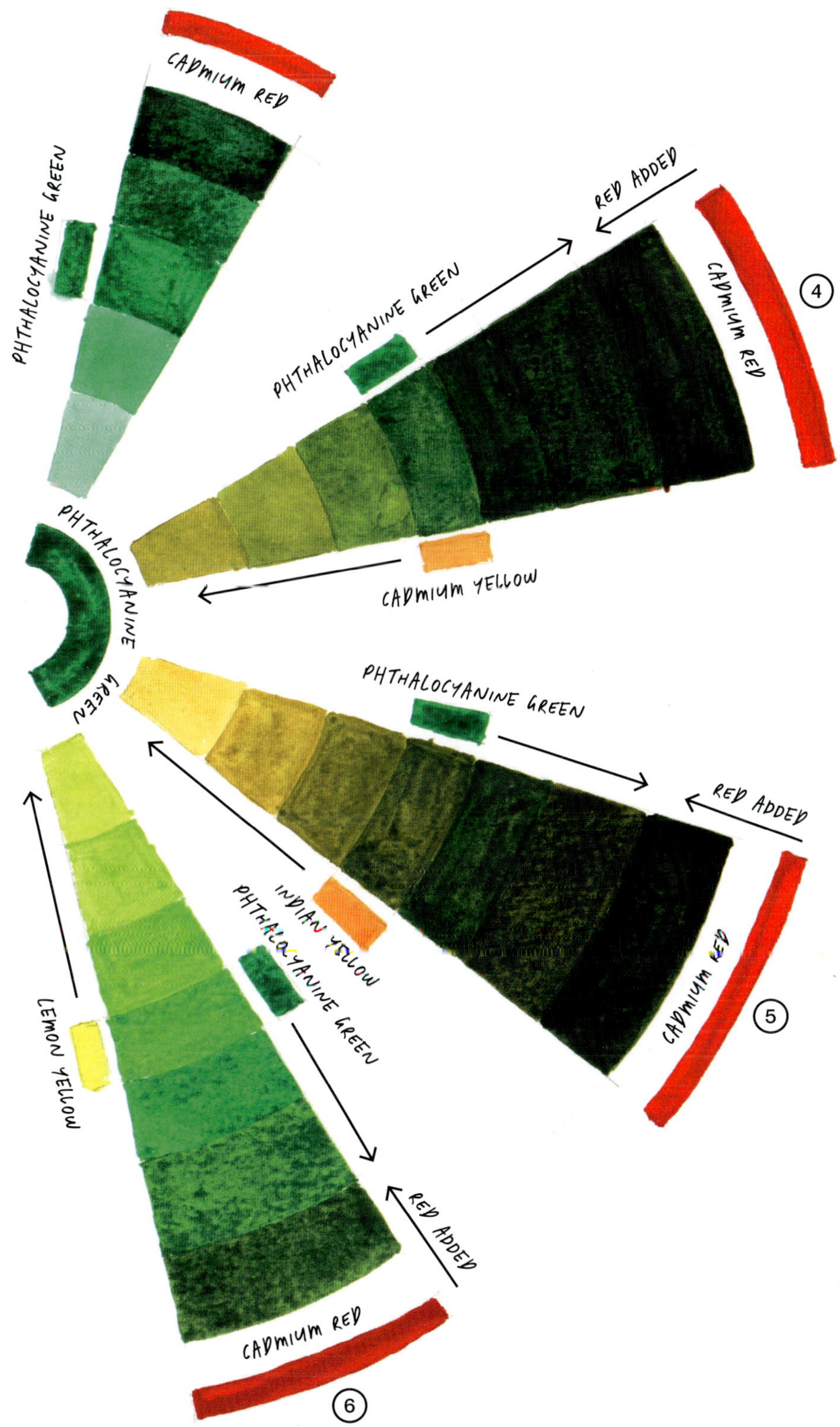

CADMIUM RED
PHTHALOCYANINE GREEN
RED ADDED
PHTHALOCYANINE GREEN
CADMIUM RED
4
CADMIUM YELLOW
PHTHALOCYANINE GREEN
PHTHALOCYANINE GREEN
RED ADDED
INDIAN YELLOW
PHTHALOCYANINE GREEN
CADMIUM RED
5
LEMON YELLOW
RED ADDED
CADMIUM RED
6


(4) In the middle of the column is a mixture of Phthalocyanine Green and Cadmium Yellow, lightened towards the center by adding increasingly diluted Cadmium Yellow. Moving outwards from the middle mixture, pure Phthalocyanine Green is added to the mix, darkening the color in stages. Cadmium Red is added at the very last stages.

(5) In the middle of the column is a mixture of Phthalocyanine Green and Indian Yellow. Increasing amounts of diluted Indian Yellow are added in stages towards the center of the circle. Moving outwards from the middle mix, pure Phthalocyanine Green is added to the mix in stages with Cadmium Red being added at the final stages.

(6) In the middle of the column is a mixture of Phthalocyanine Green and Lemon Yellow. Increasing quantities of diluted Lemon Yellow are added towards the center, lightening the tone. Moving outwards, increasing quantities of Phthalocyanine Green are added, darkening the tone. Cadmium Red is added at the final stages, darkening the green without altering its integrity too much.

***In this visual "snapshot" of a group of tulips, blues and greens dominate the background, pushing the lighter petals forward. The variety of different greens is clear.***

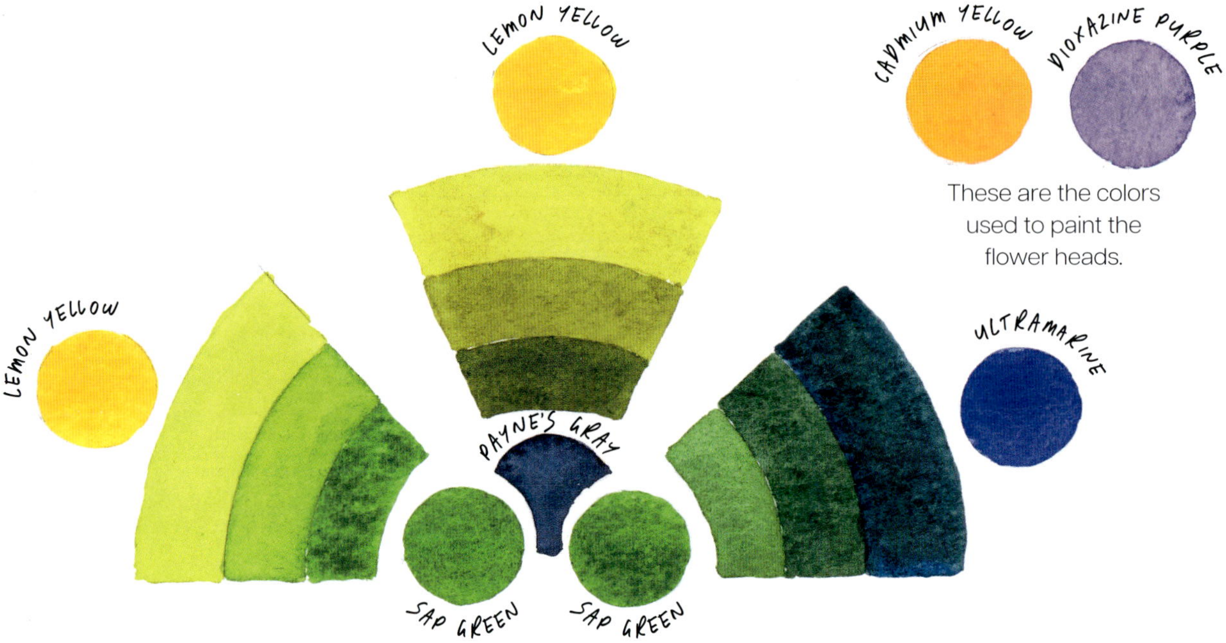
LEMON YELLOW
CADMIUM YELLOW
DIOXAZINE PURPLE
LEMON YELLOW
ULTRAMARINE
PAYNE'S GRAY
SAP GREEN
SAP GREEN

These are the colors used to paint the flower heads.

This chart illustrates the color mixes that I have used to create the wealth of tones seen in the green leaves and stems of this composition.

STAGE 1

The key colors were applied to damp paper in this stage and allowed to bleed, doing some of the color mixing for me. These were allowed to dry to become the highlights.

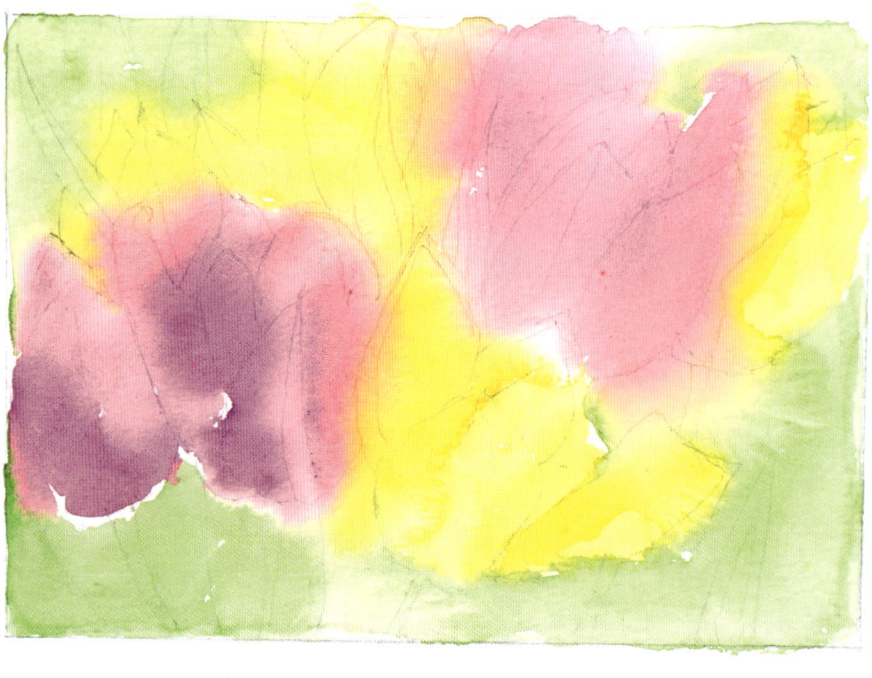

STAGE 2

In this stage I mixed some of the darker colors and painted around the highlights, visually pushing them forward.

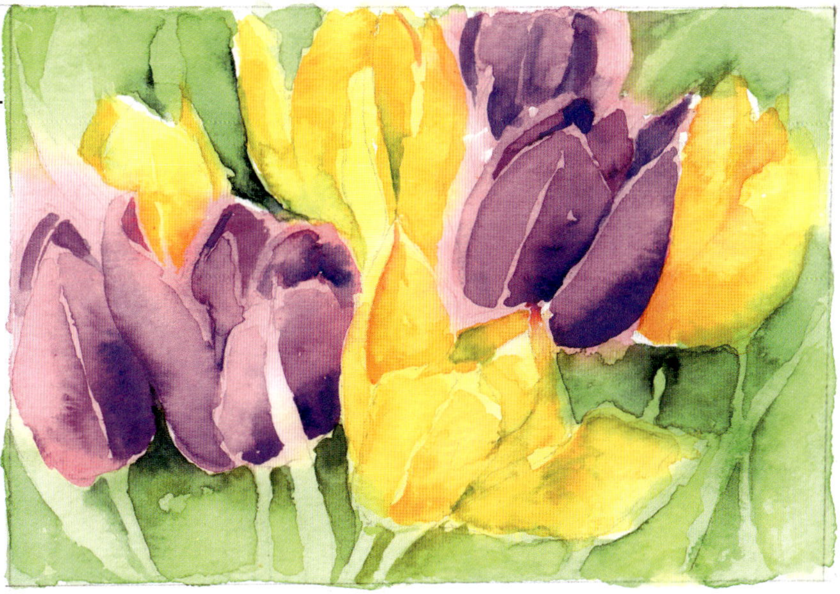

FINAL PAINTING

In this stage the deepest, darkest colors were added "behind" the mid-tones of Stage 2, pushing them forward even further in the composition.

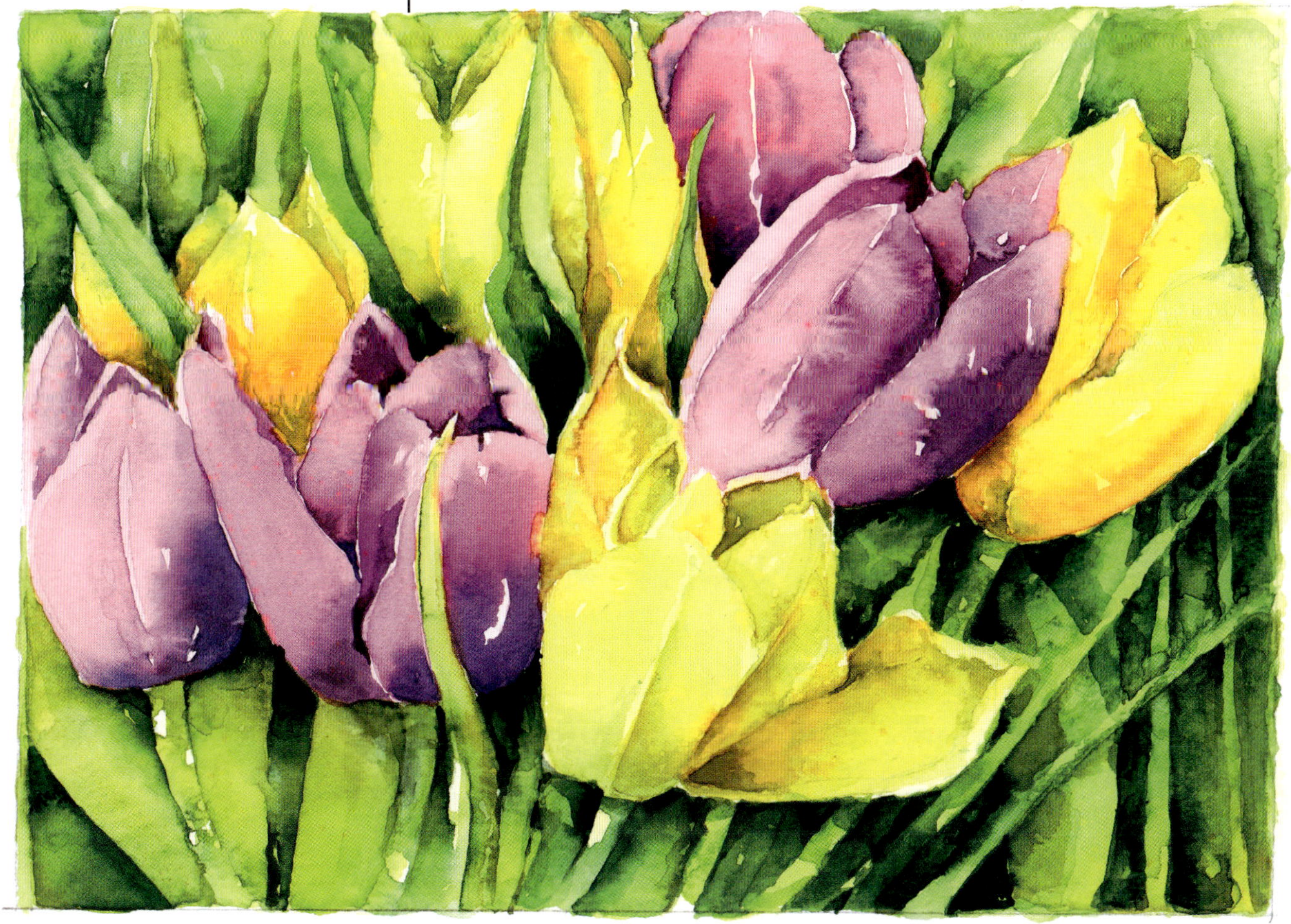

# *Part 3:* LIGHT & SHADE

The concept of light and shade is one of the most important for artists – second only, possibly, to an understanding of color. These two considerations, however, are reliant upon each other.

This section will explore how you can use color to best effect to help create shade and shadows, enhancing the three-dimensional effect that we first looked at in the Watercolor Basics chapter.

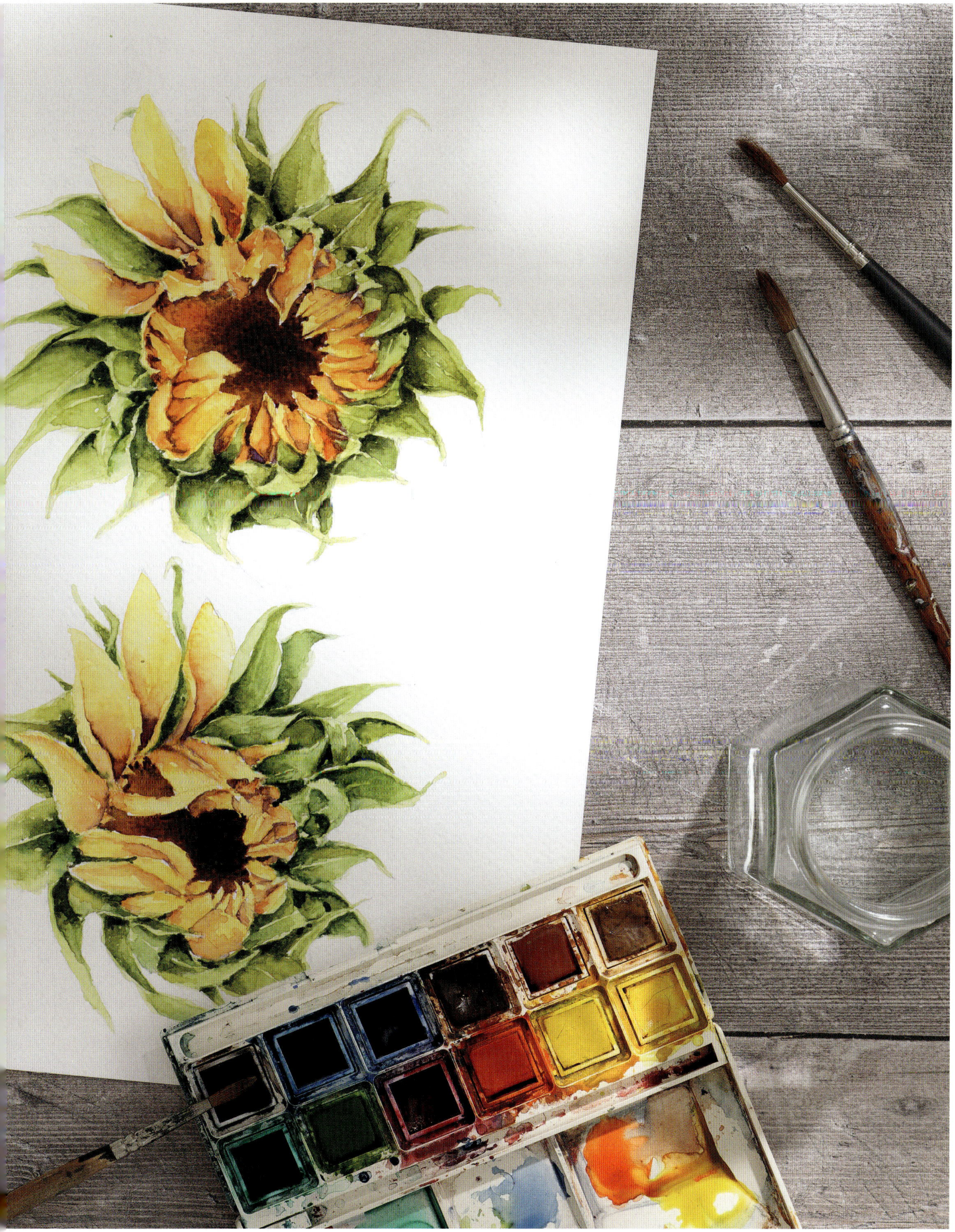

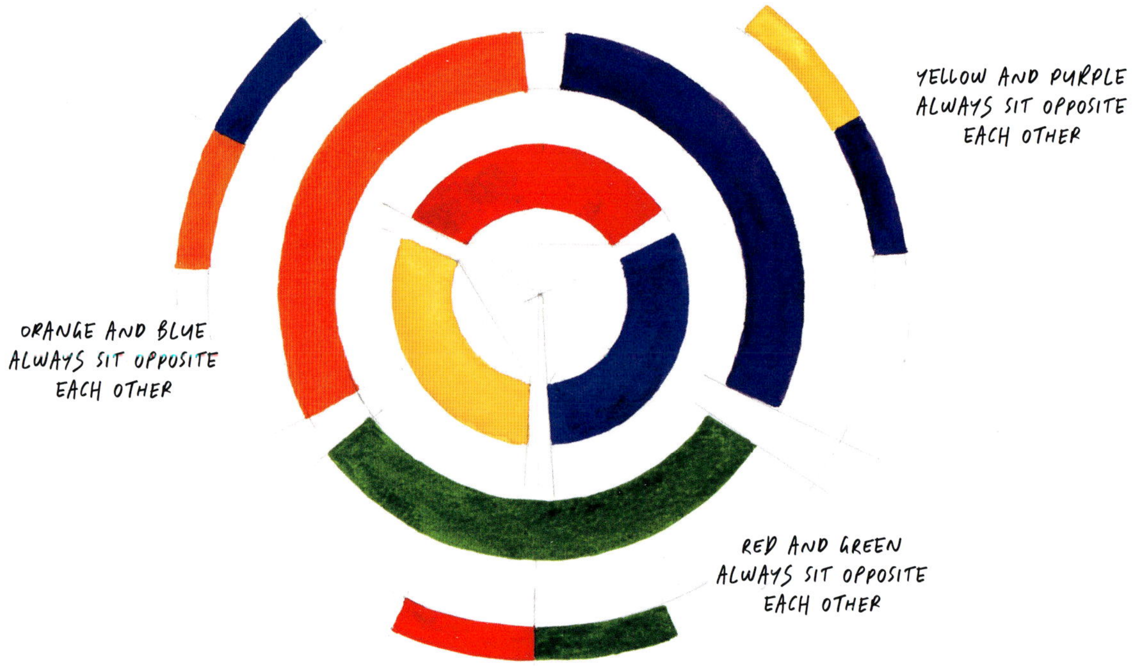
YELLOW AND PURPLE ALWAYS SIT OPPOSITE EACH OTHER
ORANGE AND BLUE ALWAYS SIT OPPOSITE EACH OTHER
RED AND GREEN ALWAYS SIT OPPOSITE EACH OTHER

# The Three Stages

So far, we have actively explored the many ways in which you can change the appearance of a whole range of colors using a selection of paints. We will now explore how you can use your knowledge of the color wheel to create effective shade and shadows.

## COMPLEMENTARIES

On the pages on primary and secondary colors we explored the structure of the color wheel and the immutable law of optics which dictates which colors will always be opposite others. For purposes of consistency and, I believe, clarity, I shall now refer to these colors as "complementaries." These colors have two key uses. When placed next to each other they create a remarkable visual dynamic. This system was often used by the French Impressionists to depict the sharp, transitory effects of light through small flashes of complementaries – red geraniums set against green foliage for example.

***The three stage approach of light (water added), medium (straight from the tube or pan) and dark (complementary color added) can help to create a real sense of form within your paintings.***

## CREATING SHADOWS

The other technique we learned from that group of revolutionary painters was the creation of shadows by mixing complementaries. While it might not be the first natural choice, the most effective way of making yellow, for example, darker, is to add a small touch of its complementary color – purple. I appreciate that this may seem an odd, and slightly scary, prospect – adding such a strong dominant color as purple to such a fragile color as yellow – but it really does work! Other colors would darken yellow, but they would change the natural integrity of the paint. Its complementary will allow the nature of the color to remain unchanged but just a little darker. This does require some sensitivity and subtlety with your paint mixing however. Be gentle and add as little of the complementary as you possibly can to start off. You can always add more of the complementary to the primary to make it darker, but you can't take it away to make it lighter.

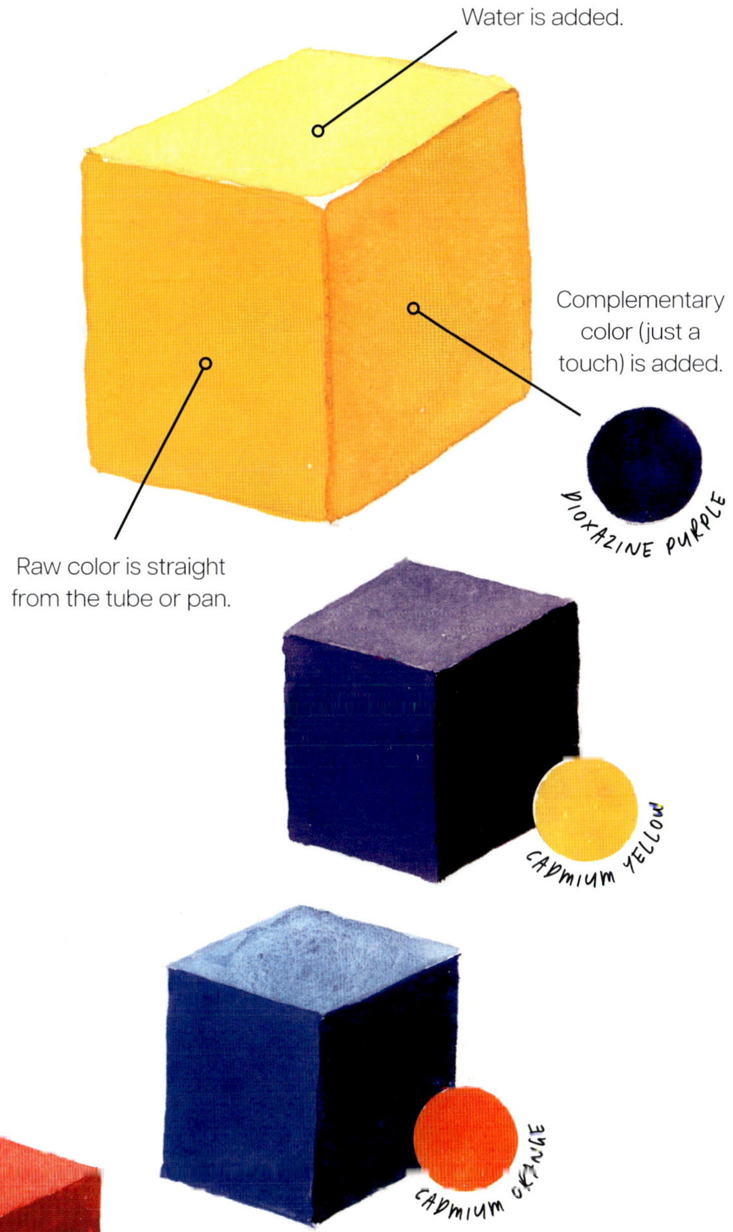
Water is added.
Complementary color (just a touch) is added.
Raw color is straight from the tube or pan.
DIOXAZINE PURPLE
CADMIUM YELLOW
CADMIUM ORANGE

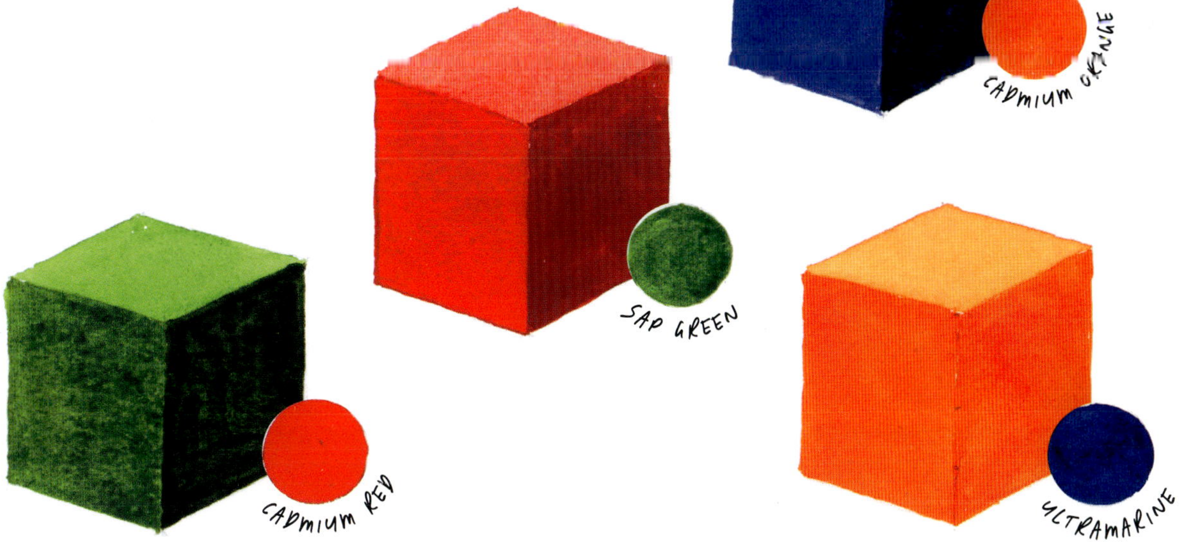
SAP GREEN
CADMIUM RED
ULTRAMARINE

# Reflected Color

Reflected color is also an important element to get to grips with in order to create effective watercolor paintings. This involves exploring a little more optical theory and some simple watercolor painting techniques.

## MAKING CONNECTIONS

The theory is that light bounces from every object that it hits and, from the painter's point of view, picks up a little of the color and carries it onto the next object it hits. This is not something that we can actually see in action, but when you place a red and a yellow object together, you will be able to see a little "yellow light" catching the red object and a little "red light" catching the yellow object. These will visually blend to create a red orange on the red object and a yellow orange on the yellow object. This does not mean that you will need to use an orange paint to create this effect. If you simply touch a small amount of yellow onto the red object while the paper is still damp, the colors will bleed gently and create the orange tone for you. This leads us in to watercolor technique.

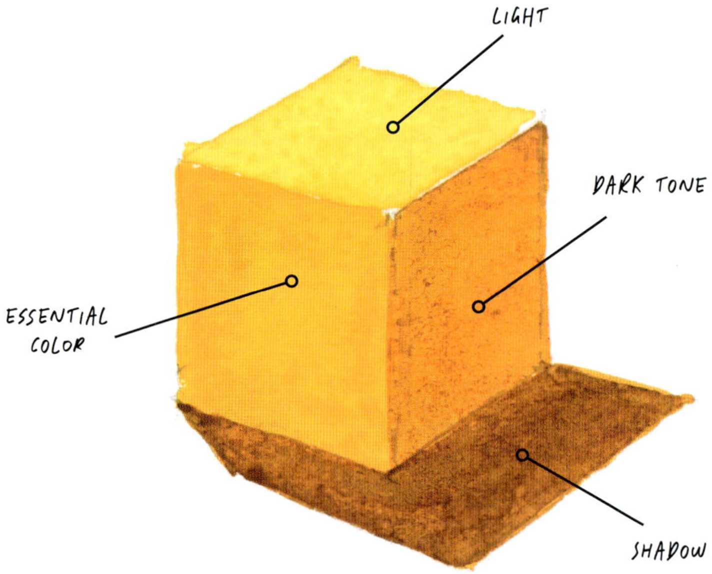

LIGHT
DARK TONE
ESSENTIAL COLOR
SHADOW


**CREATING CONNECTIONS:**
To prevent your painting from looking like a series of physically unrelated cardboard cut-outs, the colors from each object will need to be added, or bled into each other, creating a visual connection.

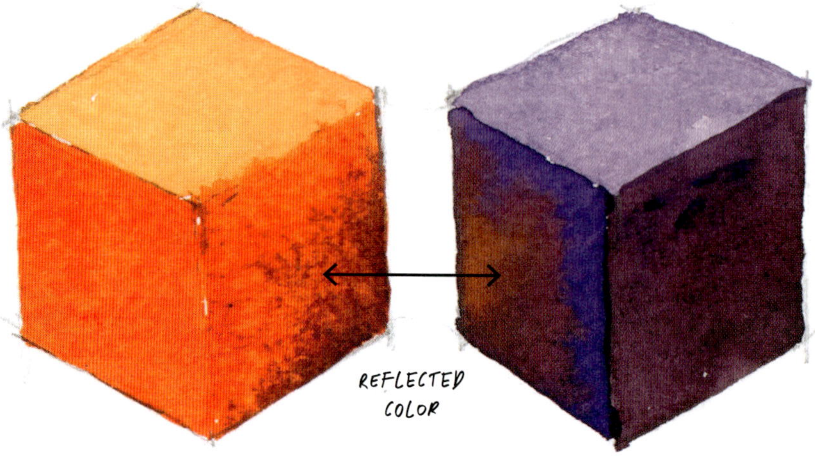

REFLECTED COLOR

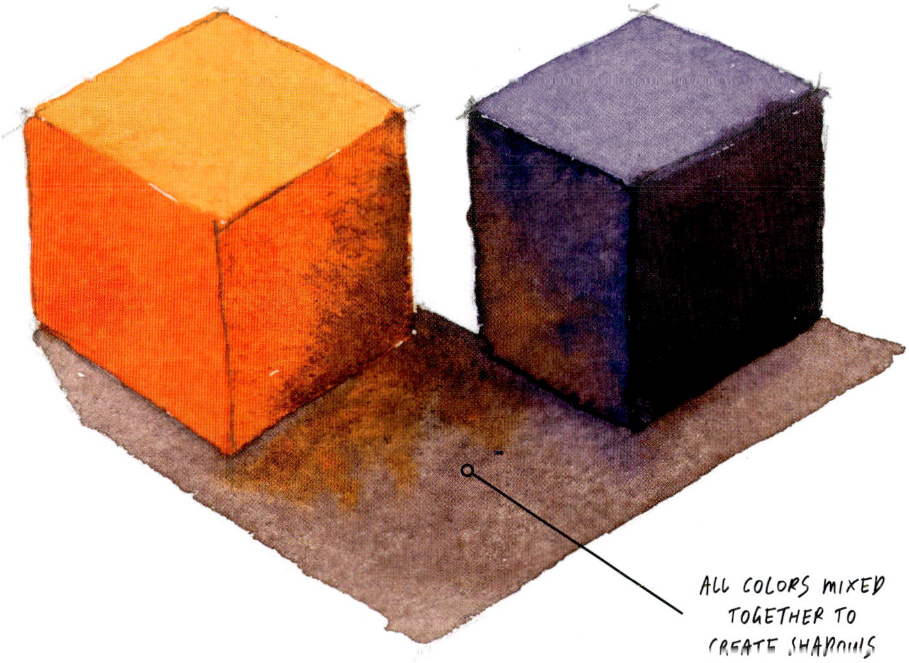
ALL COLORS MIXED
TOGETHER TO
CREATE SHADOWS

## THE RIGHT BALANCE

This works best when working onto damp paper, just before your painting has dried. If you were to paint your subjects and drop in a little of the color to your neighboring object while the paper was still very wet – that is when you can clearly see surface water on the paper – then the color would flood across the paper, altering the look and tone of everything, and resulting in you losing control of the process. The color would simply flow where the water took it. If, however, you waited until the painting is completely dry, then you would end up with blocks of color that don't really make much visual sense. So, wait until the surface water has started to soak into the fibers of the paper and is beginning to evaporate. When you can see a gentle sheen on the paper, then you will know the time is right.

## MIXING SHADOWS

Finally, we move on to shadows. In my own early years' art education, I was taught that any blue used in a sky color should be added to the shadows on the ground. Equally, any greens used in trees should also be dropped into the shadow mix. Towards the end of the process, every color used had made a contribution to the colored shadows. This is a technique that I still use, even when painting indoors. Color still spreads through light and touches everything that you can see.

**MIXING SHADOWS:** My starting point for creating effective looking shadows is to take the color of the object casting the shadows and then add a small amount of its complementary color. Then, I will look at the other surrounding objects and pick up a small amount of these and add them to the watery mix. This will give an indistinct but tinted watercolor wash that catches all the colors' reflections and will help to visually anchor them onto the surface on which they are positioned.

*"Towards the end of the process, every color used had made a contribution to the colored shadows."*

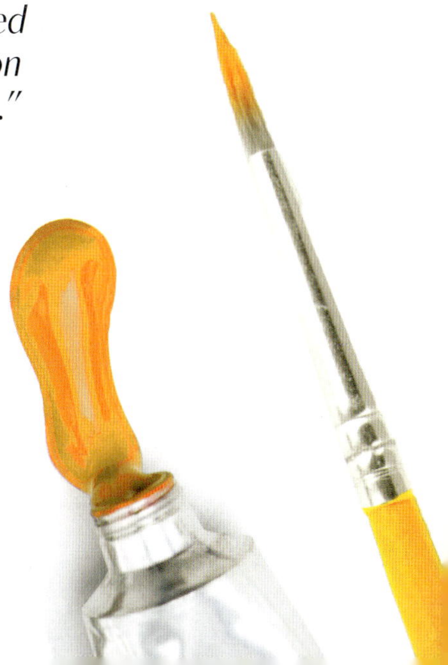

# Still Life Studies

Now that we have looked at the theory of light and shade in color, we can look at that theory in practice through the following still life studies. You will see both The Three Stages and Reflected Color in action.

**LEAVES**

This segment shows the colors used for the sunflower leaves.

Purple has been added as yellow's complementary color, to give an extra dimension and bring the painting alive.

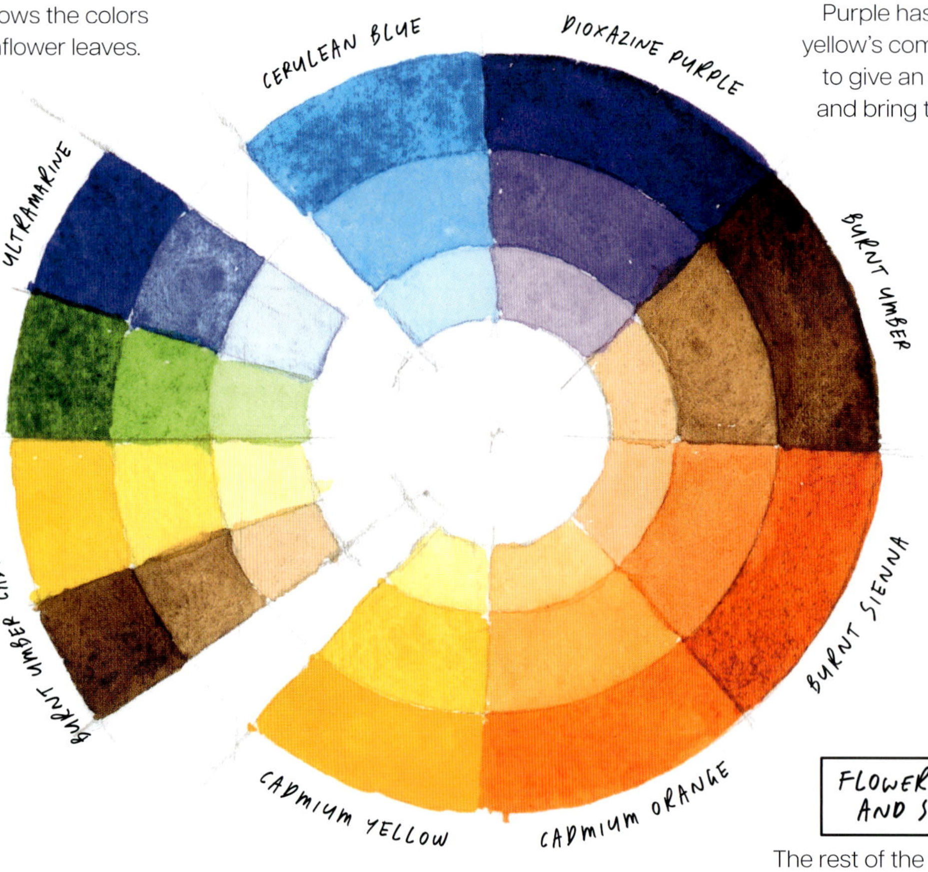

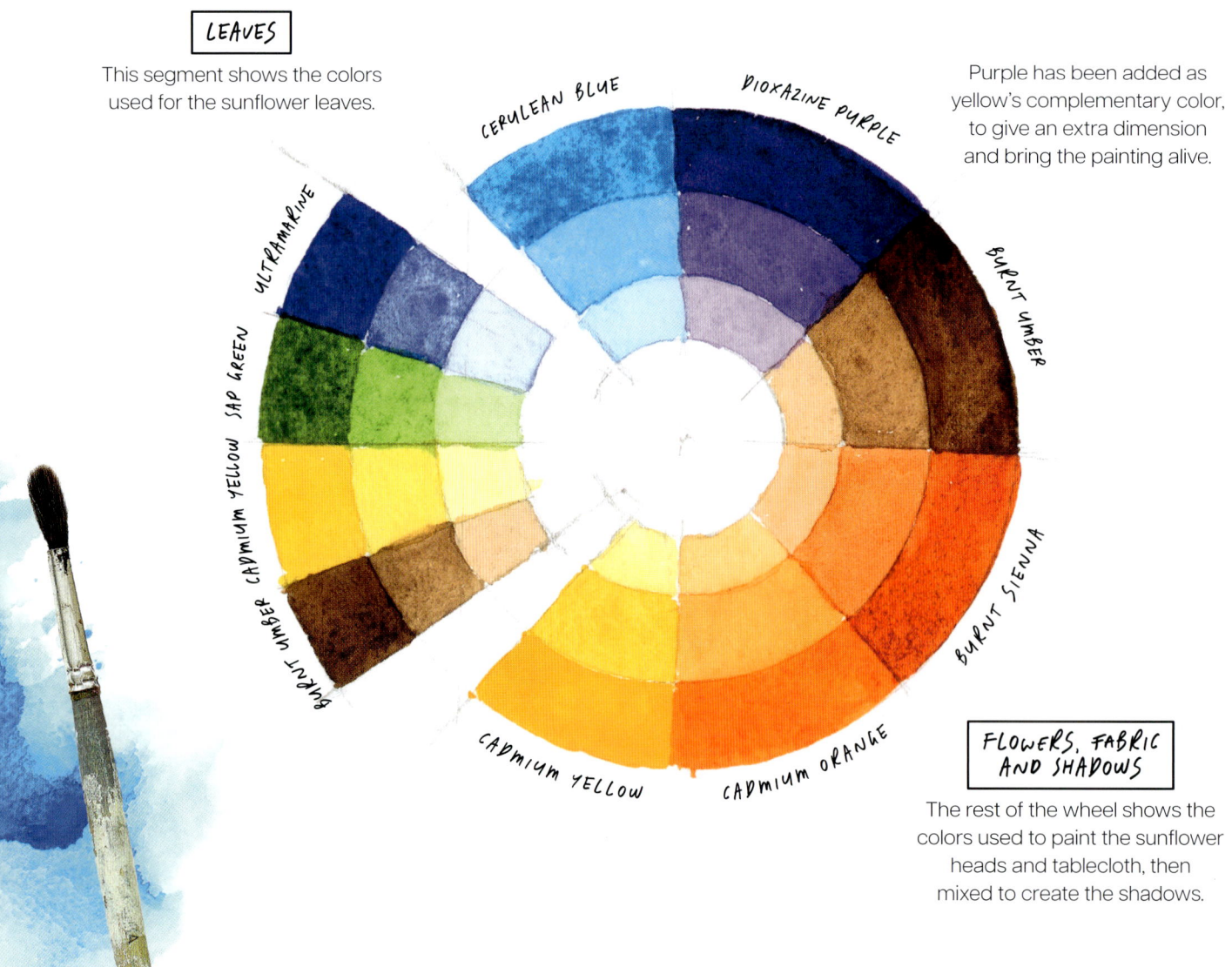

CERULEAN BLUE
DIOXAZINE PURPLE
BURNT UMBER
BURNT SIENNA
CADMIUM ORANGE
CADMIUM YELLOW
BURNT UMBER
CADMIUM YELLOW
SAP GREEN
ULTRAMARINE


**FLOWERS, FABRIC AND SHADOWS**

The rest of the wheel shows the colors used to paint the sunflower heads and tablecloth, then mixed to create the shadows.

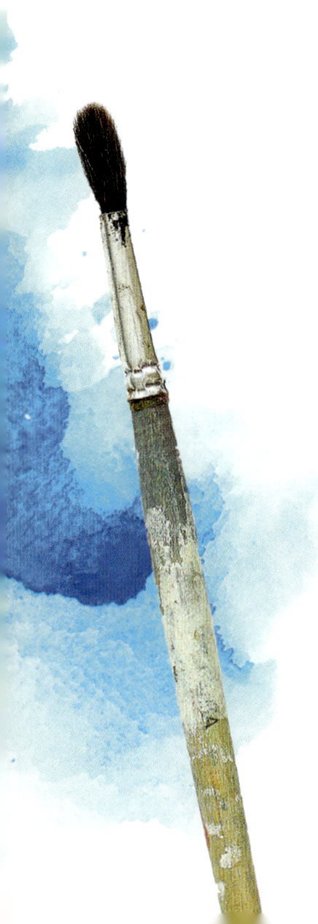

***In this study, the white vase and the shadow on the tablecloth are created using a mixture of the colors used across the rest of the painting.***

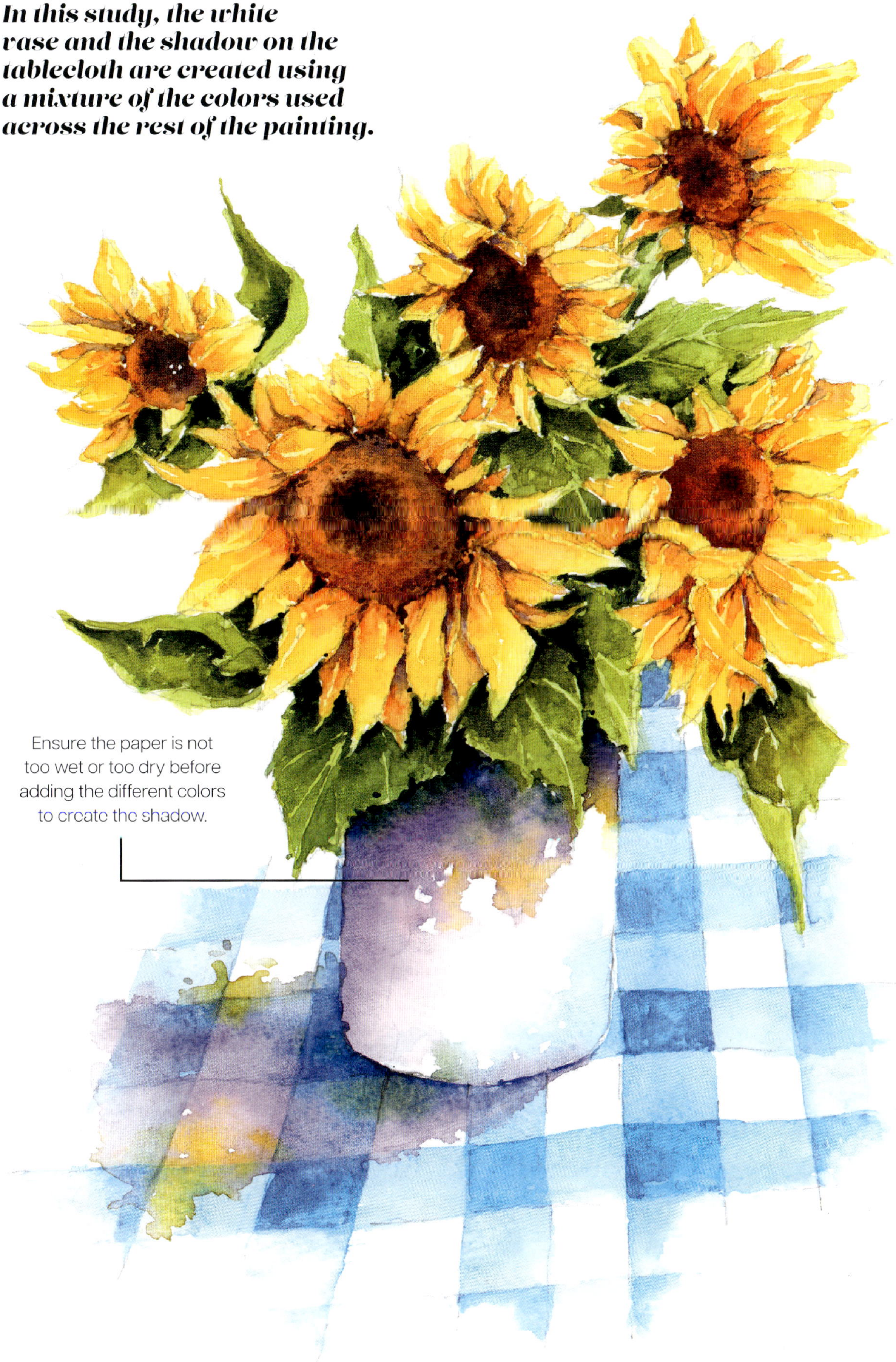

Ensure the paper is not too wet or too dry before adding the different colors to create the shadow.

***The studies featured here illustrate the three-stage approach in action, and the technique of bleeding colors into each other.***

This study shows the step-by-step approach to painting an object using the three-stage approach. The lightest tones are the first to be applied. Another color is introduced to help establish the mid-tones. The darker tones – the green leaves in particular – are created by the addition of a very small touch of red – the complementary color to green.

FLOWER

The top semicircle of colors are those used on the tulip head.

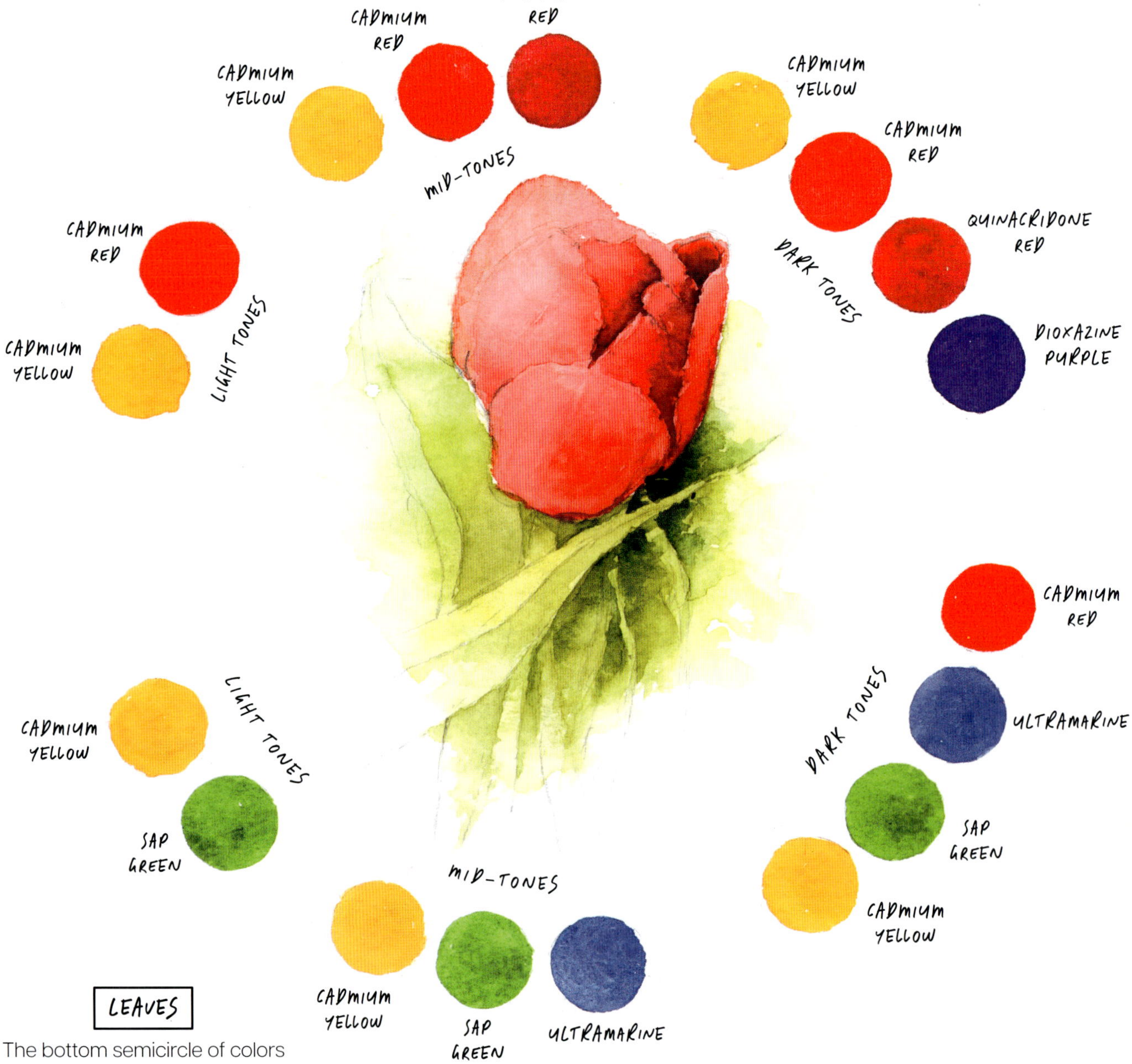

LIGHT TONES
CADMIUM RED
CADMIUM YELLOW
MID-TONES
CADMIUM YELLOW
CADMIUM RED
QUINACRIDONE RED
DARK TONES
CADMIUM YELLOW
CADMIUM RED
QUINACRIDONE RED
DIOXAZINE PURPLE
LIGHT TONES
CADMIUM YELLOW
SAP GREEN
MID-TONES
CADMIUM YELLOW
SAP GREEN
ULTRAMARINE
DARK TONES
CADMIUM RED
ULTRAMARINE
SAP GREEN
CADMIUM YELLOW


LEAVES

The bottom semicircle of colors are those used on the leaves.

This study makes full use of the variety of green tones that can be mixed by adding yellows and blues to a pre-mixed green. The tulip heads show the effect that allowing colors to bleed into each other can have, binding the scene together.

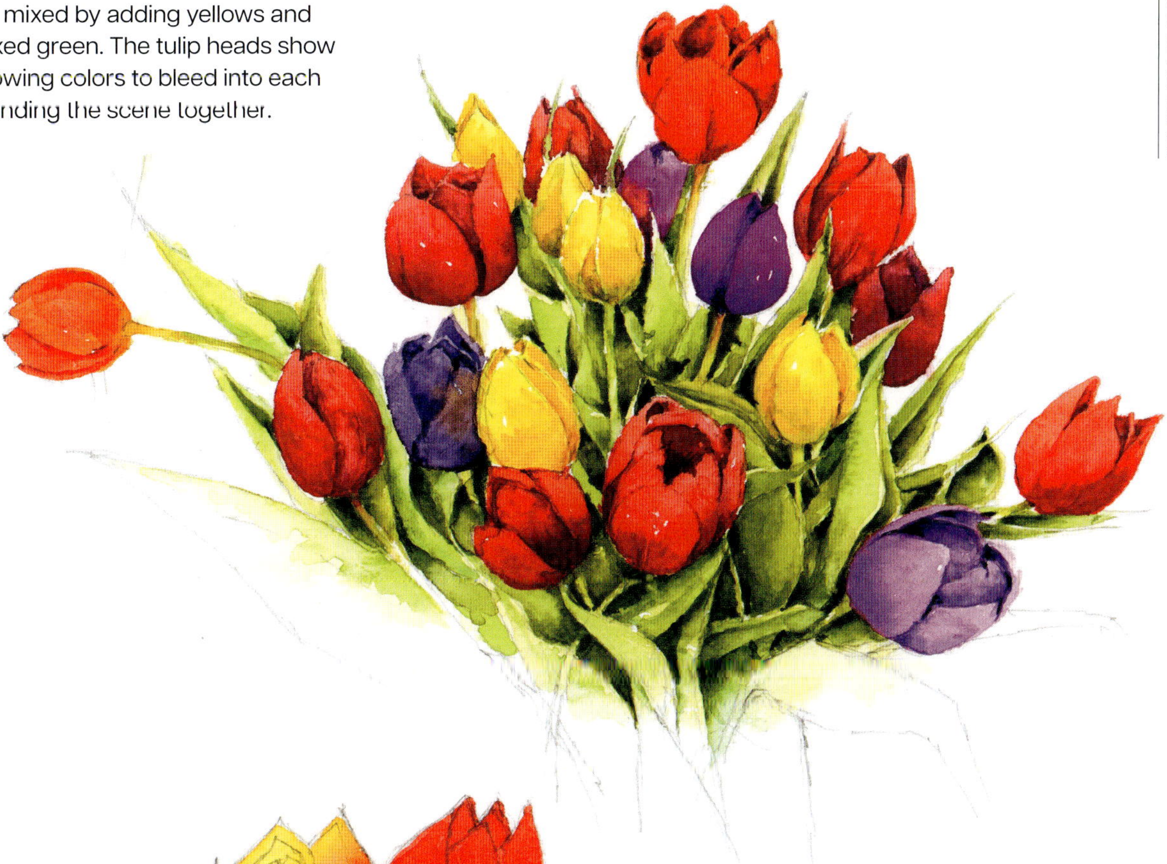

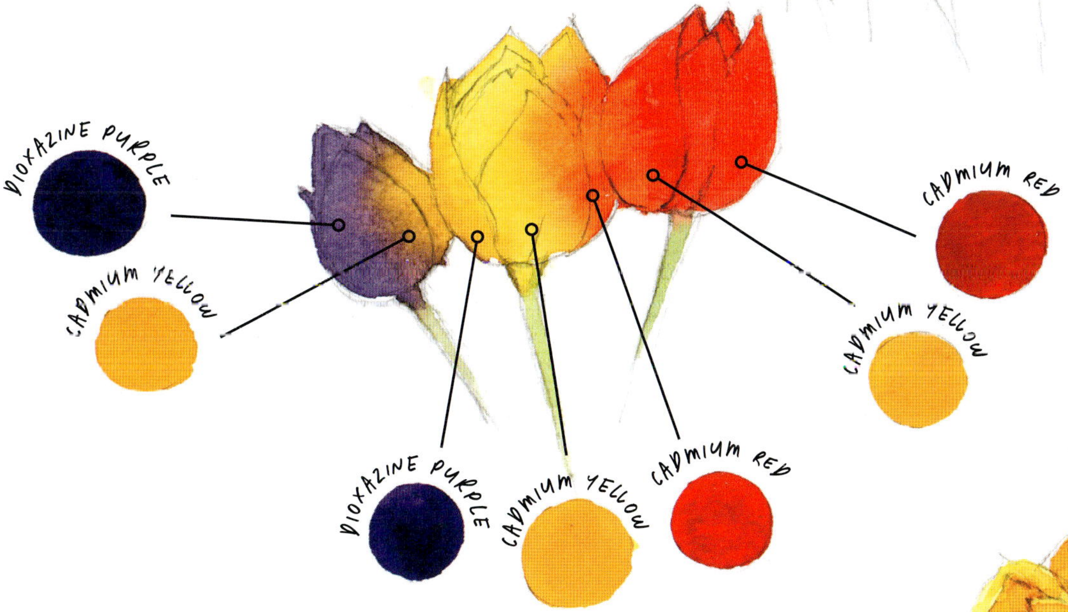
DIOXAZINE PURPLE
CADMIUM YELLOW
CADMIUM RED
CADMIUM YELLOW
DIOXAZINE PURPLE
CADMIUM YELLOW
CADMIUM RED

The technique of bleeding colors is illustrated in these two studies. As each paint is placed next to another, a little is encouraged to bleed into the color next to it. This binds the objects being painted together as they are all being viewed through the same light.

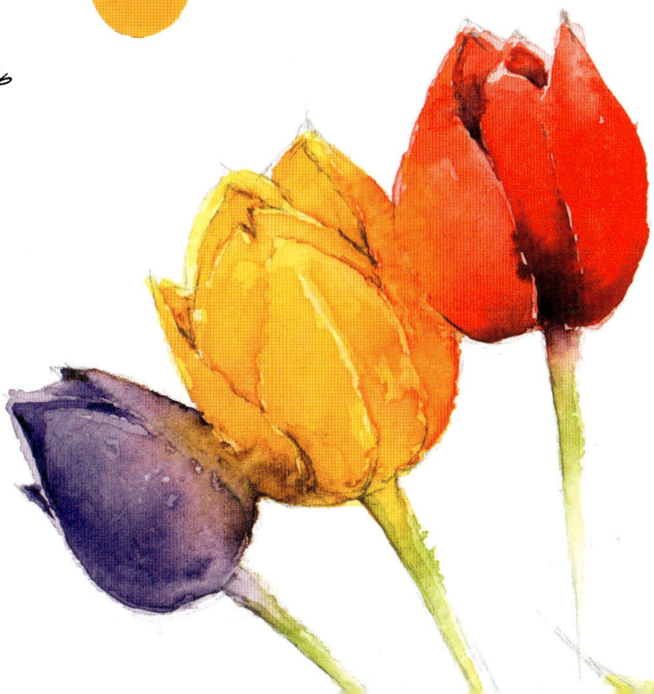

***These studies explore how you might use colors when painting a small group within one color "family" – yellows and oranges.***

**TONAL STUDIES:** I started by mxing tones I thought I might need, using the main colors that I chose.

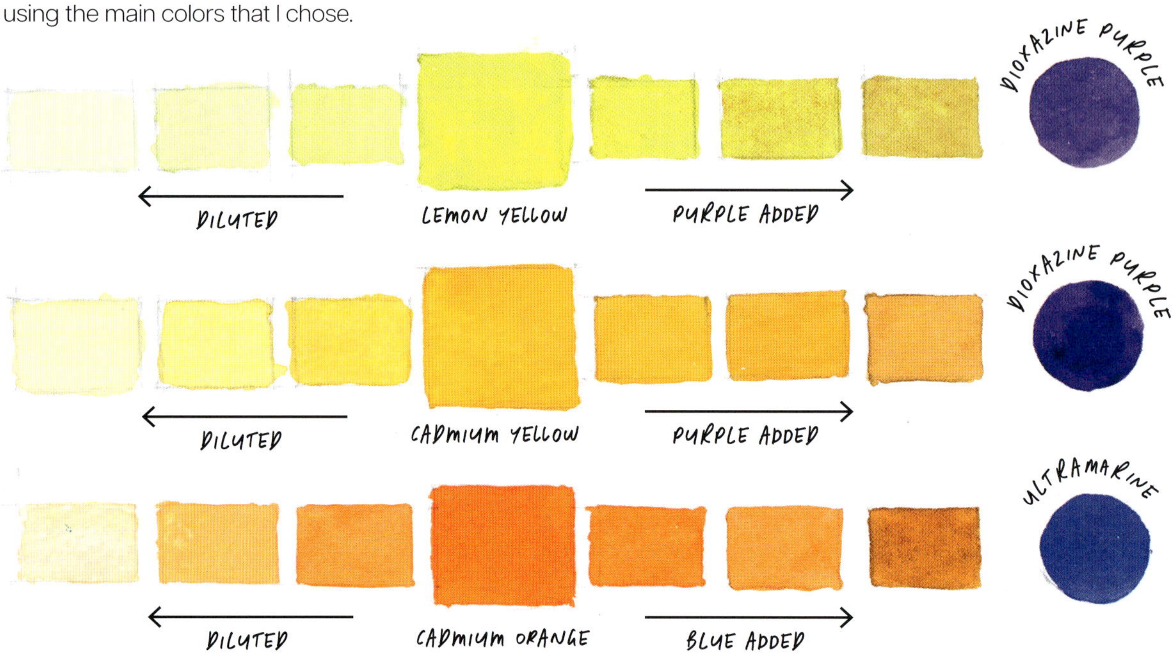

DIOXAZINE PURPLE
DILUTED
LEMON YELLOW
PURPLE ADDED
DIOXAZINE PURPLE
DILUTED
CADMIUM YELLOW
PURPLE ADDED
ULTRAMARINE
DILUTED
CADMIUM ORANGE
BLUE ADDED


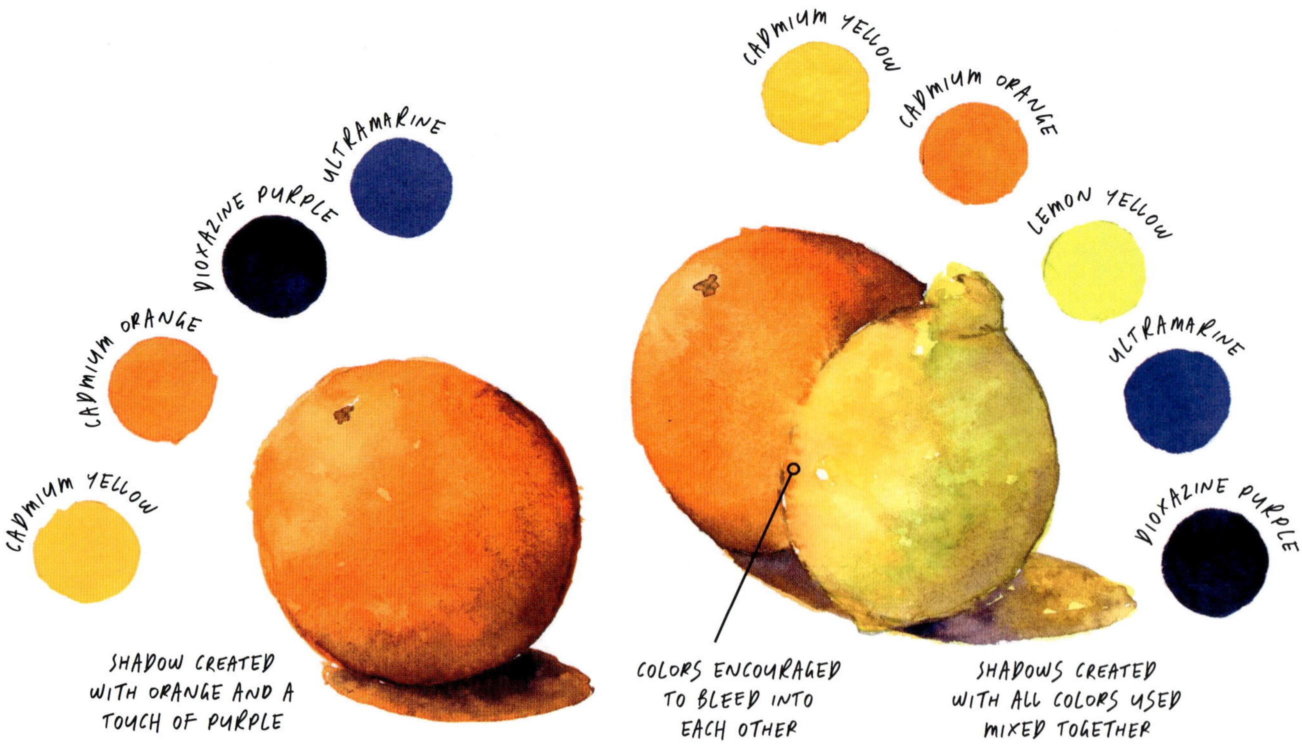

ULTRAMARINE
DIOXAZINE PURPLE
CADMIUM ORANGE
CADMIUM YELLOW
SHADOW CREATED WITH ORANGE AND A TOUCH OF PURPLE
CADMIUM YELLOW
CADMIUM ORANGE
LEMON YELLOW
ULTRAMARINE
DIOXAZINE PURPLE
COLORS ENCOURAGED TO BLEED INTO EACH OTHER
SHADOWS CREATED WITH ALL COLORS USED MIXED TOGETHER

**MIXING WITH A LIMITED PALETTE:** Small still life groups such as this fruit study allow you to practice your mixing skills within a limited color range. Choose objects that share the same color base – here they are all yellows and oranges. To begin with, limit yourself to three or four simple objects for your still life.

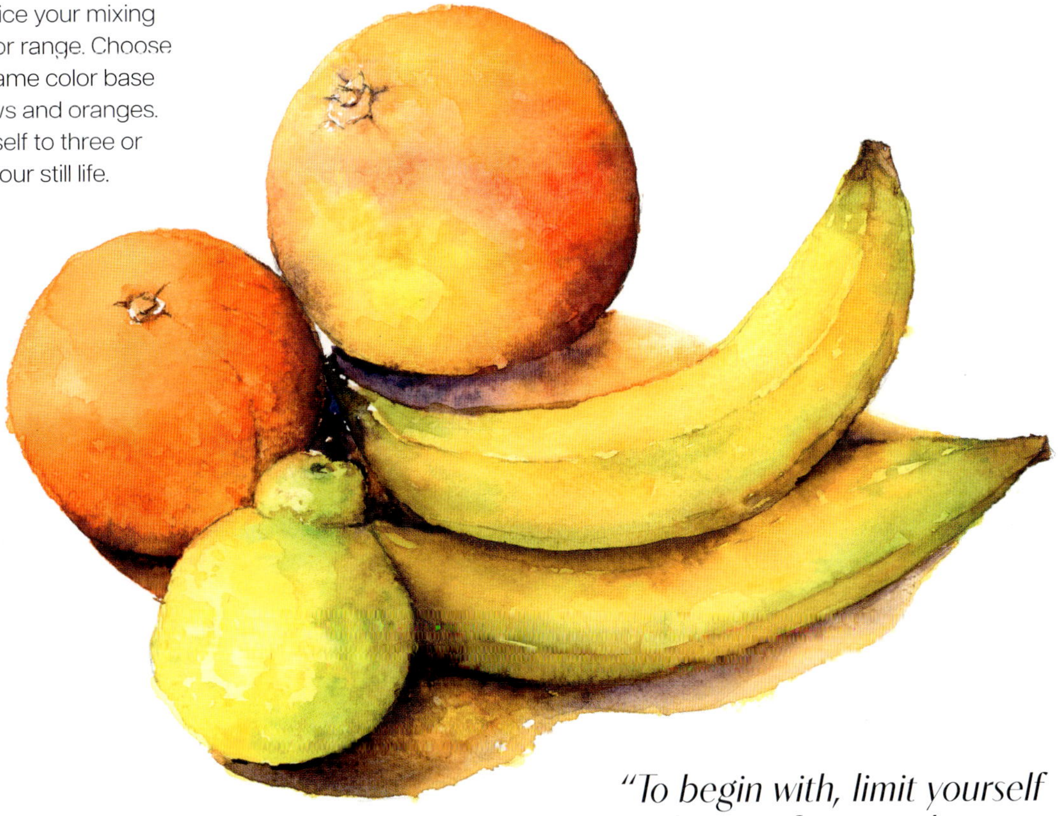

*"To begin with, limit yourself to three or four simple objects for your still life."*

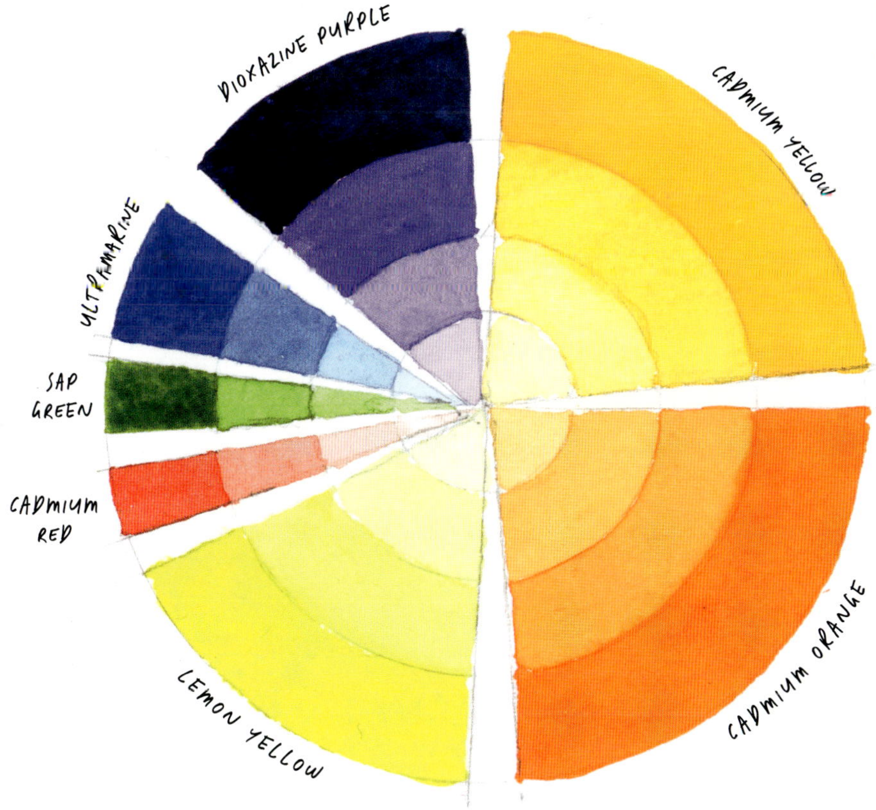
DIOXAZINE PURPLE
CADMIUM YELLOW
ULTRAMARINE
SAP GREEN
CADMIUM RED
LEMON YELLOW
CADMIUM ORANGE

**COLOR PROPORTIONS:** This chart illustrates all the colors in the final fruit study. It represents the approximate proportion of each paint used – although painting is not a precise science!

***This study is a trial run for the vegetable painting. All objects were, in a way, curved, allowing me to practice multiple color blending and bleeding.***

**MIXING COLOR FAMILIES:** These illustrations show how you might begin mixing and blending colors from different color families. Nothing changes just because you introduce a different group of colors. It just becomes more fun!

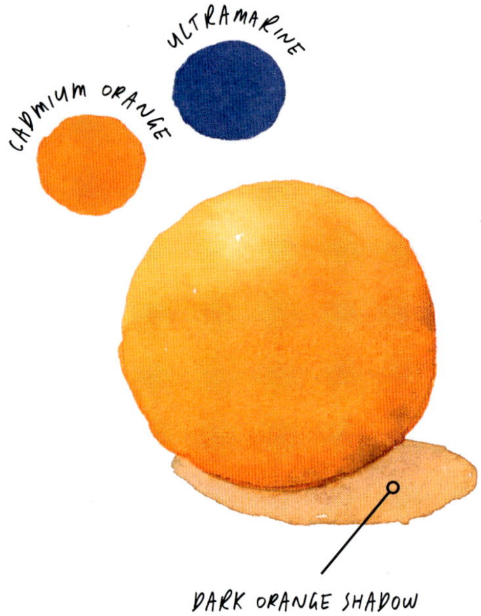
ULTRAMARINE
CADMIUM ORANGE
DARK ORANGE SHADOW

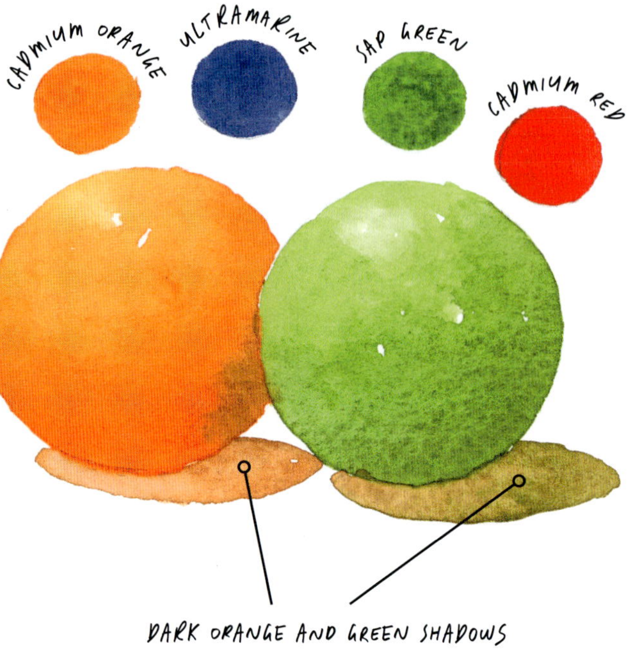
CADMIUM ORANGE
ULTRAMARINE
SAP GREEN
CADMIUM RED
DARK ORANGE AND GREEN SHADOWS

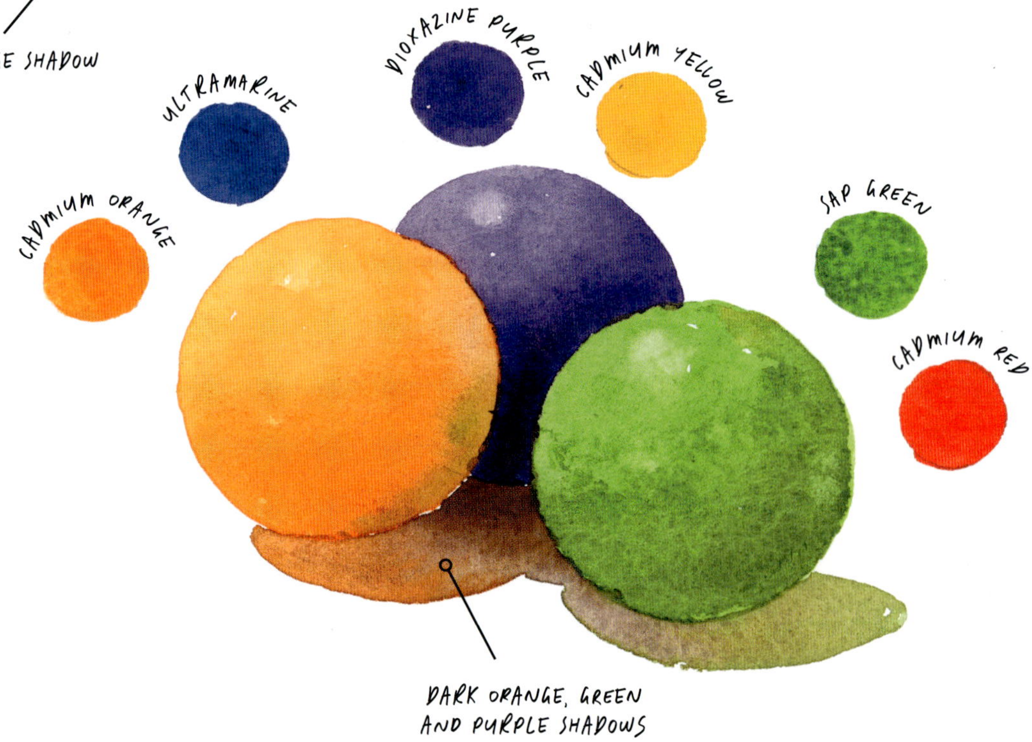
DIOXAZINE PURPLE
CADMIUM YELLOW
ULTRAMARINE
CADMIUM ORANGE
SAP GREEN
CADMIUM RED
DARK ORANGE, GREEN
AND PURPLE SHADOWS

### GRADUATING COLOR VALUES:

This vegetable group contains more objects than the previous fruit still life, but I chose subjects that were all, essentially, rounded. This allowed me to experiment with graduated light and dark values – hence the spheres used for practice purposes.

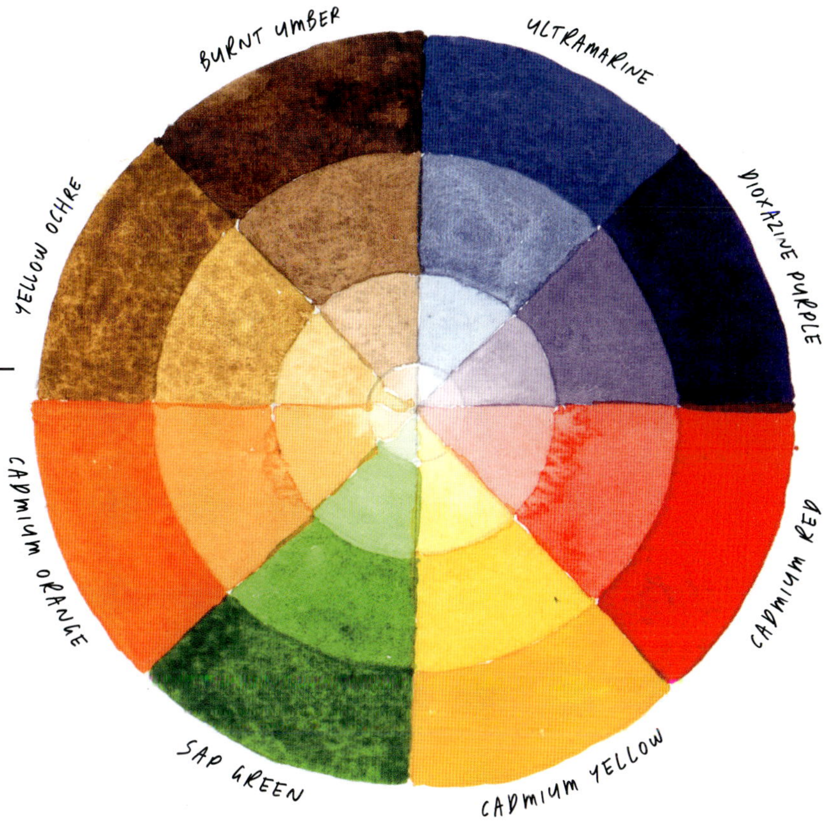
BURNT UMBER
ULTRAMARINE
DIOXAZINE PURPLE
CADMIUM RED
CADMIUM YELLOW
SAP GREEN
CADMIUM ORANGE
YELLOW OCHRE

This chart represents all the colors used in the final vegetables study.

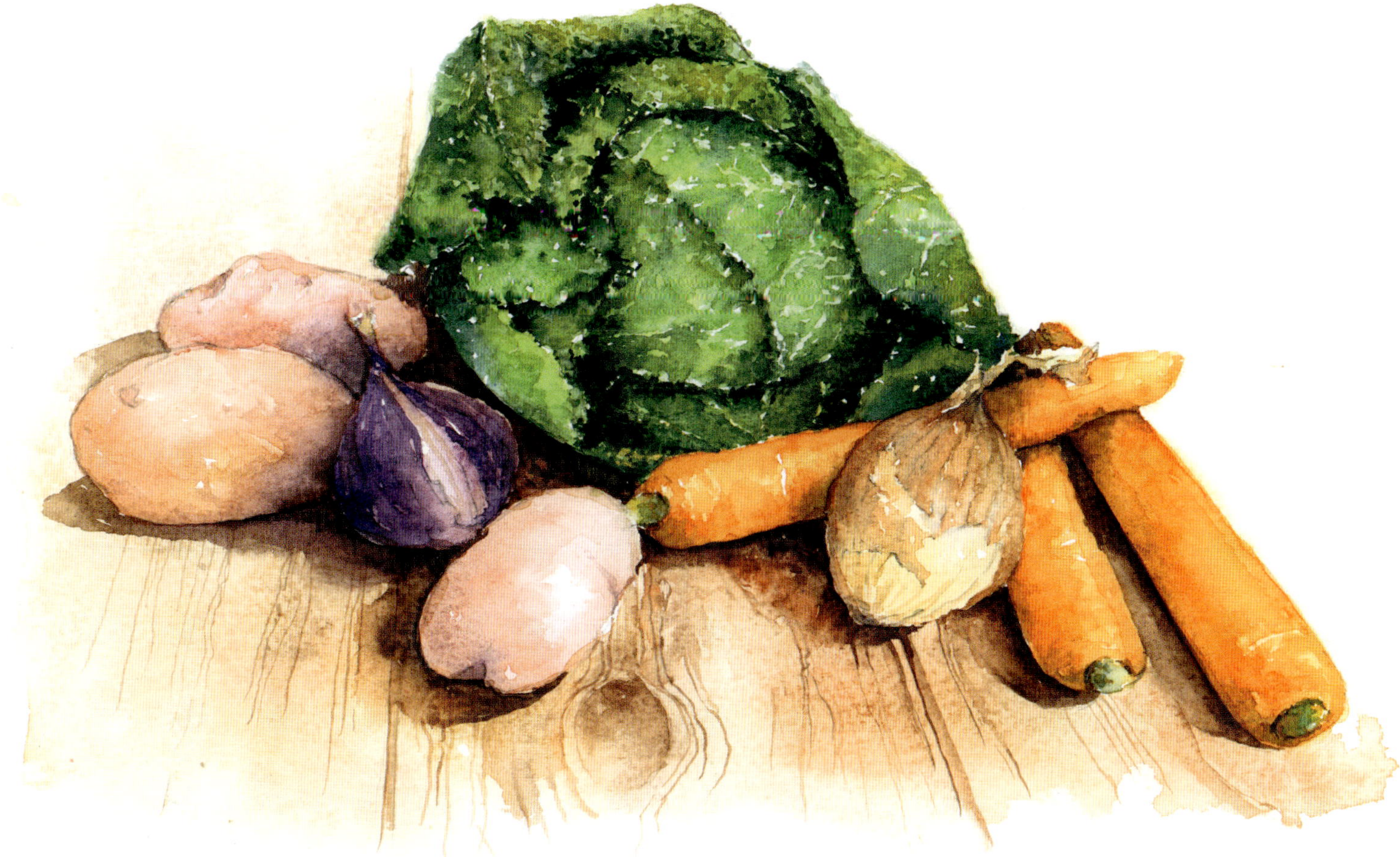

# *Part 4:* WARM & COLD

Colors can be used to appeal to the senses in many ways – these pages will explore the idea of temperature, or its illusion. The "signage" industry does not always help us as embryonic artists – red images are typically used for warnings of heat and fire, and blue lettering for cold and freezing. These are highly effective for safety, but do the "rules" of warm and cold apply equally when we start to explore paints?

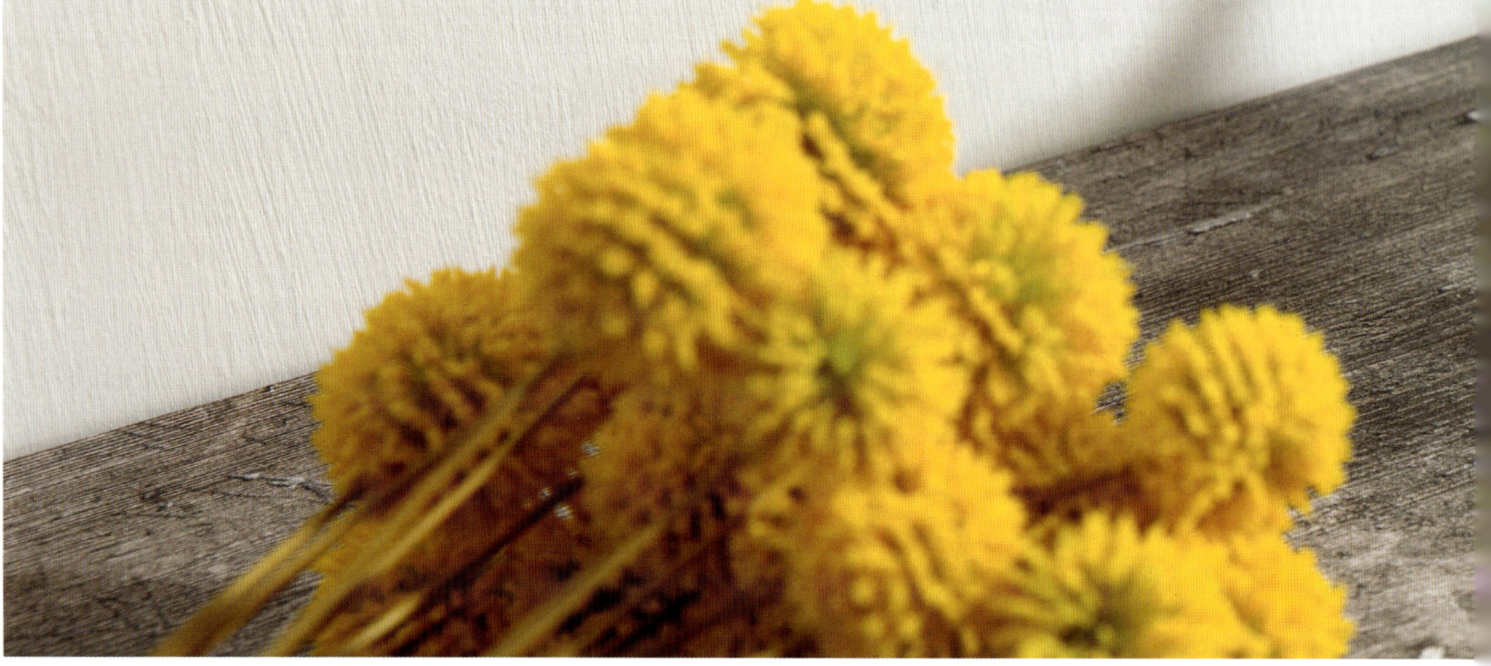

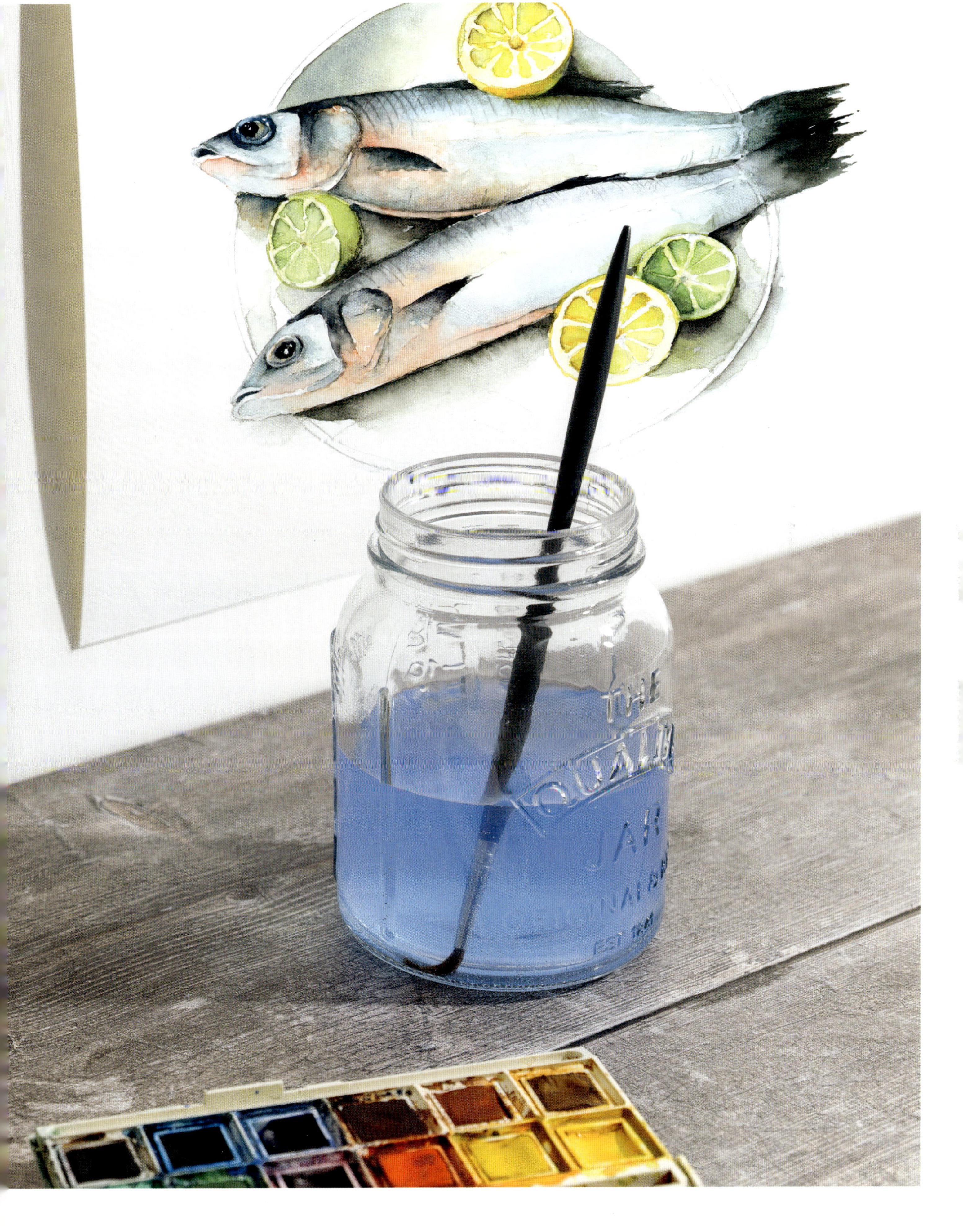
THE
JAR

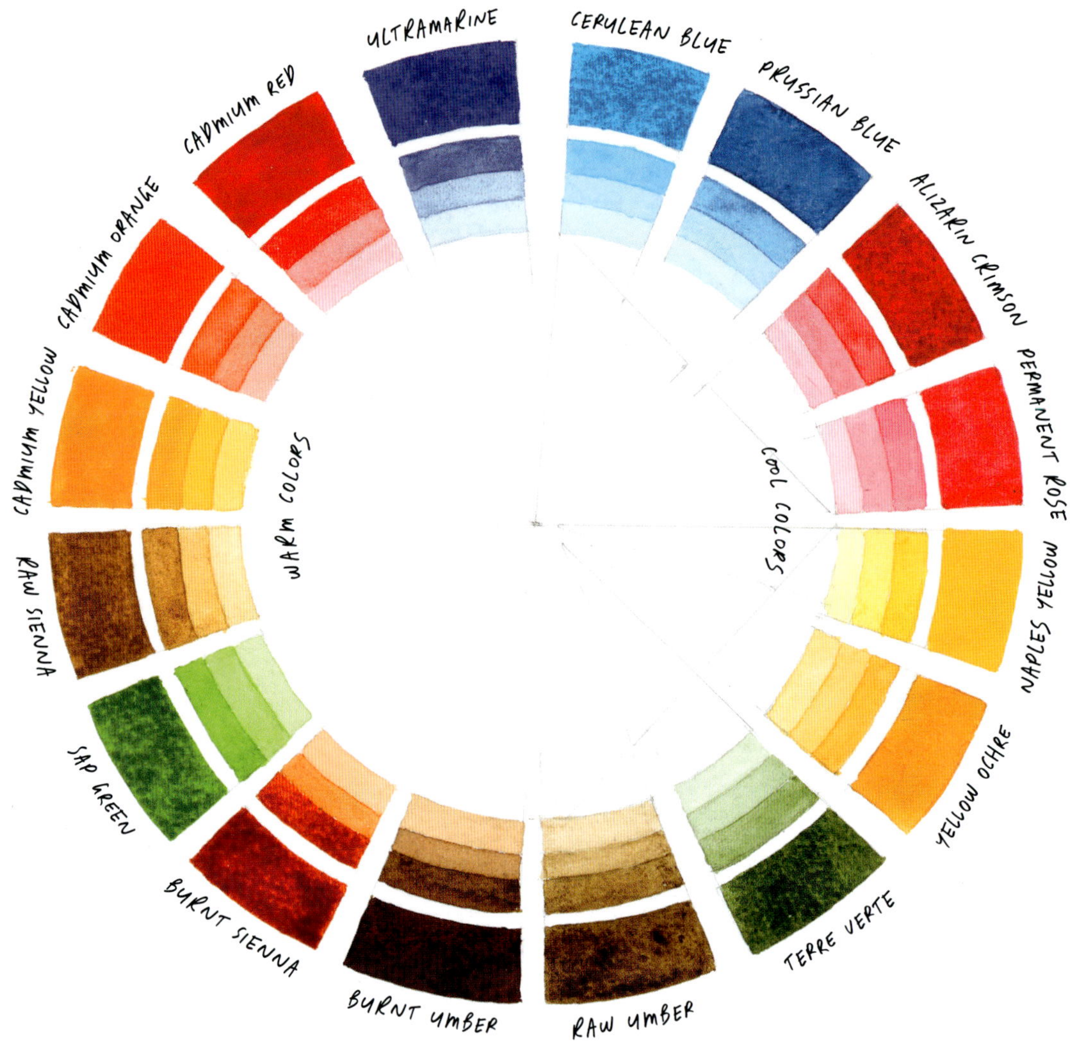
ULTRAMARINE
CERULEAN BLUE
PRUSSIAN BLUE
ALIZARIN CRIMSON
PERMANENT ROSE
NAPLES YELLOW
YELLOW OCHRE
TERRE VERTE
RAW UMBER
BURNT UMBER
BURNT SIENNA
SAP GREEN
RAW SIENNA
CADMIUM YELLOW
CADMIUM ORANGE
CADMIUM RED
WARM COLORS
COOL COLORS

# The Theory

Paints themselves do not hold any physical qualities of heat or cold – this is purely a matter of perception or optical sensations. Some of this, however, may be learned through pre-conceived concepts. Reds are warm and blues are cold, surely?

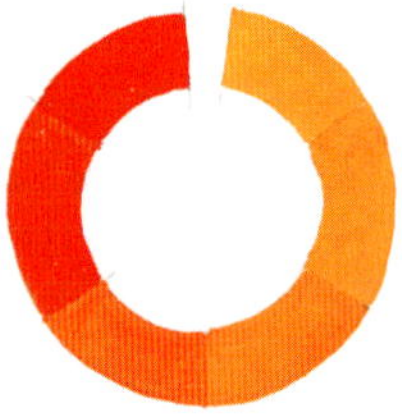

**TEMPERATURE CIRCLES:** The first circle moves from warm yellow to hot red, creating four classic "warm" oranges. The other travels from yellow to blue, creating four different greens en route. But are these greens warm or cold?

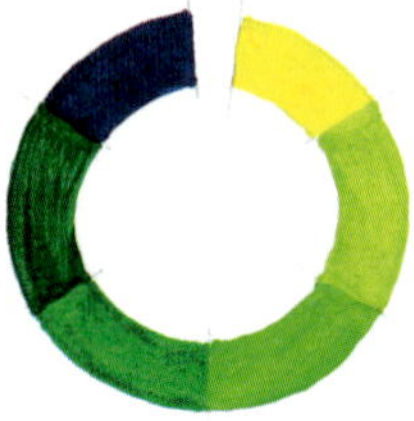

## PERCEIVED WISDOM

The subjectivity of these sensations may sometimes cause us to question the perceived wisdom that all blues are cold colors and that all reds are warm. This is something that is often engendered by advertisers for a wealth of commercial products. But as artists, we know better. The next few pages will consider this with examples of reds that could be considered to be within the cooler section of the color spectrum and blues that can be considered to be within the warmer section.

## WARM OR COLD?

The warm colors/cool colors temperature chart takes a look at some of these myths and lays out the colors on the left-hand side as those that we usually associate with the visual sensation of warmth. While many blues do in fact tend towards the cooler end of the spectrum, not all do.

Ultramarine, for example, certainly does impart the sensation of warmth, and is particularly valuable in Mediterranean scenes with sun-drenched shadows. The right-hand side contains those colors that we usually associate with the cooler end of the color spectrum. Both Cerulean Blue and Prussian Blue are clear examples of this.

Several colors, however, manage to maintain dual identity. Alizarin Crimson, for example, is one of those colors that can take on a distinctly chilled appearance once diluted, yet in its raw state can appear quite warm.

## THINKING SUBJECTIVELY

In the examples of the small temperature circles, the first color circle is made up of yellows, oranges and reds – most would agree that these colors are in the "warm" category. The small circle on the right, however, is not quite so straightforward. Having mixed yellow with blue, some of the greens created could easily fit into the "warm" category, while those close to the blue may appear "colder." So, let's not harbor too many assumptions about color temperature and instead start to make our own decisions.

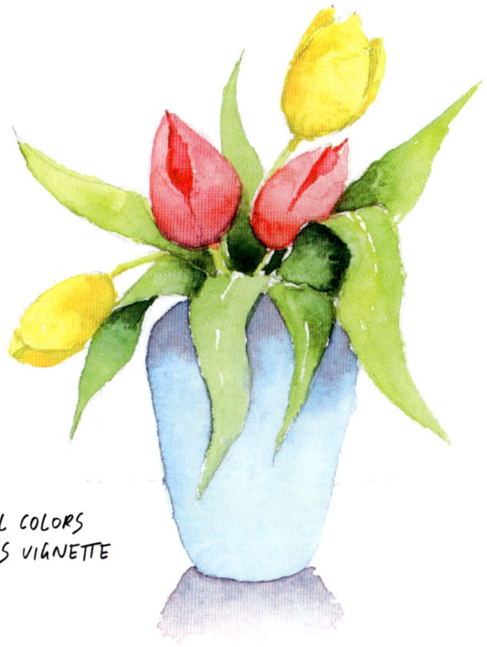

COOL COLORS TULIPS VIGNETTE

**SETTING THE TEMPERATURE:** For the two small tulip vignettes, I used two different sets of paints. The warm colors tulips vignette uses predominantly Ultramarine, Cadmium Yellow and Cadmium Red and so, by comparison to the cool colors vignette, it appears to be much "warmer." The cool colors tulip vignette was painted with Prussian Blue, Naples Yellow and Alizarin Crimson and consequently, has a much "cooler" feel to it.

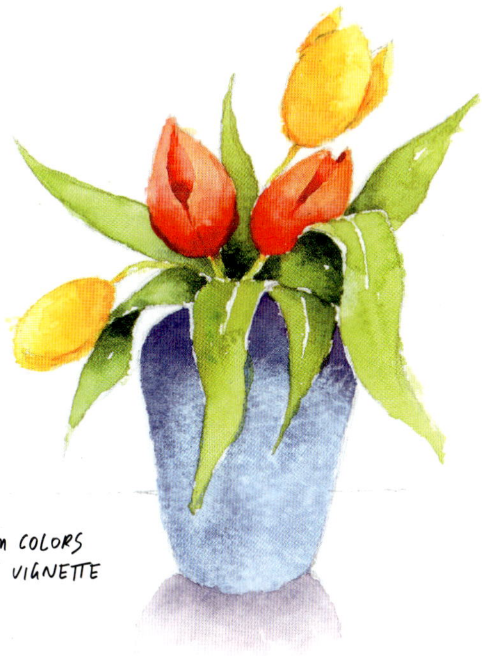

WARM COLORS TULIPS VIGNETTE

# Still Life Studies

Having explored the theory of temperature in color, we can look at a few still life studies that demonstrate that theory in practice. This also includes choosing shades according to your preference and own perception of warm and cool.

***To begin, I raided my garden for a selection of spring flowers that hadn't yet acquired any feeling of summer warmth. Chiefly "cold" colors record the flowers in loose sketch form.***

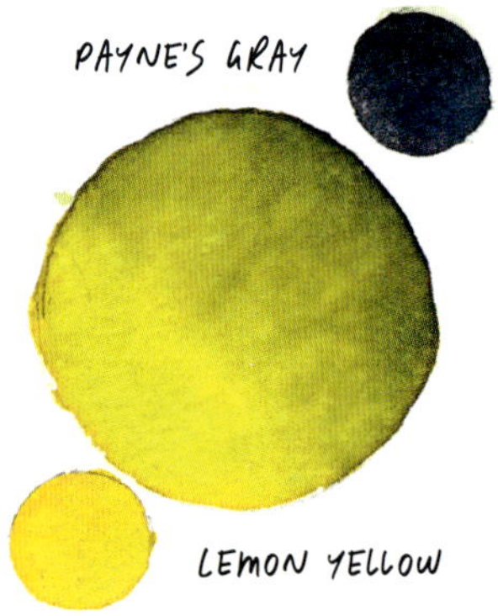
PAYNE'S GRAY
LEMON YELLOW

I used a valuable mix, already considered – Lemon Yellow and a small touch of Payne's Gray – to create those cool, acidic greens of the leaves. The blue in Payne's Gray reacts very quickly with yellow to change its original color. I also introduced a touch of Hooker's Green, a light, thin color that tends towards blue, hence the "cooling" effect that it can have in a mix.

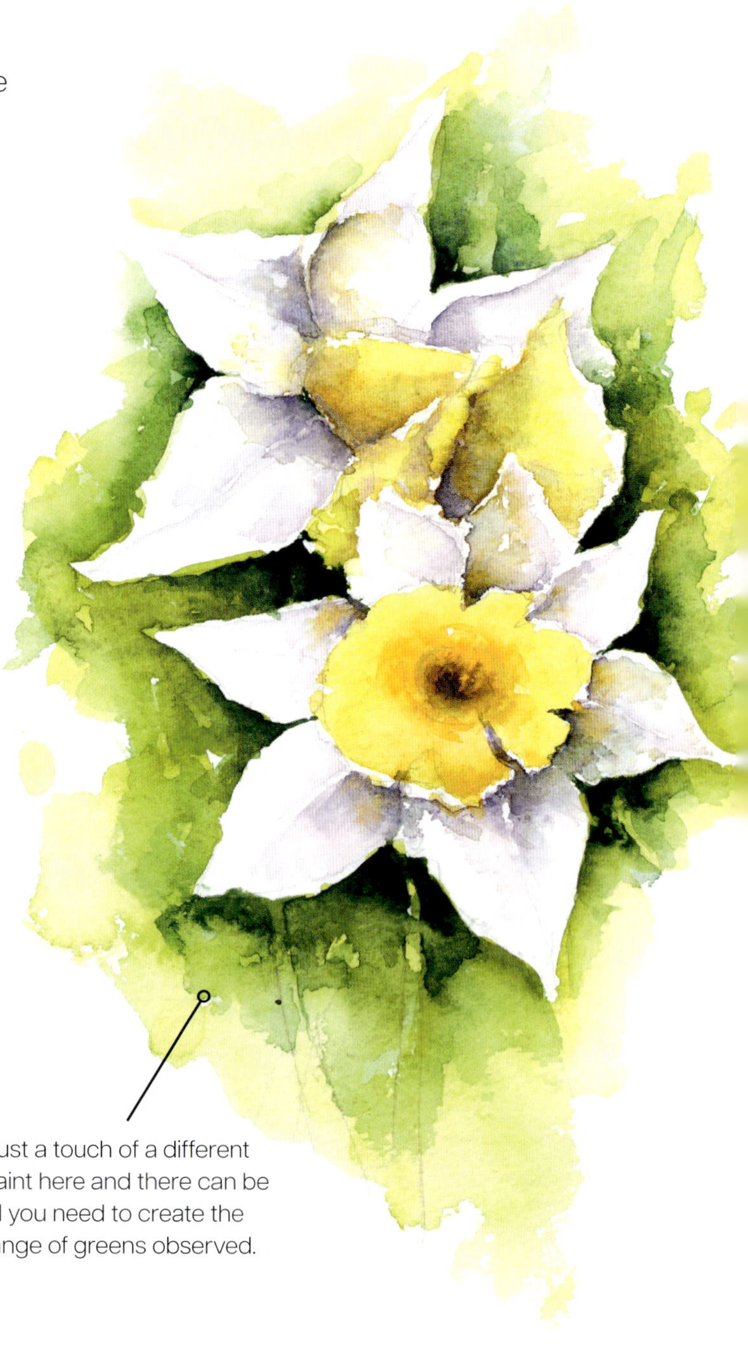

Just a touch of a different paint here and there can be all you need to create the range of greens observed.

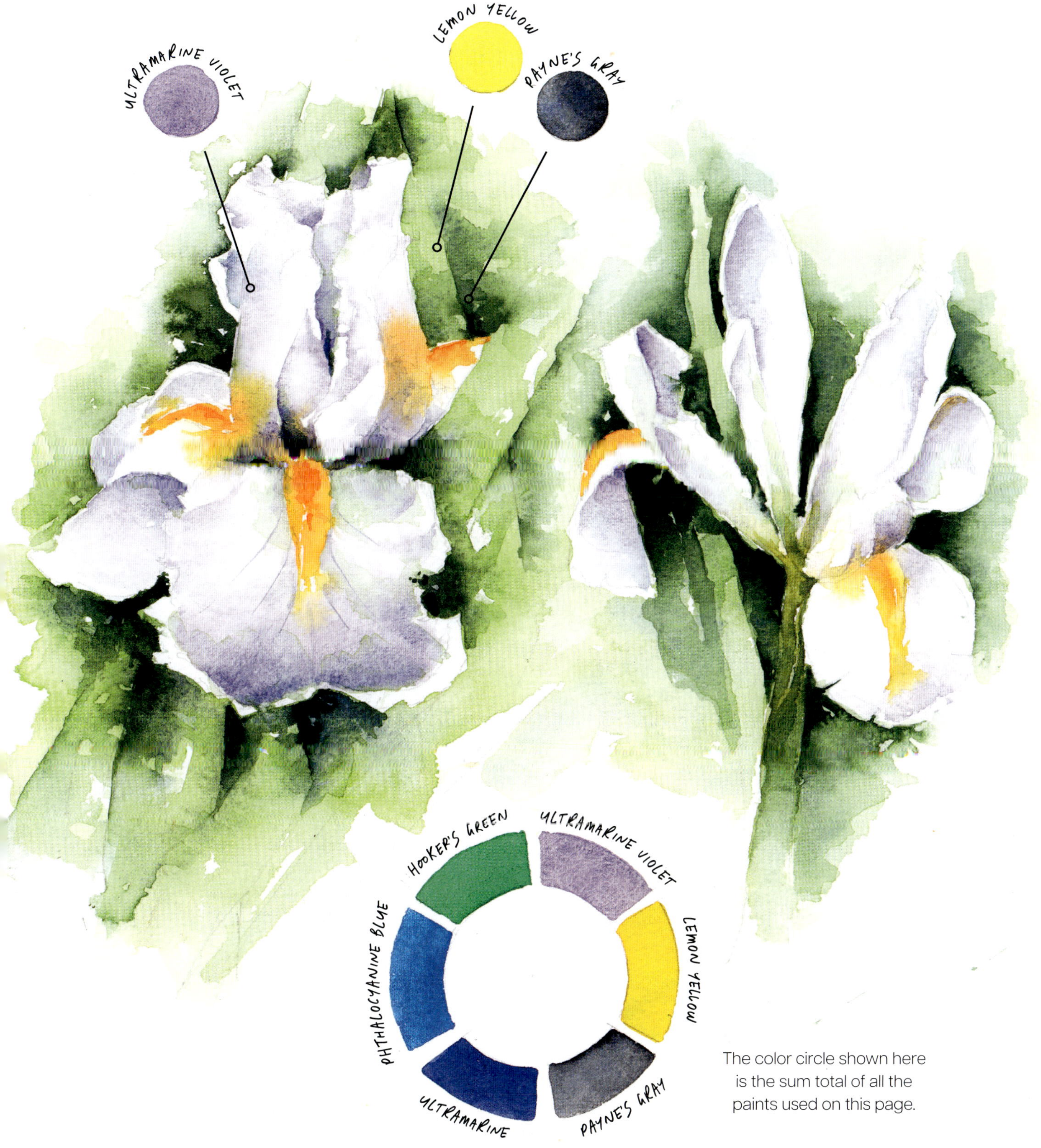
ULTRAMARINE VIOLET
LEMON YELLOW
PAYNE'S GRAY
HOOKER'S GREEN
ULTRAMARINE VIOLET
LEMON YELLOW
PAYNE'S GRAY
ULTRAMARINE
PHTHALOCYANINE BLUE

The color circle shown here is the sum total of all the paints used on this page.

***Now, moving on to a slightly different approach to using color: these still lifes of glistening fresh fish were painted to illustrate how you can utilize color to serve your own personal choices.***

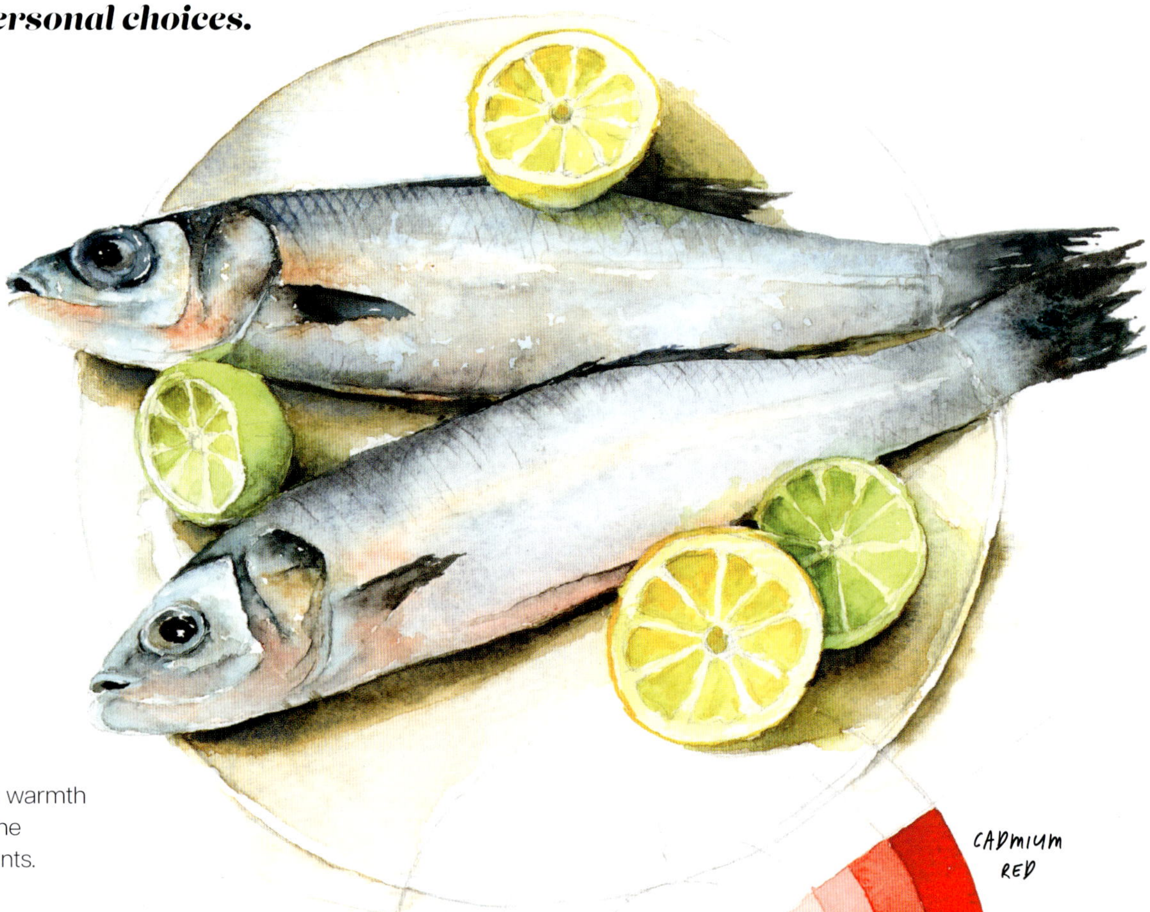

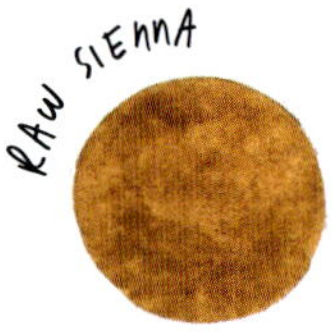
RAW SIENNA

Raw Sienna added warmth when mixed with the lemon and lime paints.

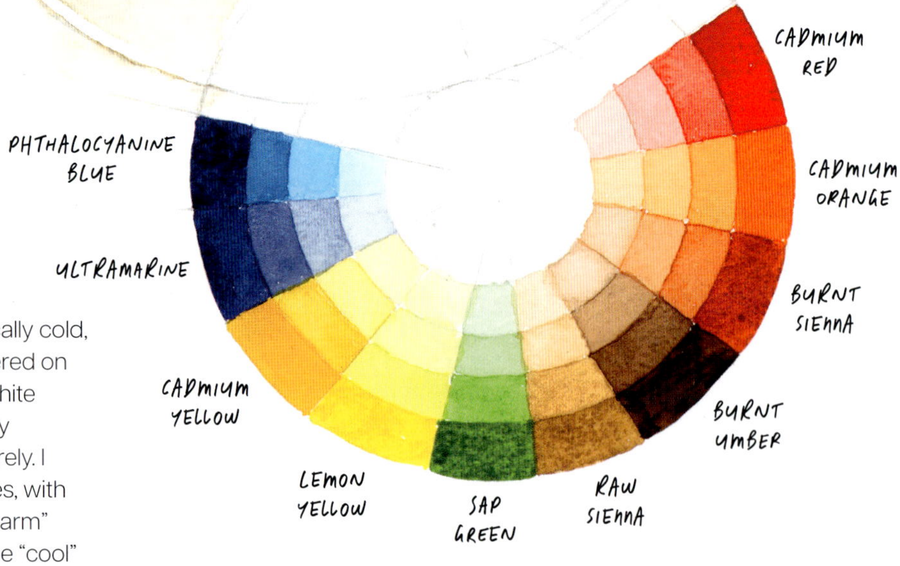
CADMIUM RED
CADMIUM ORANGE
BURNT SIENNA
BURNT UMBER
RAW SIENNA
SAP GREEN
LEMON YELLOW
CADMIUM YELLOW
ULTRAMARINE
PHTHALOCYANINE BLUE

The wet fish were naturally and physically cold, while the lemons and limes also bordered on the "cold" side of the spectrum. The white plates held no color values. So, the only colors used would be my choices entirely. I used the same palette for both pictures, with the exception of two paints. For the "warm" image, I introduced Raw Sienna. For the "cool" image, I introduced Prussian Blue. This let me add a "warming" tone to the shadows for one, and a "cooling" tone to the other. Your paper, your paints. You are in charge!

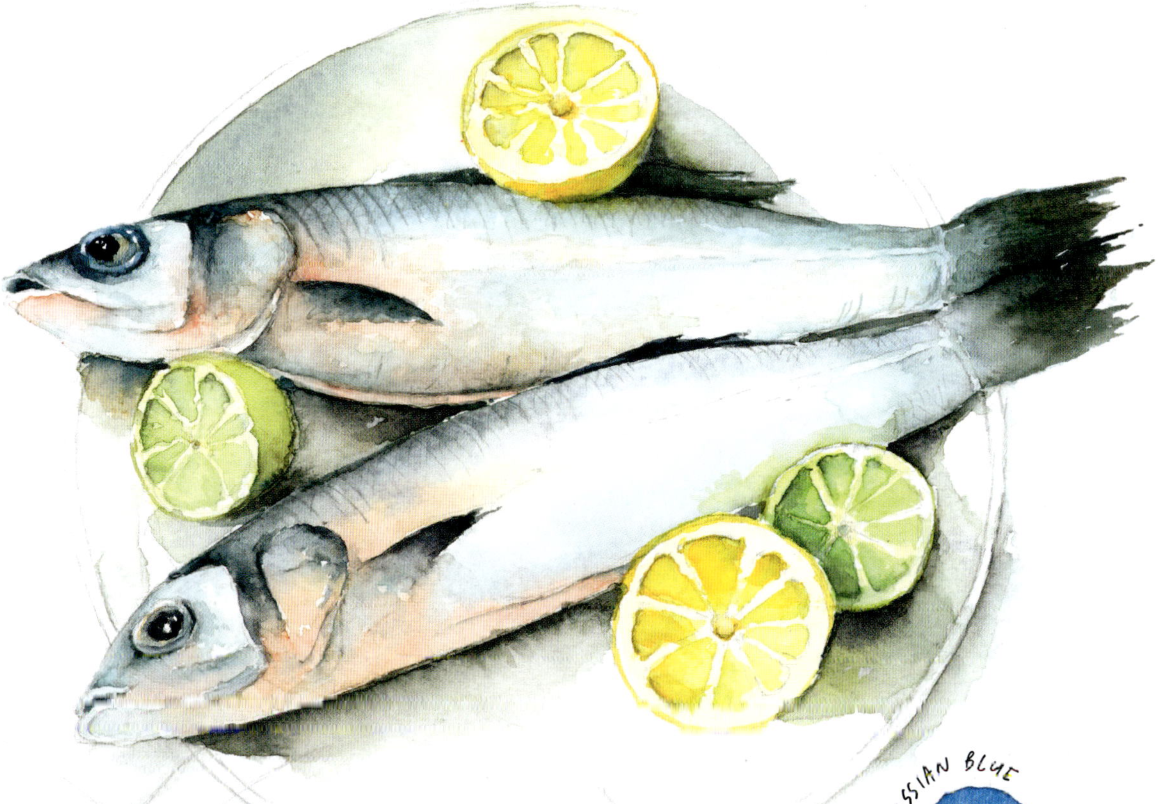

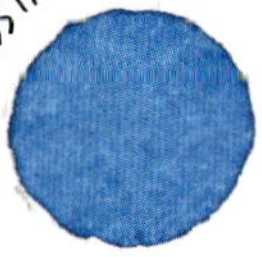
PRUSSIAN BLUE

Prussian Blue was used to create cooler shadows.

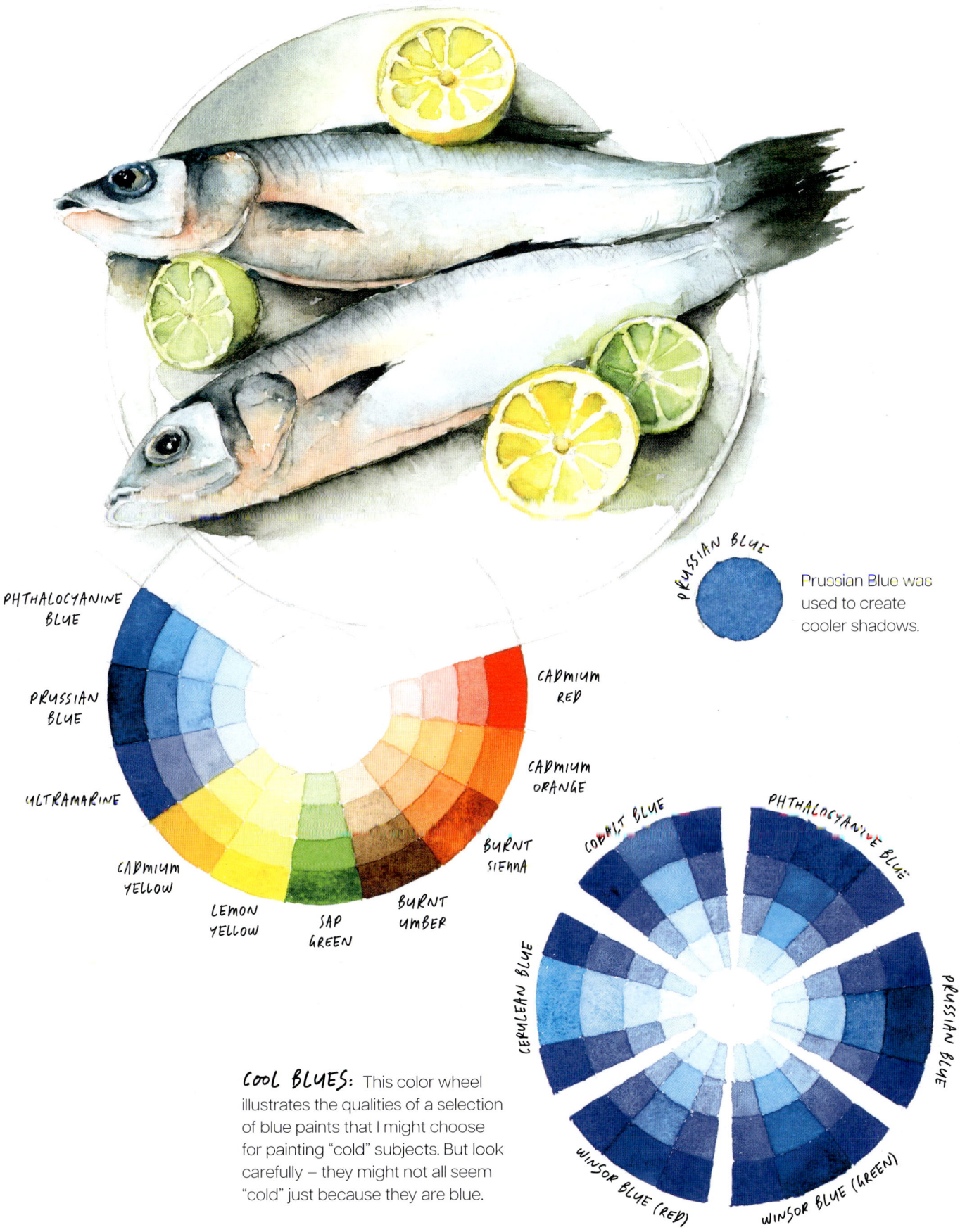

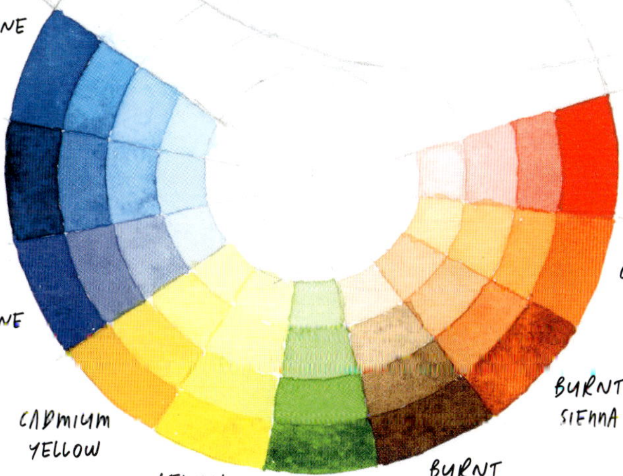
PHTHALOCYANINE BLUE
PRUSSIAN BLUE
ULTRAMARINE
CADMIUM YELLOW
LEMON YELLOW
SAP GREEN
BURNT UMBER
BURNT SIENNA
CADMIUM ORANGE
CADMIUM RED

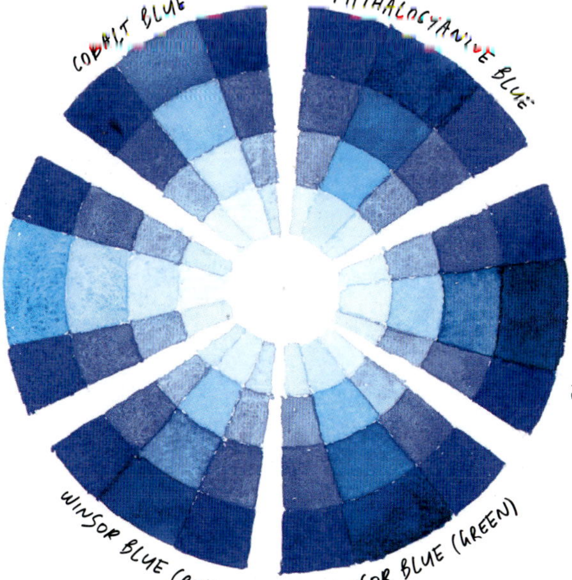
COBALT BLUE
PHTHALOCYANINE BLUE
PRUSSIAN BLUE
WINSOR BLUE (GREEN)
WINSOR BLUE (RED)
CERULEAN BLUE

**COOL BLUES:** This color wheel illustrates the qualities of a selection of blue paints that I might choose for painting “cold” subjects. But look carefully – they might not all seem “cold” just because they are blue.

***For the next sketchbook page, I raided my garden for the rich, earthy browns and golds of the leaves in fall. I used predominantly "warm" colors, the clear choice to do justice to these seasonal subjects.***

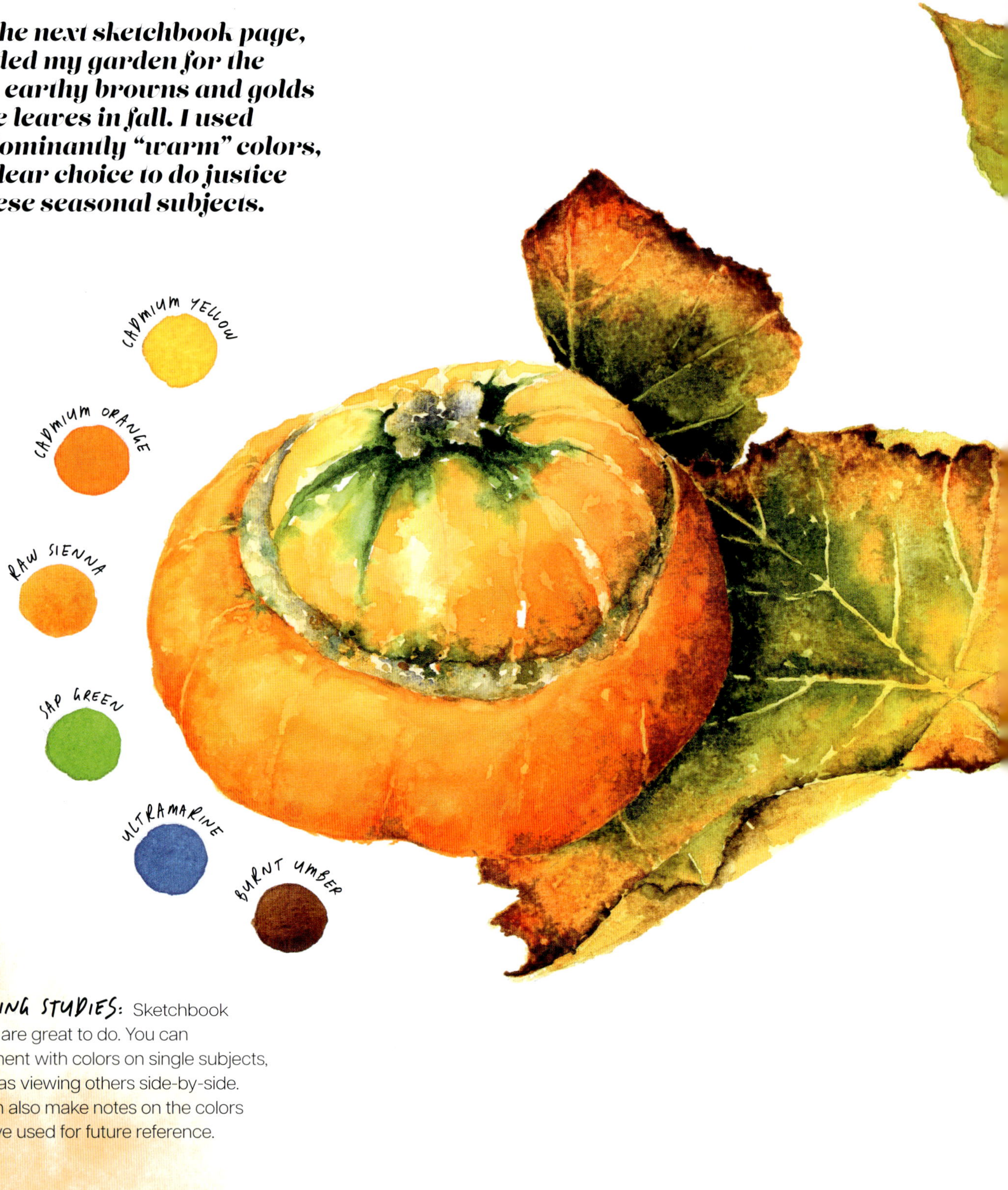

CADMIUM YELLOW
CADMIUM ORANGE
RAW SIENNA
SAP GREEN
ULTRAMARINE
BURNT UMBER


**CREATING STUDIES:** Sketchbook studies are great to do. You can experiment with colors on single subjects, as well as viewing others side-by-side. You can also make notes on the colors you have used for future reference.

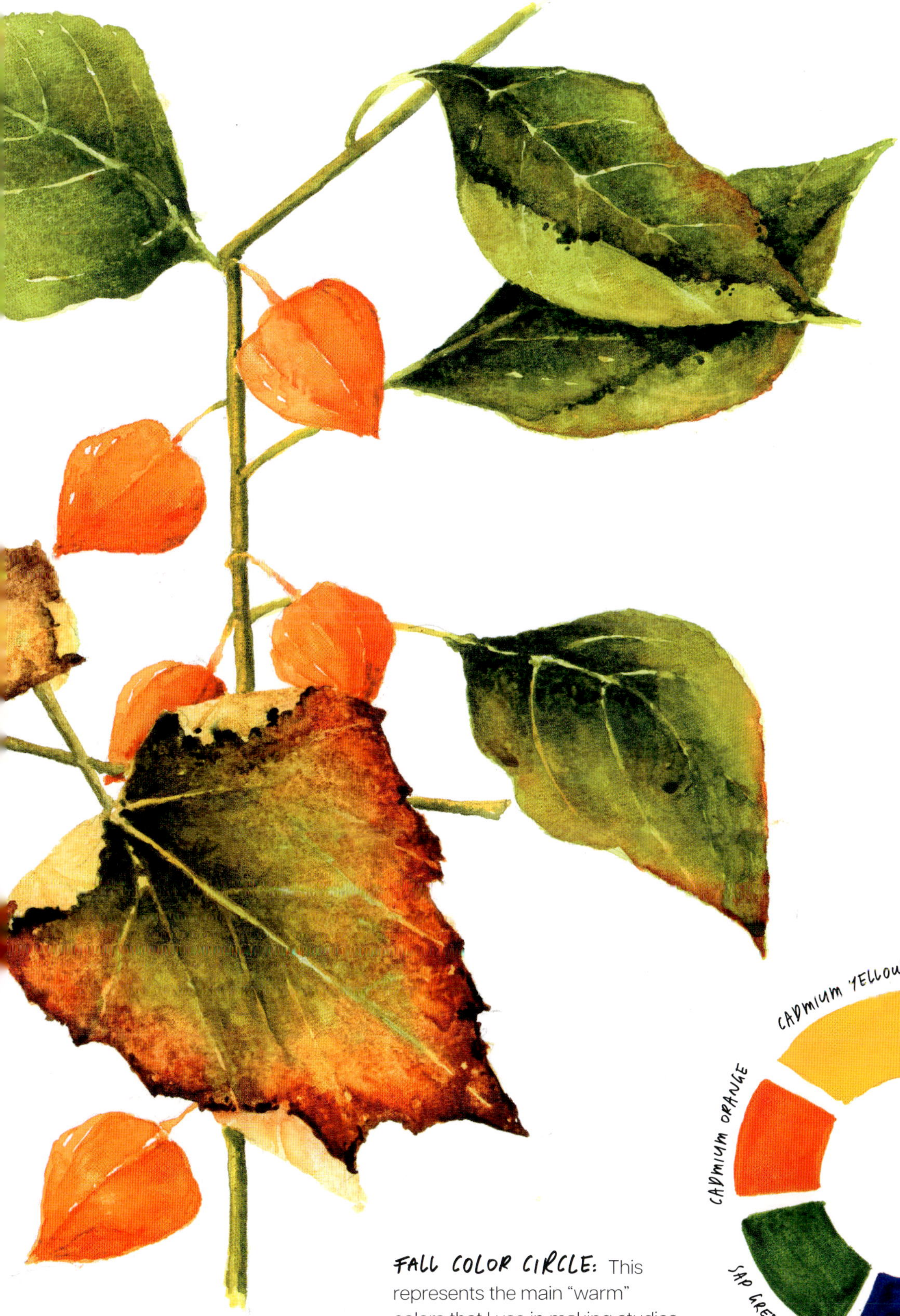

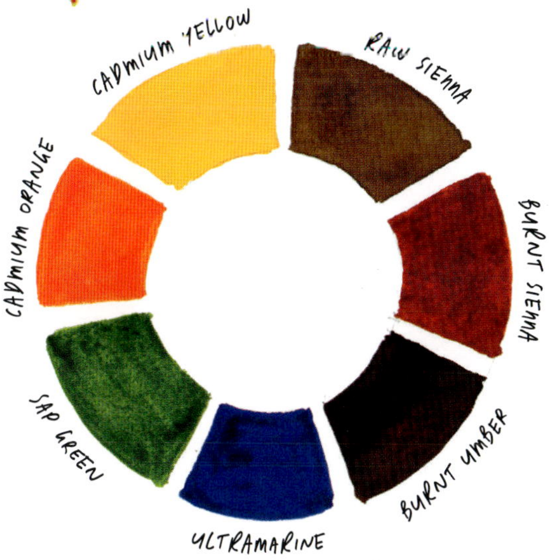
CADMIUM YELLOW
RAW SIENNA
BURNT SIENNA
BURNT UMBER
ULTRAMARINE
SAP GREEN
CADMIUM ORANGE

**FALL COLOR CIRCLE:** This represents the main "warm" colors that I use in making studies of objects found in woods and gardens at the turning of the year.

***For the blue flowerpots studies, it again fell to me to take control of the painting and color mixing process.***

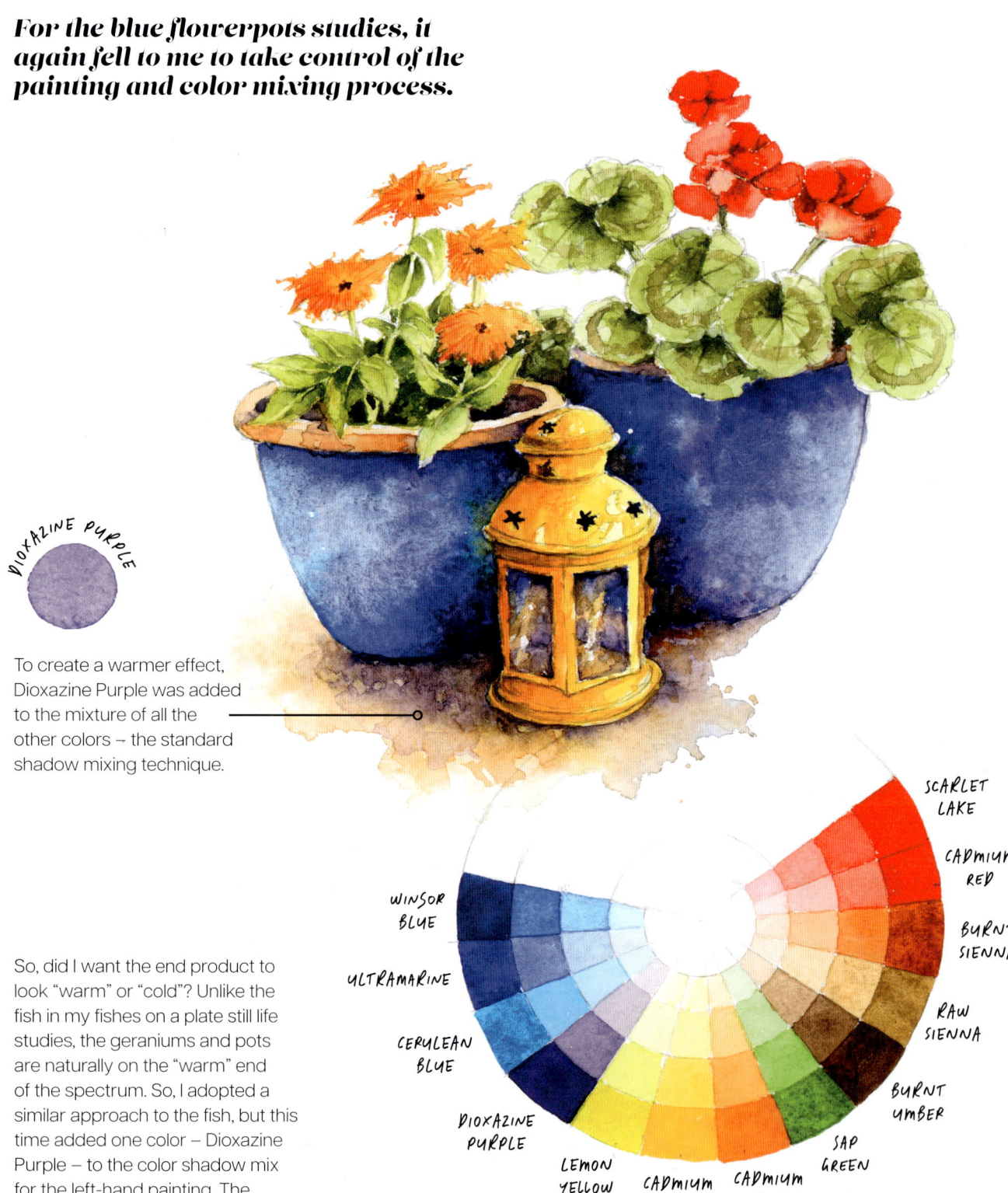

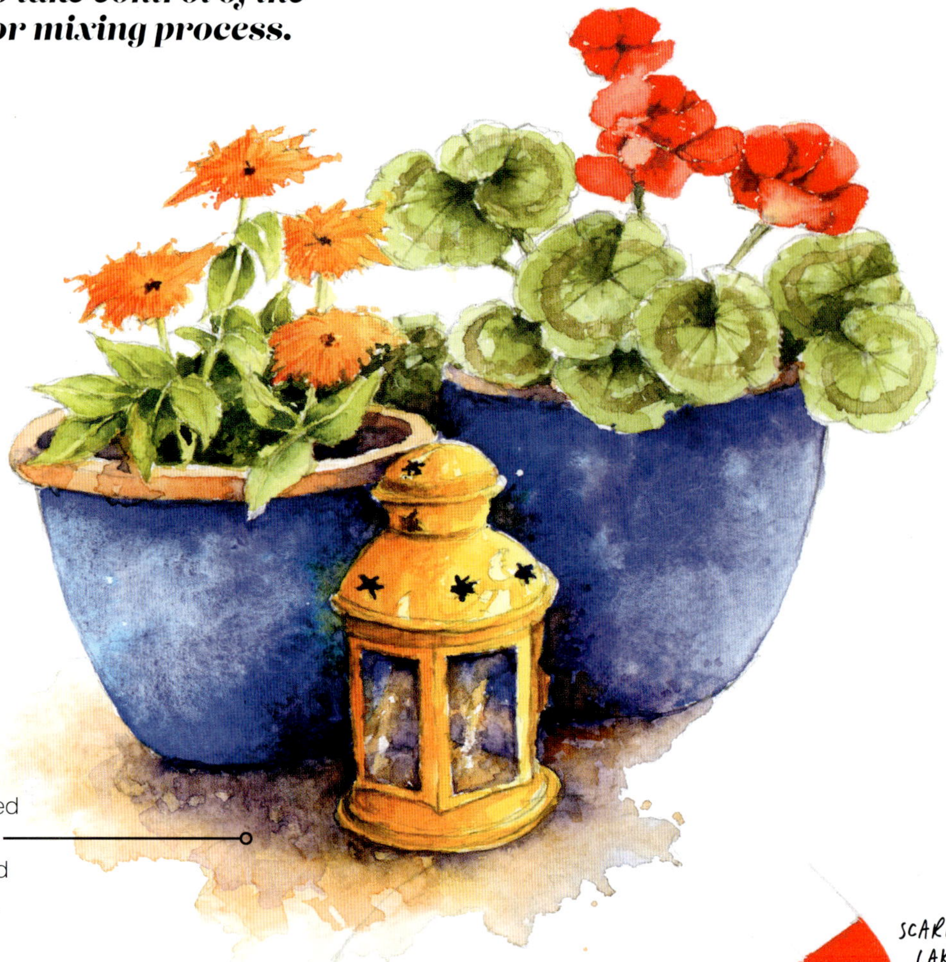

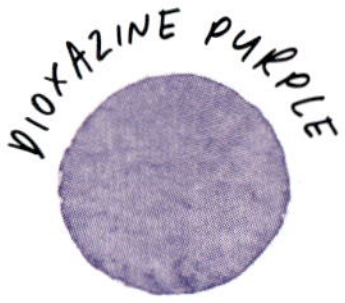
DIOXAZINE PURPLE

To create a warmer effect, Dioxazine Purple was added to the mixture of all the other colors – the standard shadow mixing technique.

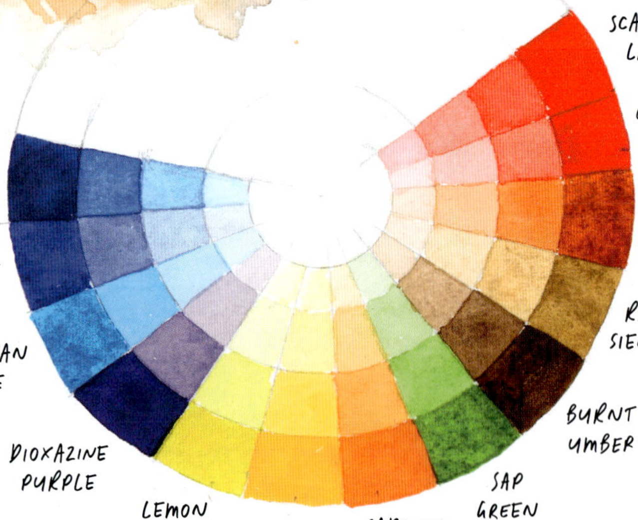
SCARLET LAKE
CADMIUM RED
BURNT SIENNA
RAW SIENNA
BURNT UMBER
SAP GREEN
CADMIUM ORANGE
CADMIUM YELLOW
LEMON YELLOW
DIOXAZINE PURPLE
CERULEAN BLUE
ULTRAMARINE
WINSOR BLUE

So, did I want the end product to look "warm" or "cold"? Unlike the fish in my fishes on a plate still life studies, the geraniums and pots are naturally on the "warm" end of the spectrum. So, I adopted a similar approach to the fish, but this time added one color – Dioxazine Purple – to the color shadow mix for the left-hand painting. The right-hand painting relied on blues added to the other colors when mixing the shadows, leaving a much "colder" feel to the deeper, darker shadows on the floor.

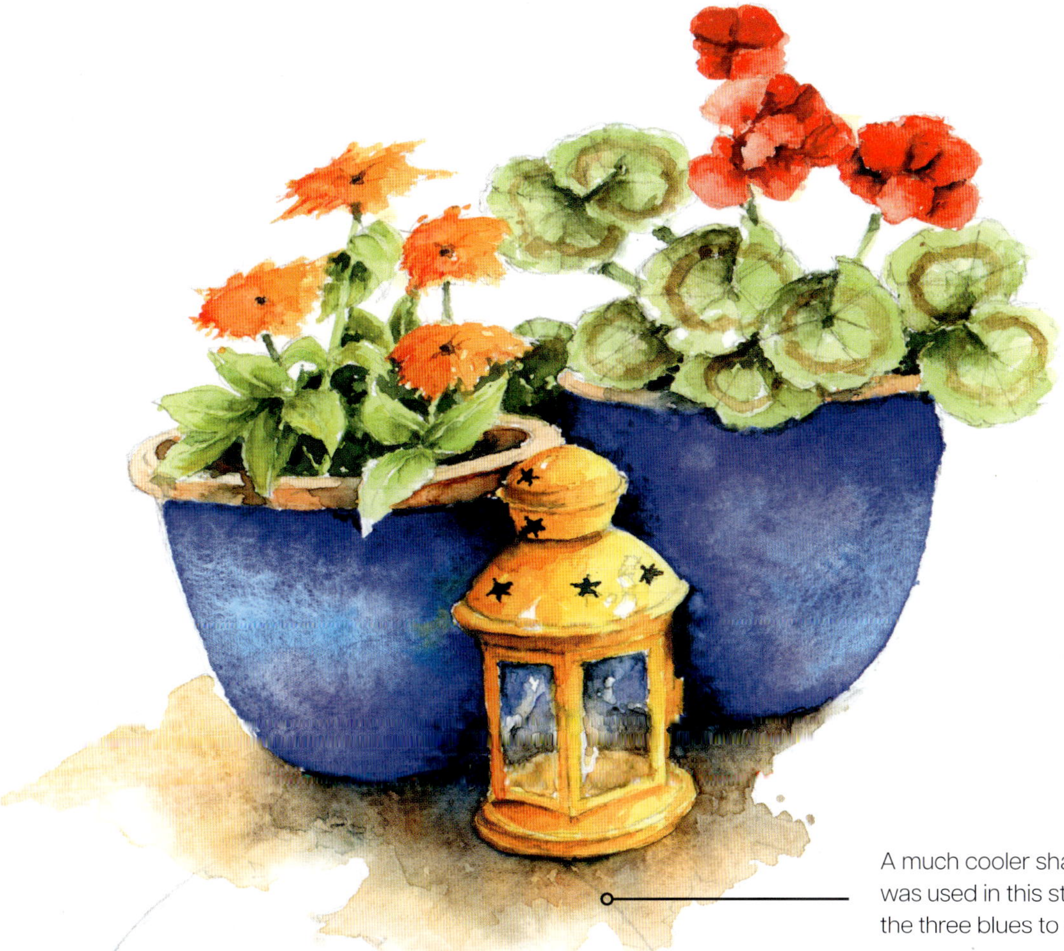

A much cooler shadow mix was used in this study, allowing the three blues to dominate.

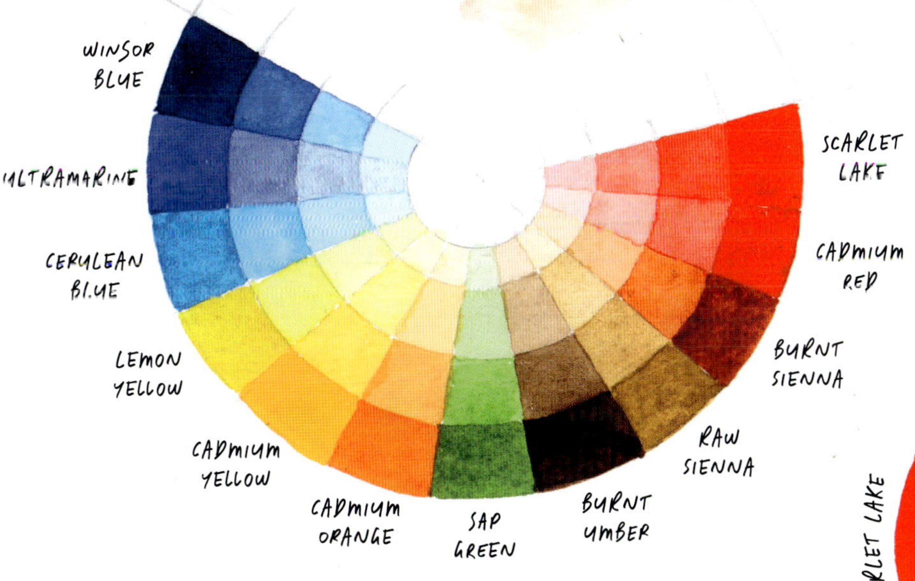
WINSOR BLUE
ULTRAMARINE
CERULEAN BLUE
LEMON YELLOW
CADMIUM YELLOW
CADMIUM ORANGE
SAP GREEN
BURNT UMBER
RAW SIENNA
BURNT SIENNA
CADMIUM RED
SCARLET LAKE

**FOCUS ON REDS:** This color wheel represents an assortment of reds for painting "warm" objects. When diluted, some clearly have a warmer feel than others, so choose carefully.

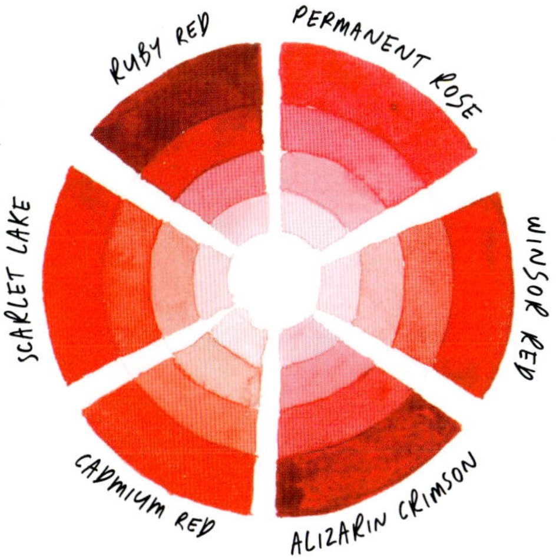
RUBY RED
PERMANENT ROSE
WINSOR RED
ALIZARIN CRIMSON
CADMIUM RED
SCARLET LAKE

# *Part 5:*

# COLOR IN ACTION

So, now we have an insight into the temperature imparting qualities of colors, and we can move on to bringing all the past pages together and undertaking some extended projects. This section is an insight into my own methods of painting – observe, record and experiment in "sketch" form before beginning a larger scale composition.

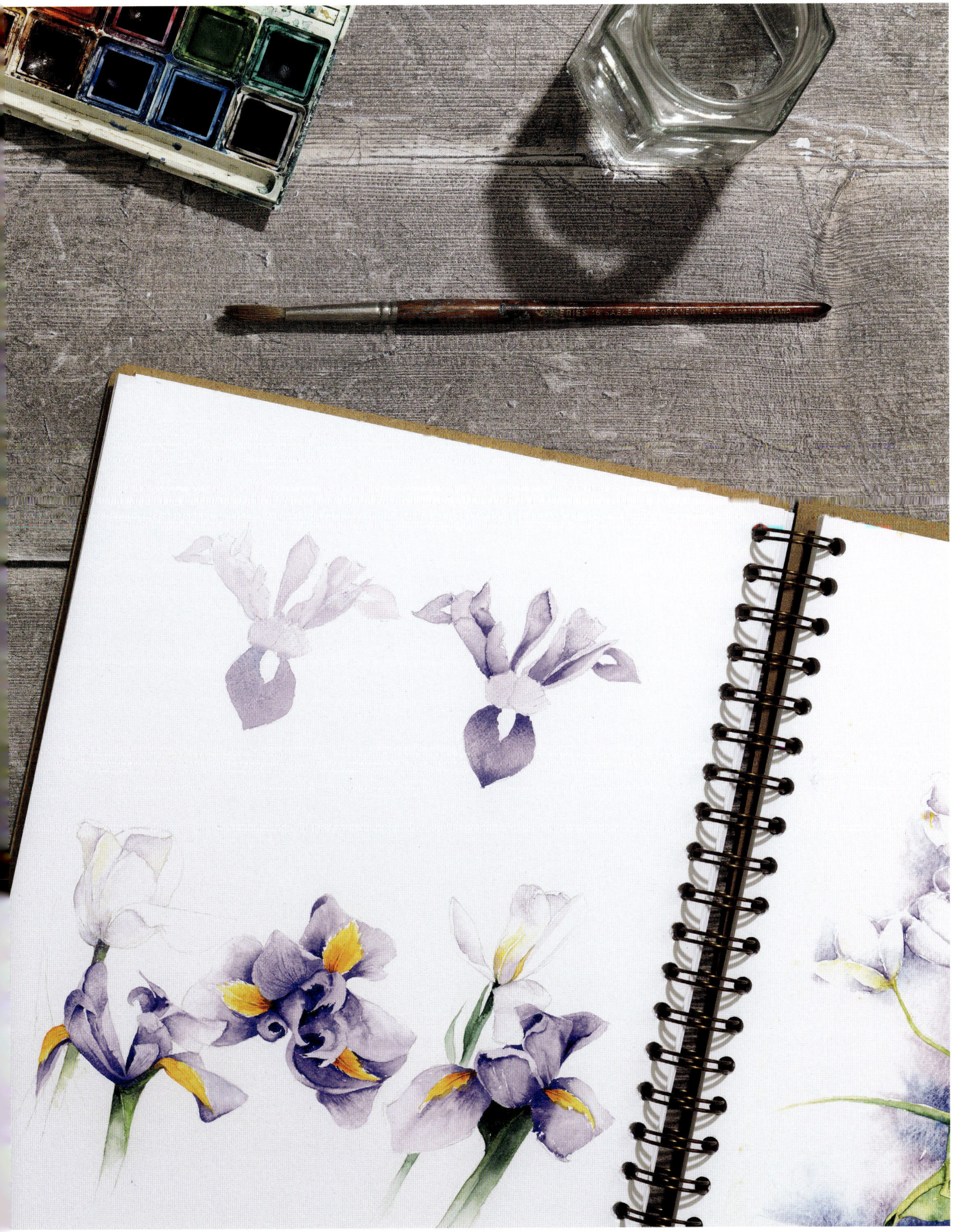

# Sketchbook Studies

Having explored the basics of watercolor painting, the types of colors available to us, the grays and neutral paints, the color family "filing system," light, shade and shadows, and color temperature, it's now time to bring all of these experiences together and embark on some painting projects in which color really is the key component.

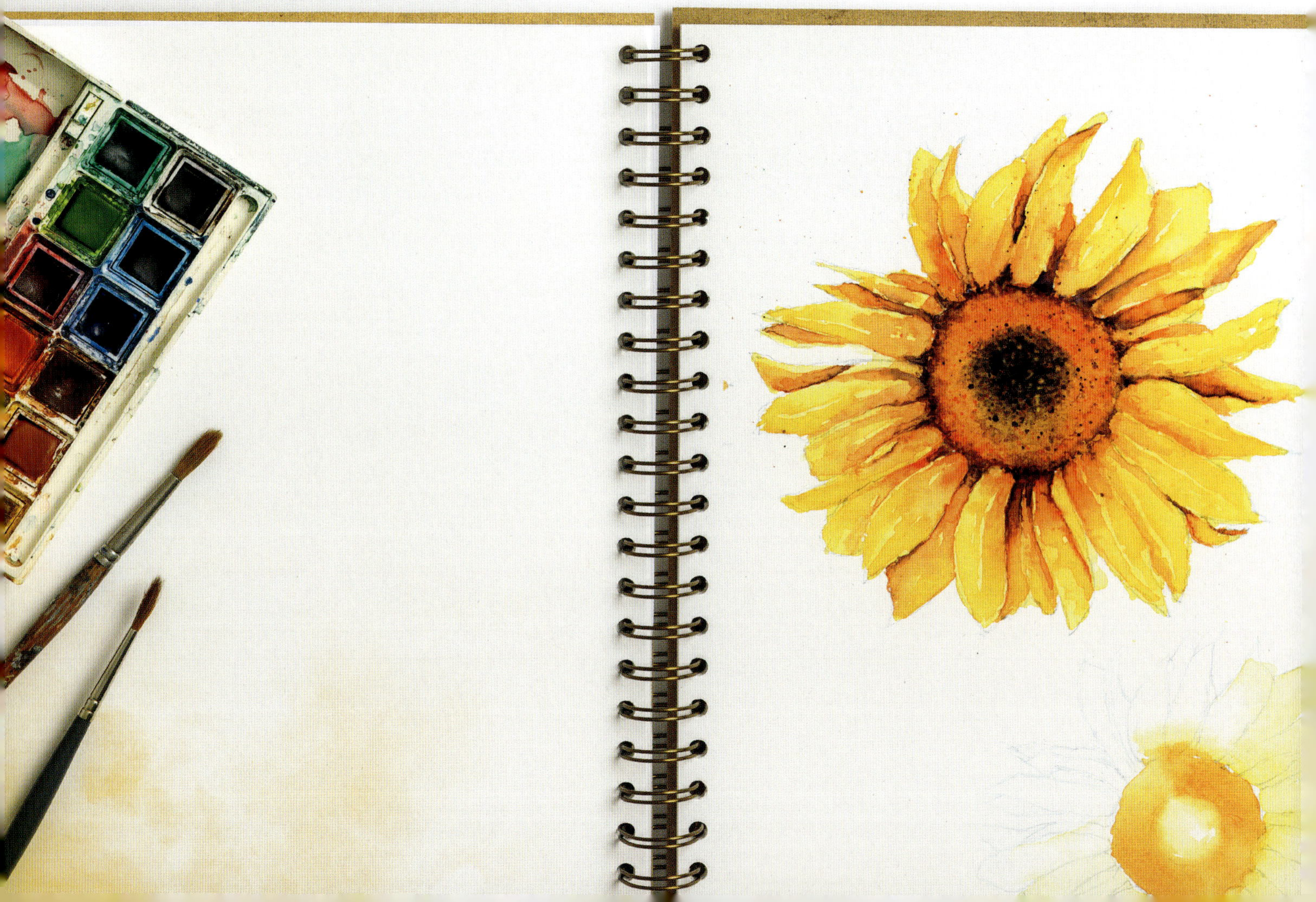

## GET TO KNOW YOUR SUBJECT

How subjects are structured will affect the light and shade, so I always start by making some studies of them in sketchbook format. These are not meant to be finished paintings – they are simply investigations to better inform me as to exactly how these subjects will look when put together in a group. It also allows me to get to grips with the colors that I am likely to need to make a finished piece of work.

The chance to try different colors without worrying about getting it wrong is invaluable. Out of place colors on a sketchbook page are never as bad as a color so glaringly out of place in a finished composition. For that reason, I always make a point of exploring the front, back, top and bottom of my subjects. So often the natural colors will vary in tone underneath and not necessarily from any lack of light. The underside of the sunflower heads, for example, are a notably lighter green than the actual leaves.

Making studies of individual objects also allows you to get a really good feel for where the shadows fall within the objects. The iris heads, for example, are considerably darker towards the center of the flower heads, whereas the longer petals are lighter at the ends. This knowledge will allow you to use the darker colors to visually push the lighter colors forward, adding to the illusion of three dimensions on a flat sheet of paper.

## COLOR WITH CONFIDENCE

So, this is my painting technique in watercolor – always the lightest first, working through to dark. Try the Irises and Sunflowers sketchbook studies for yourself and then set up your own still life groups. But please don't paint these timidly. Color can't hurt. And remember, when working onto damp paper your colors will always dry much lighter than when you first see them. So, apply with confidence. The only way to get colors to work for you is to take charge of them yourself.

## THE THREE STAGES

In each of the Irises and Sunflowers sketchbook studies, pages of individual studies are followed by step-by-step guides to the compositions. I have broken down the painting process into the three stages that were introduced in Part 3: Light & Shade. The color circles underneath the examples illustrate the colors used in each stage.

**STAGE 1** Create the lightest tones which will, ultimately, become the highlights. Once this paint has dried it cannot be effectively altered – it will be the job of the next applications of paint to make it appear even lighter still.

**STAGE 2** I am building up colors as the process progresses. My aim is to show clearly just how the technique of using slightly darker colors to push forward the lighter colors really does work.

I also aim to show how effective the technique of bleeding colors can be. To avoid sharp, hard lines and create softer shadows, colors need to be applied to damp paint on the paper. These will become the mid-tones.

**STAGE 3** The final stage of applying the darkest colors can be done onto dry paper as these do not necessarily need to be watered down and softened. They need to have the maximum impact to significantly "push" the other colors and tones forward.

## THE FINISHED PAINTINGS

Now, a final word on the finished paintings. I chose to set both these groups up with no clearly discernible background. I wanted to use pure color, avoiding unnecessary visual clutter, providing a colored backdrop against which the groups could be viewed.

# Irises

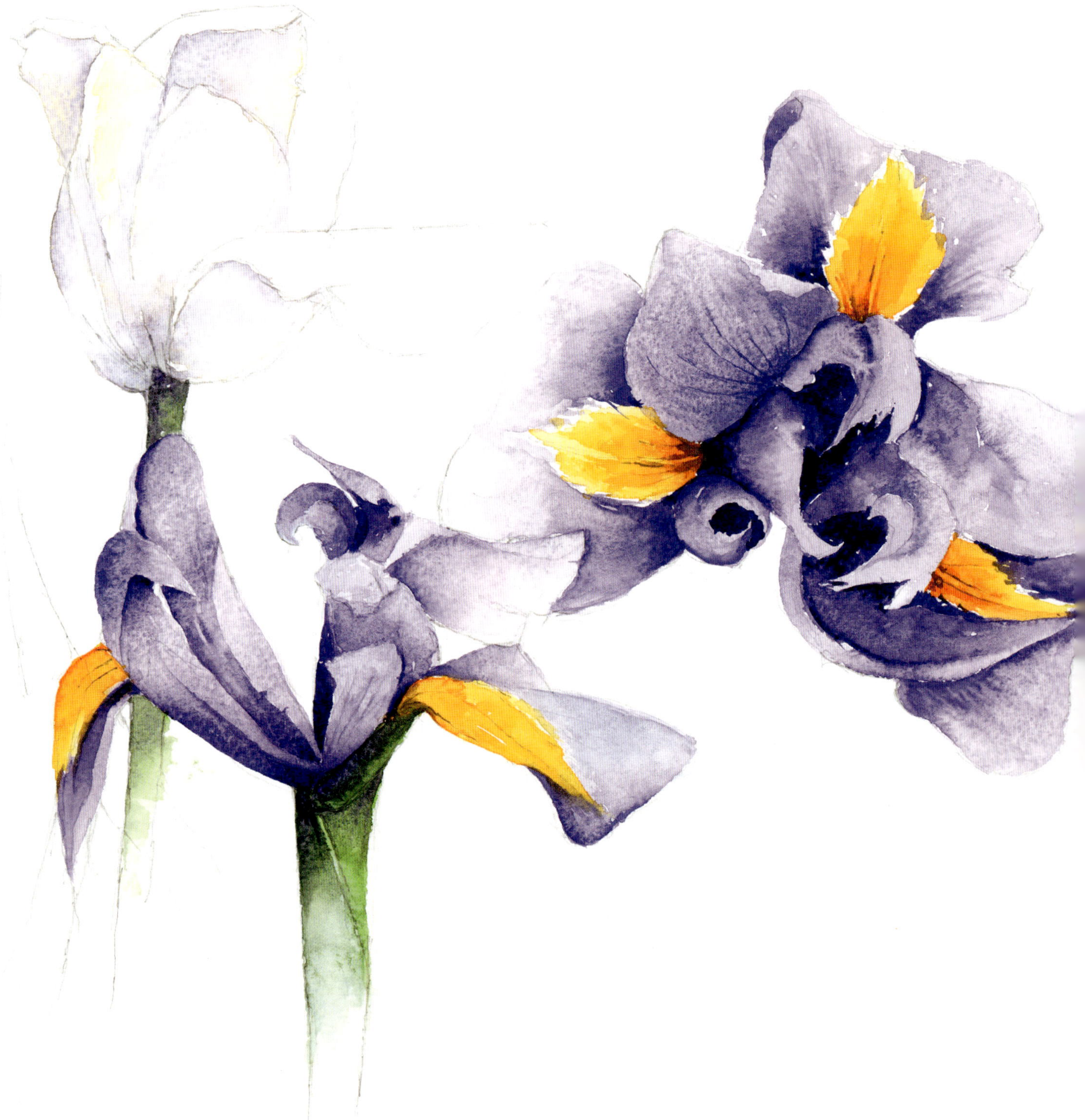

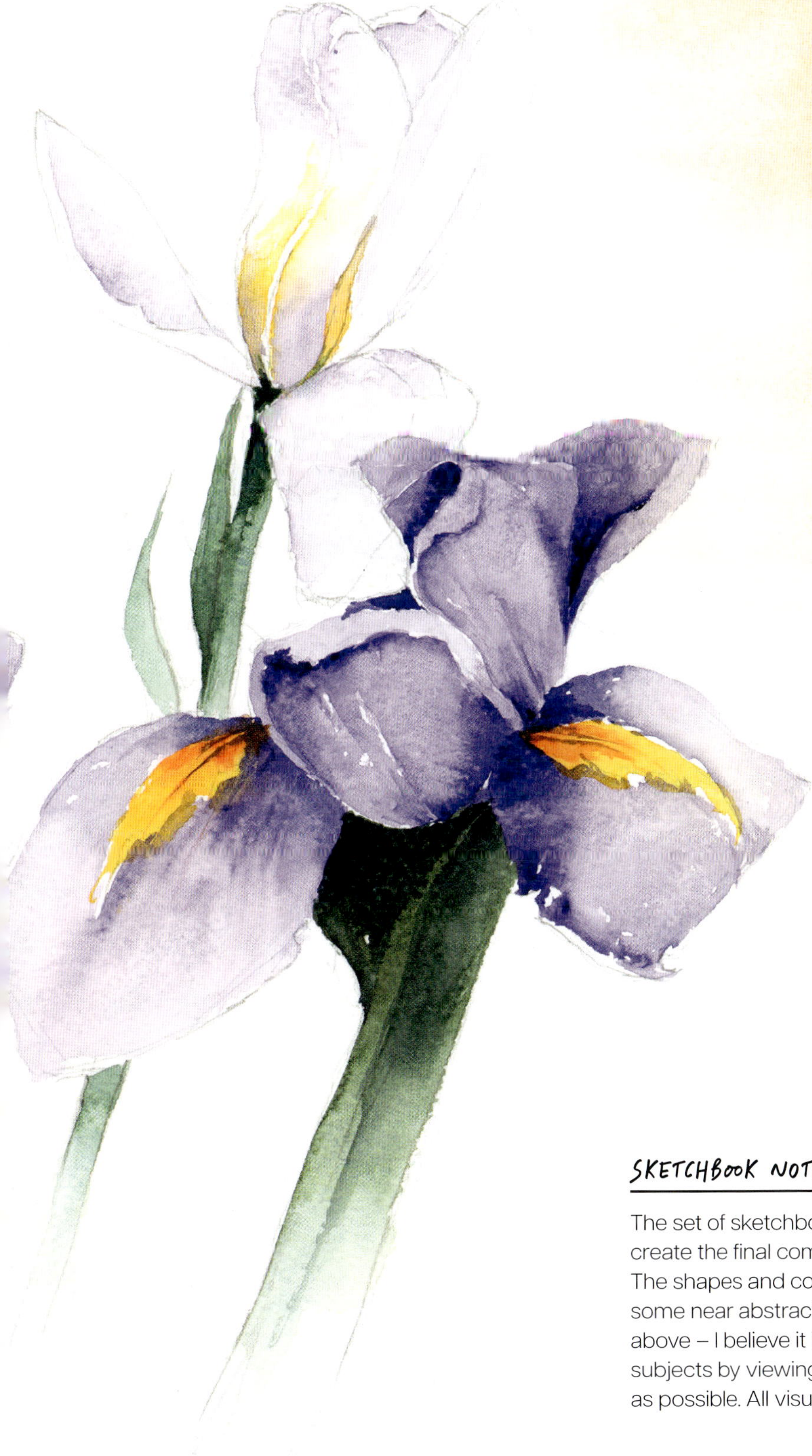

## SKETCHBOOK NOTES

The set of sketchbook studies helped me to create the final composition of the irises in a vase. The shapes and colors in the iris heads formed some near abstract shapes when viewed from above – I believe it is important to get a feel for the subjects by viewing them from as many angles as possible. All visual information is valuable!

***The studies on this page were made in preparation for a larger, more involved composition. The emphasis was on making the white flower heads stand out against the greens of the leaves and stems.***

STAGE 1

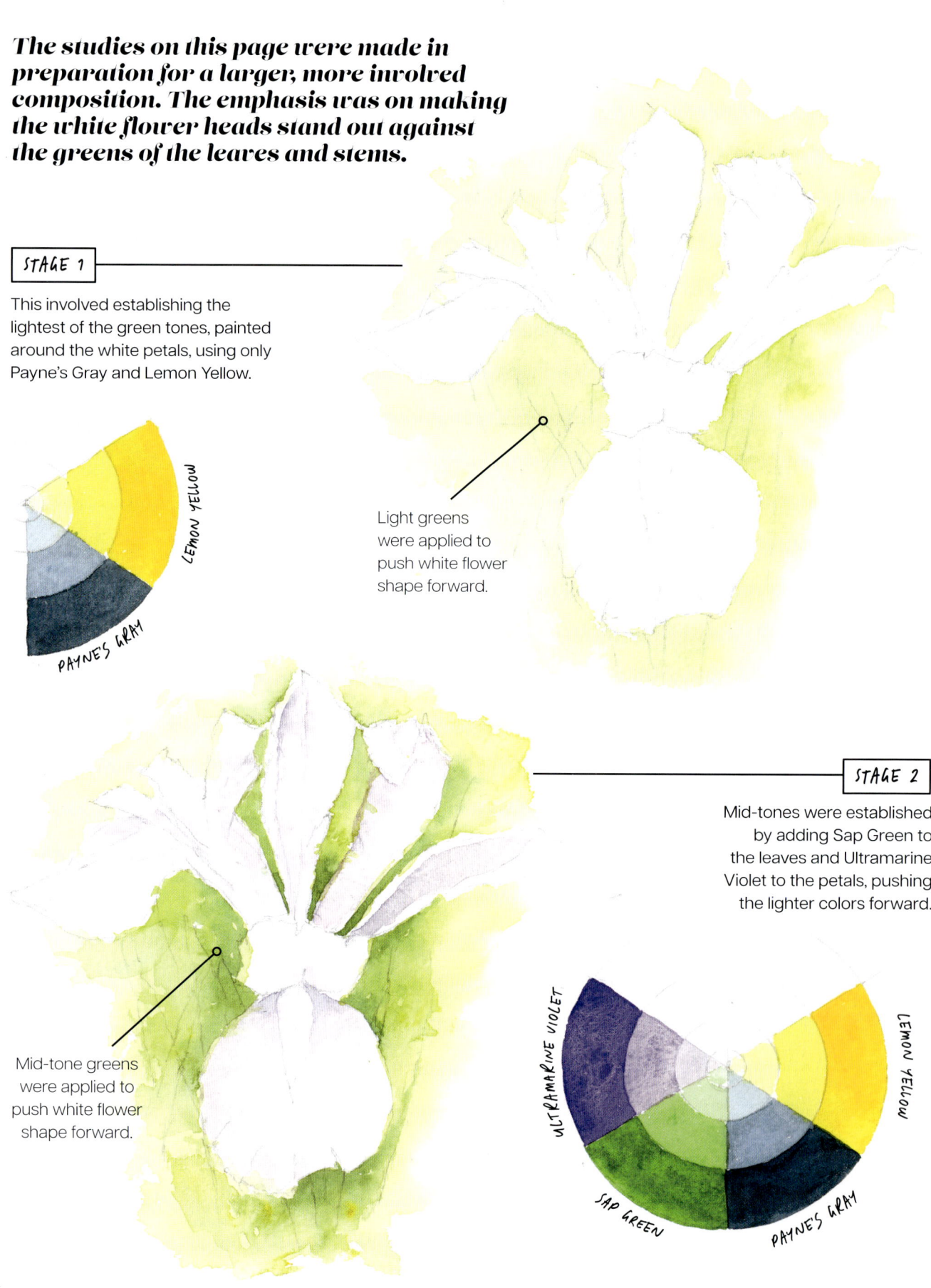

This involved establishing the lightest of the green tones, painted around the white petals, using only Payne's Gray and Lemon Yellow.

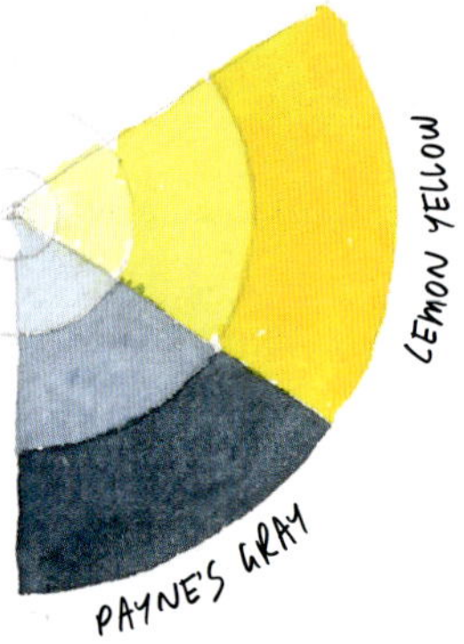
LEMON YELLOW
PAYNE'S GRAY

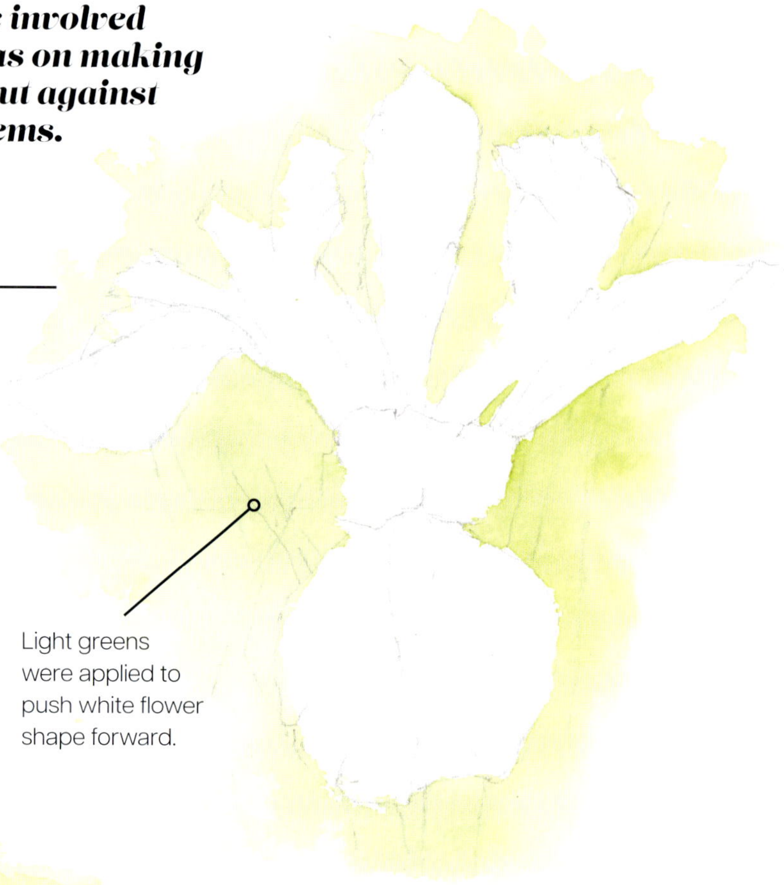

Light greens were applied to push white flower shape forward.

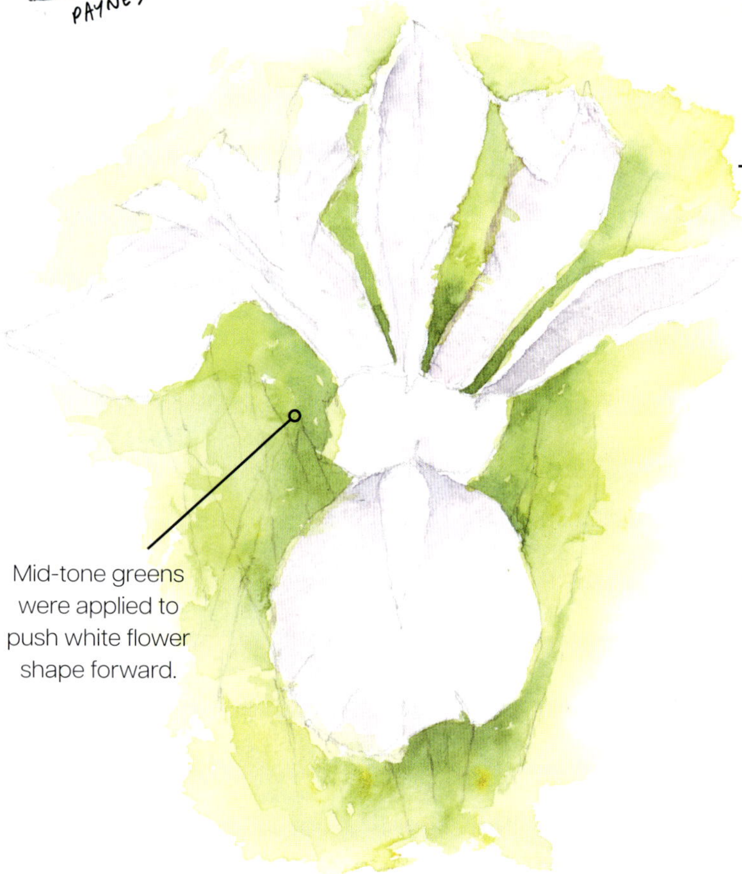

Mid-tone greens were applied to push white flower shape forward.

STAGE 2

Mid-tones were established by adding Sap Green to the leaves and Ultramarine Violet to the petals, pushing the lighter colors forward.

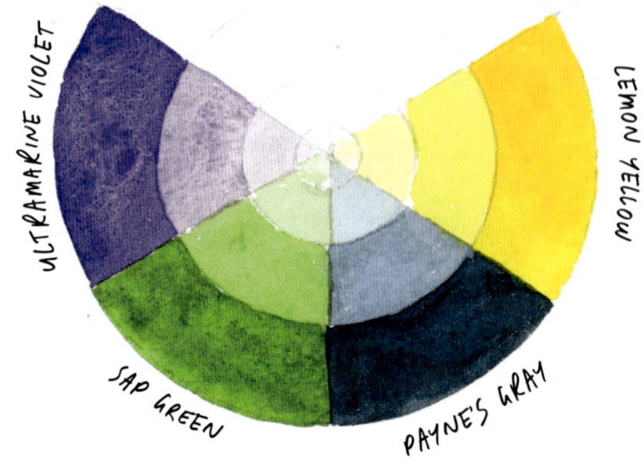
ULTRAMARINE VIOLET
LEMON YELLOW
SAP GREEN
PAYNE'S GRAY

STAGE 3

Finally, Ultramarine was introduced to the green mix to darken it sufficiently to create the parts that little light could reach. Ultramarine Violet was used to give some shape to the petals.

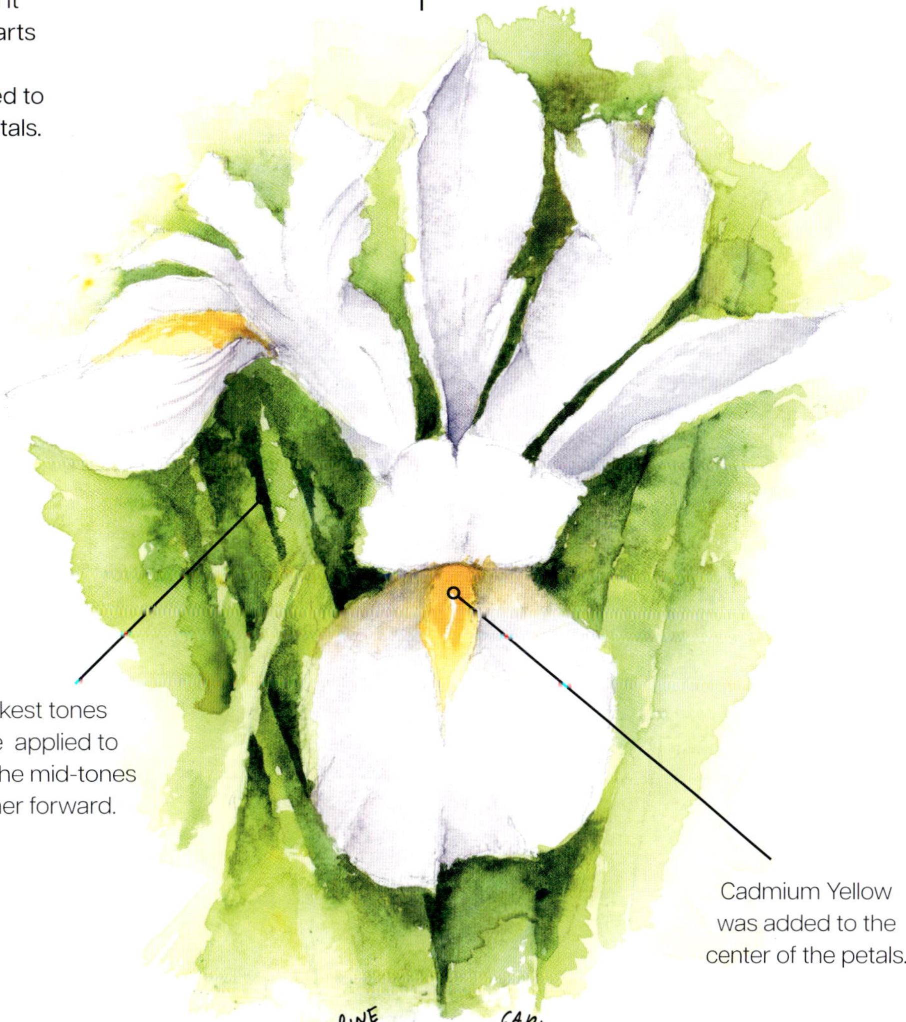

Darkest tones were applied to push the mid-tones further forward.

Cadmium Yellow was added to the center of the petals.

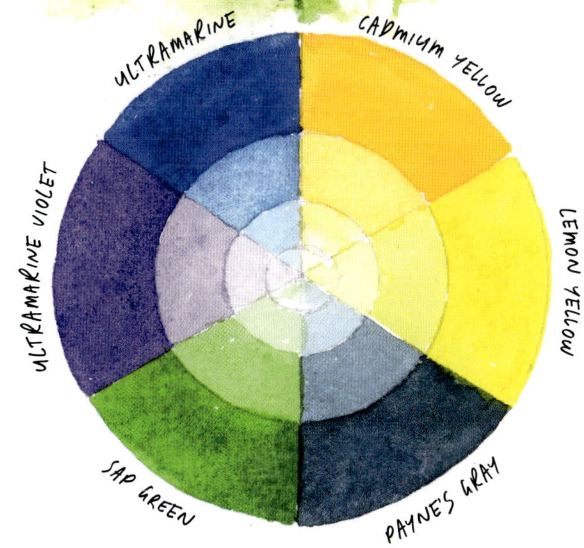
ULTRAMARINE
CADMIUM YELLOW
LEMON YELLOW
PAYNE'S GRAY
SAP GREEN
ULTRAMARINE VIOLET

***The purpose of these preparatory studies was to gauge the number of colors that would be required to paint one single iris head.***

STAGE 1

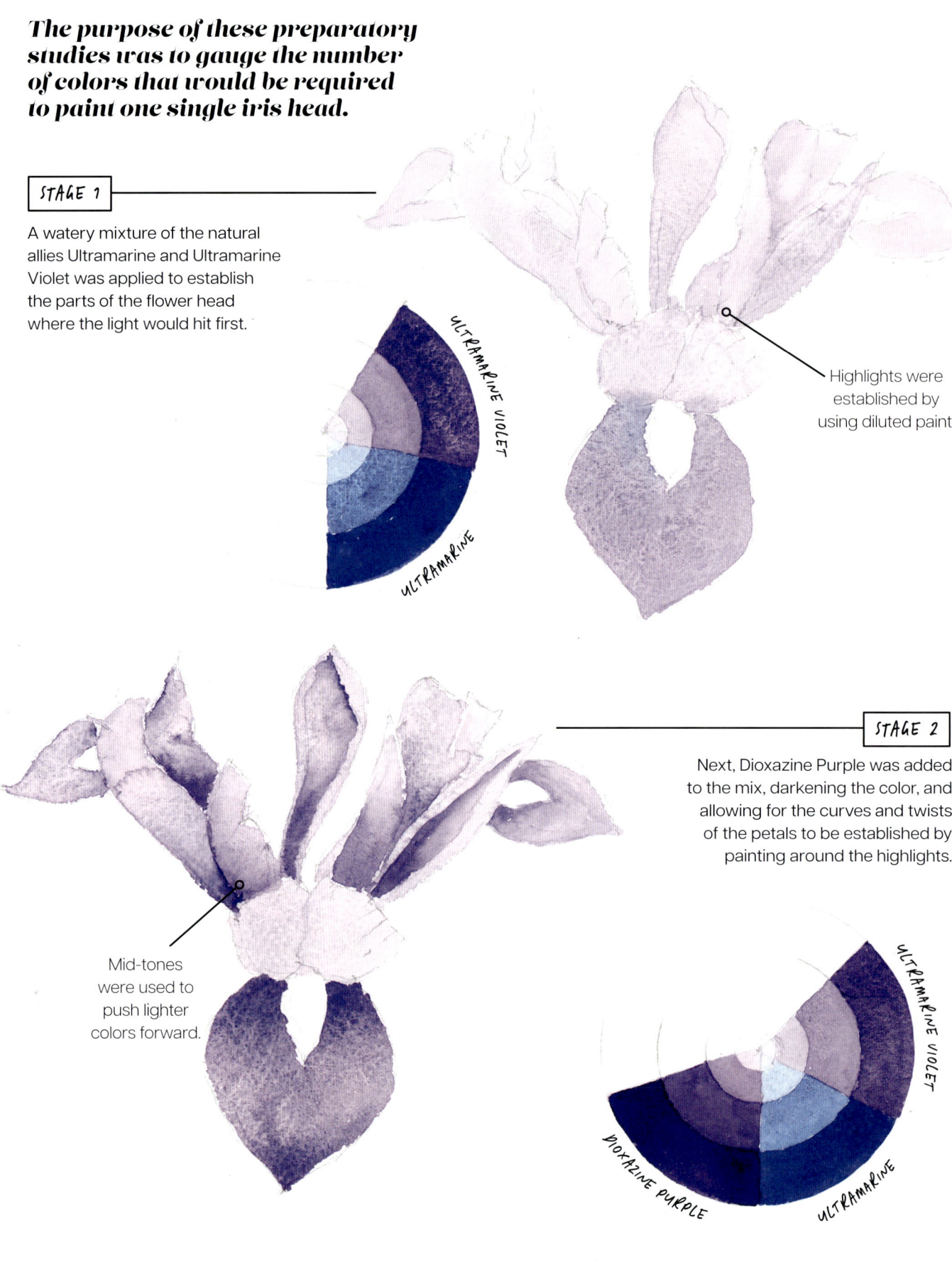

A watery mixture of the natural allies Ultramarine and Ultramarine Violet was applied to establish the parts of the flower head where the light would hit first.

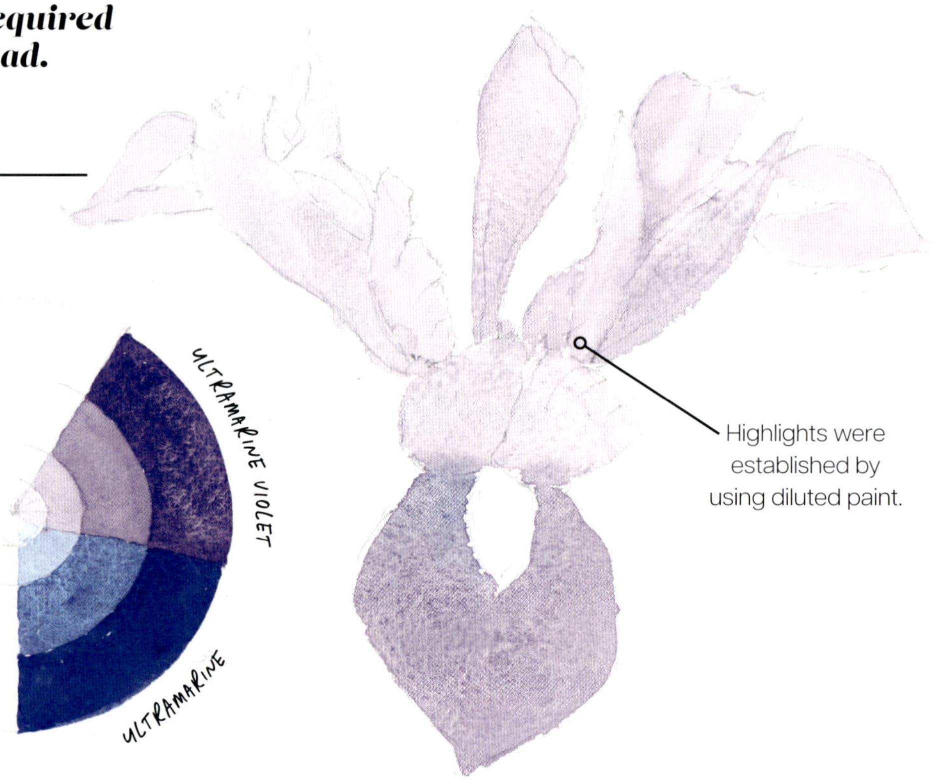
ULTRAMARINE VIOLET
ULTRAMARINE

Highlights were established by using diluted paint.

STAGE 2

Next, Dioxazine Purple was added to the mix, darkening the color, and allowing for the curves and twists of the petals to be established by painting around the highlights.

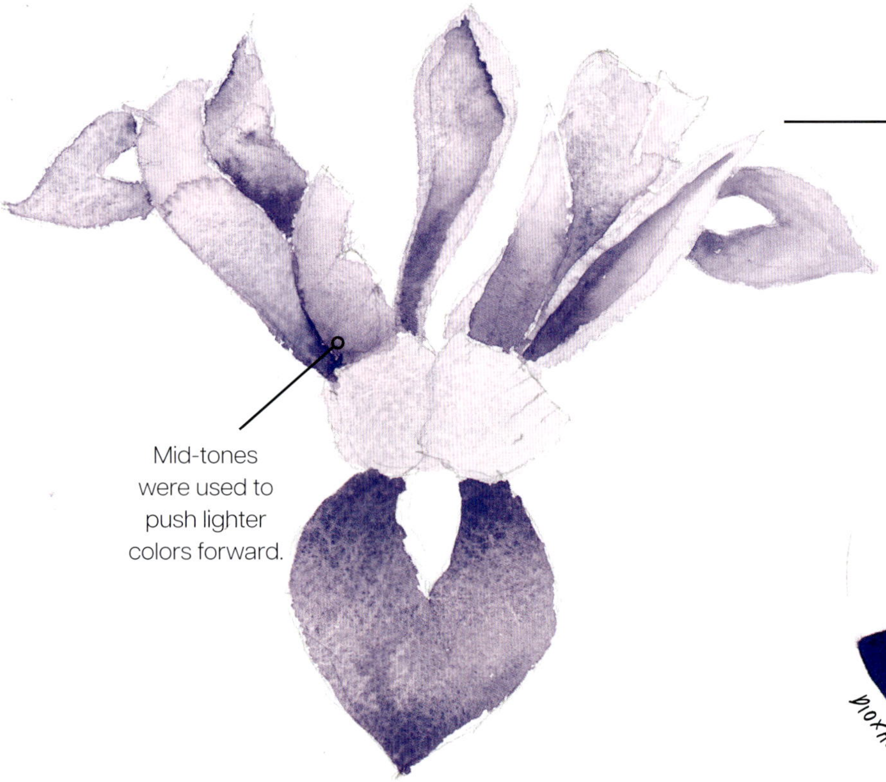

Mid-tones were used to push lighter colors forward.

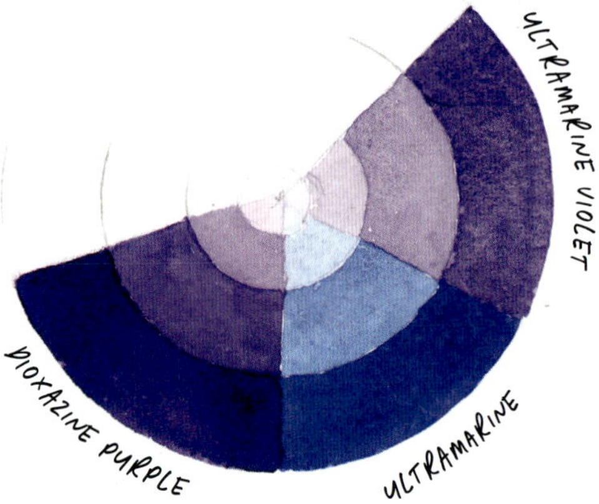
ULTRAMARINE VIOLET
ULTRAMARINE
DIOXAZINE PURPLE

STAGE 3

Finally, the mixture was "thickened" by adding even more purple to paint the deepest, darkest tones.

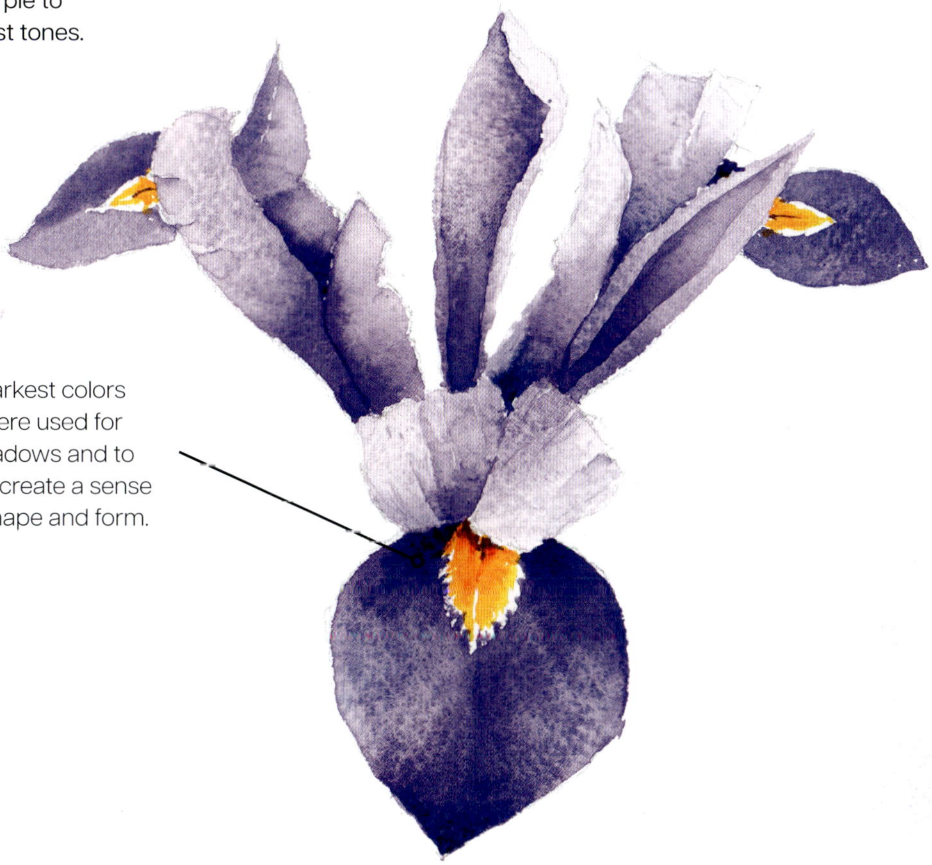

Darkest colors were used for shadows and to help create a sense of shape and form.

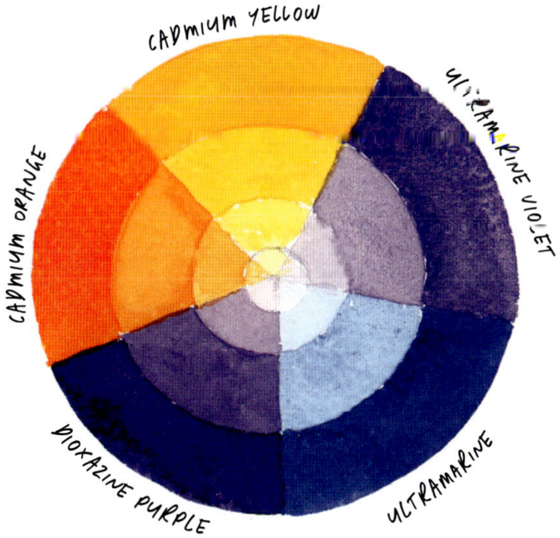
CADMIUM YELLOW
ULTRAMARINE VIOLET
CADMIUM ORANGE
DIOXAZINE PURPLE
ULTRAMARINE

***This step-by-step series shows how the main composition of spring flowers in a vase was created, building up the colors and tonal range in three stages.***

## STAGE 1

This involved washing Cerulean Blue, Ultramarine, and Ultramarine Violet, one at a time onto damp paper to create a colored backdrop with no distracting detail.

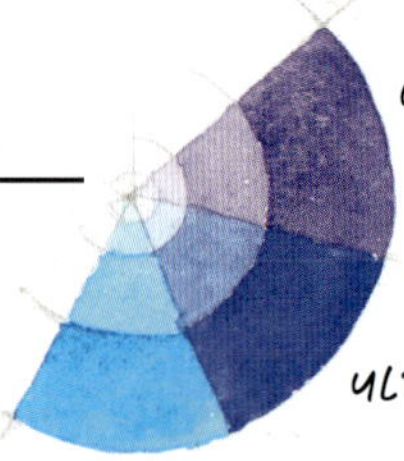
ULTRAMARINE VIOLET
ULTRAMARINE
CERULEAN BLUE

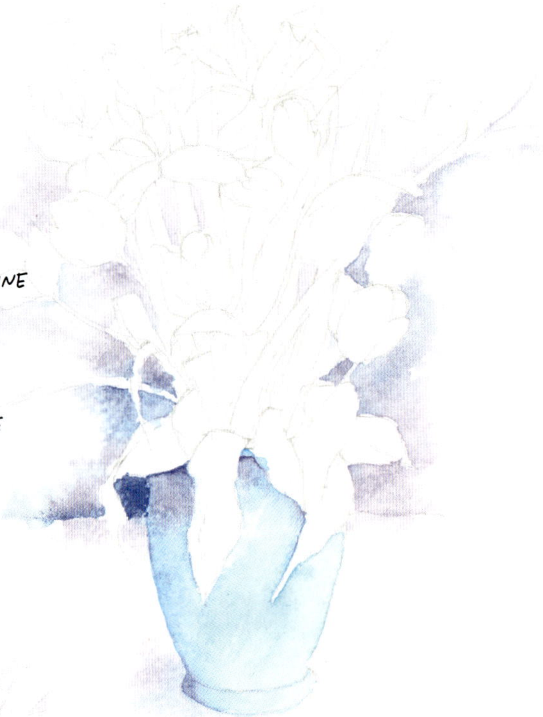

## STAGE 2

This involved using the color mixes used in the previous sets of studies.

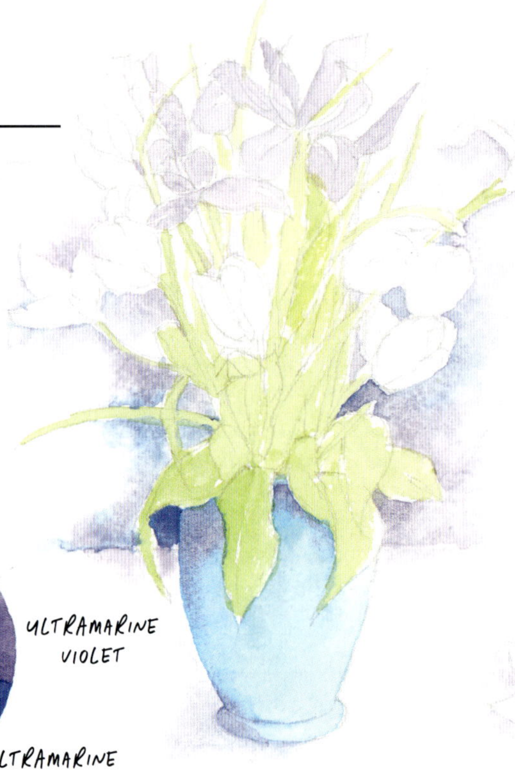

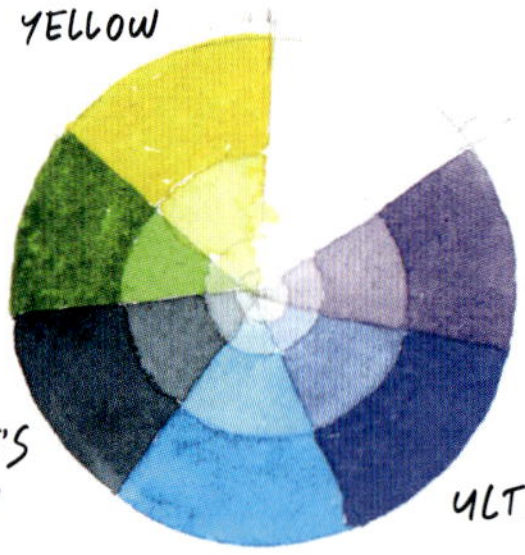
LEMON YELLOW
SAP GREEN
ULTRAMARINE VIOLET
PAYNE'S GRAY
ULTRAMARINE
CERULEAN BLUE

## STAGE 3

Finally, the darker colors were added, darkening the greens and painting with care around the mid-tones.

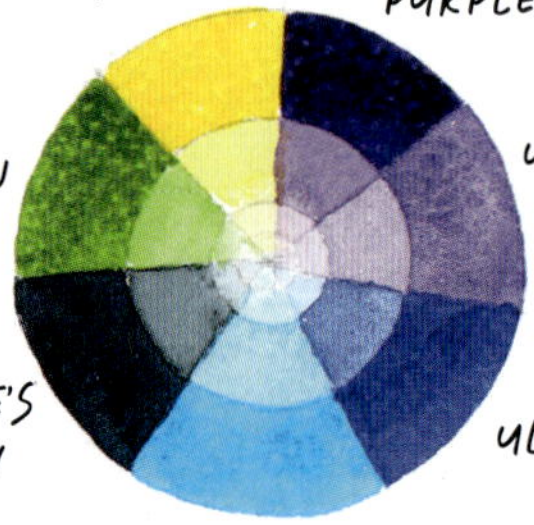
LEMON YELLOW
DIOXAZINE PURPLE
SAP GREEN
ULTRAMARINE VIOLET
PAYNE'S GRAY
ULTRAMARINE
CERULEAN BLUE

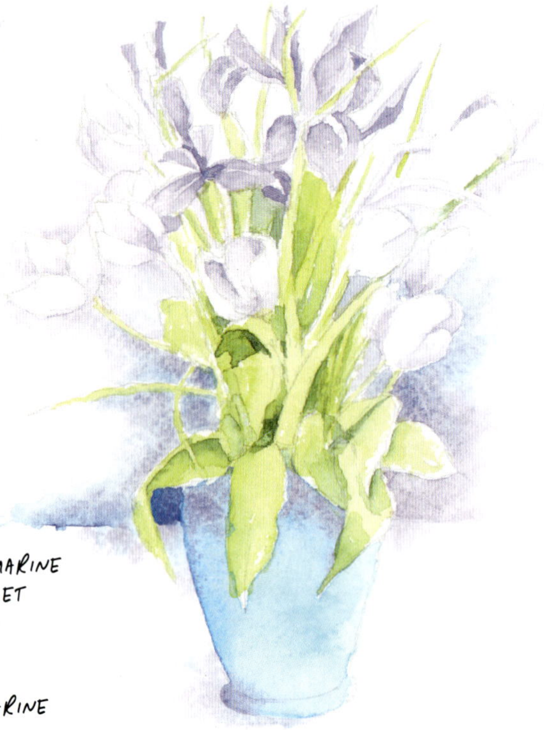

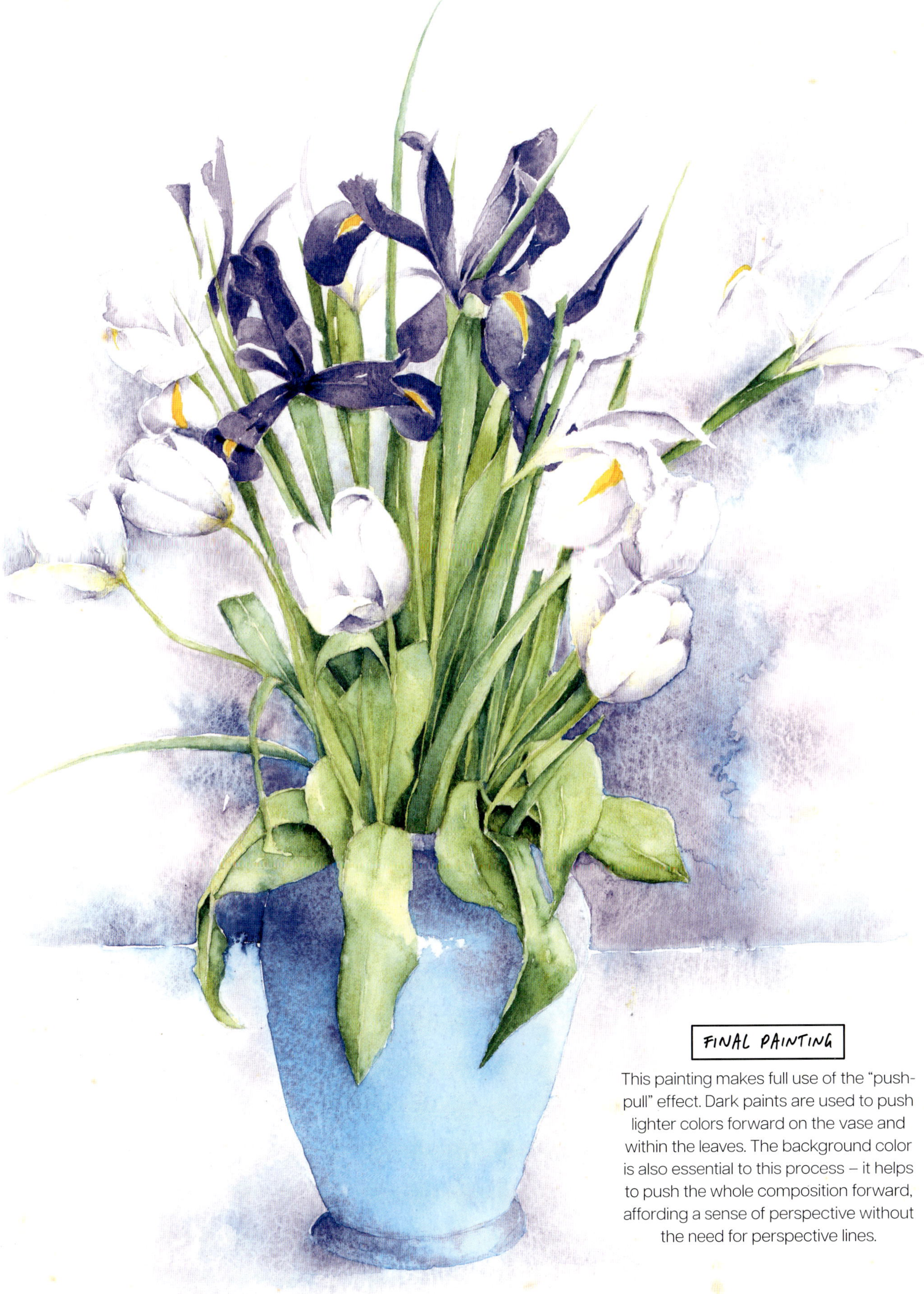

FINAL PAINTING

This painting makes full use of the "push-pull" effect. Dark paints are used to push lighter colors forward on the vase and within the leaves. The background color is also essential to this process – it helps to push the whole composition forward, affording a sense of perspective without the need for perspective lines.

# Sunflowers

## SKETCHBOOK NOTES

This page of sketchbook studies was made to explore the strange contrast between the soft coloring found in the back of the flower heads where the stem and the leaves meet to "hold" the main head, and the hard, intense coloring in the centre of the flower heads containing the seeds. This gave me the opportunity to gauge which colors I would be likely to need in a composition and to prepare for the tonal contrasts that I would have to deal with when all the sunflowers were placed together in one composition.

It also allowed me to gain a greater understanding of the tones I would need to find when painting the petals against the dark "eye" of the flower head. All this information proved valuable in creating the following pages.

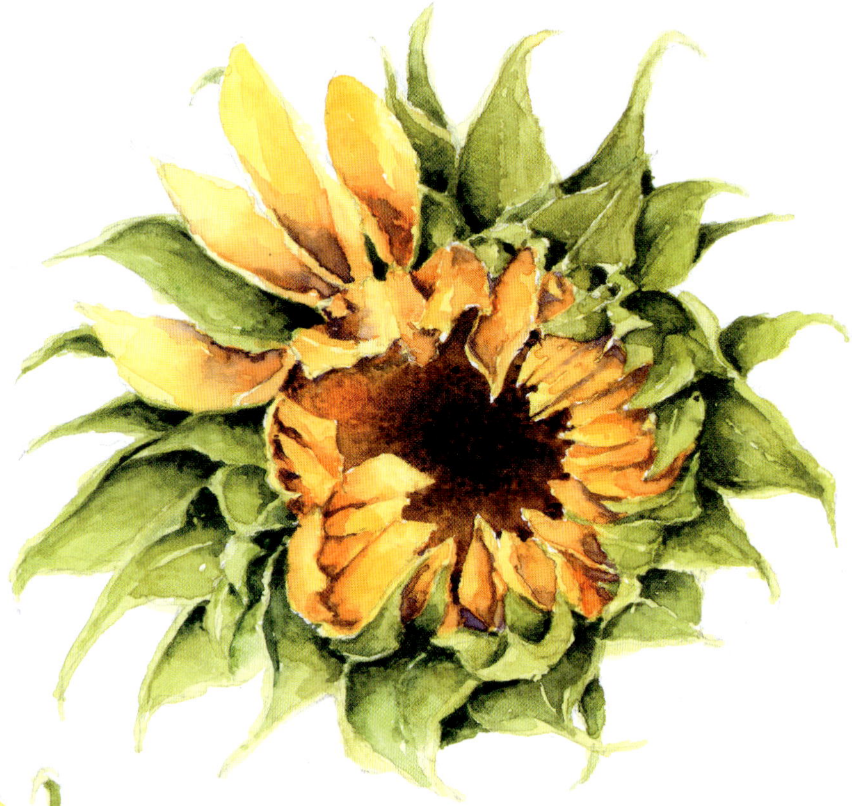

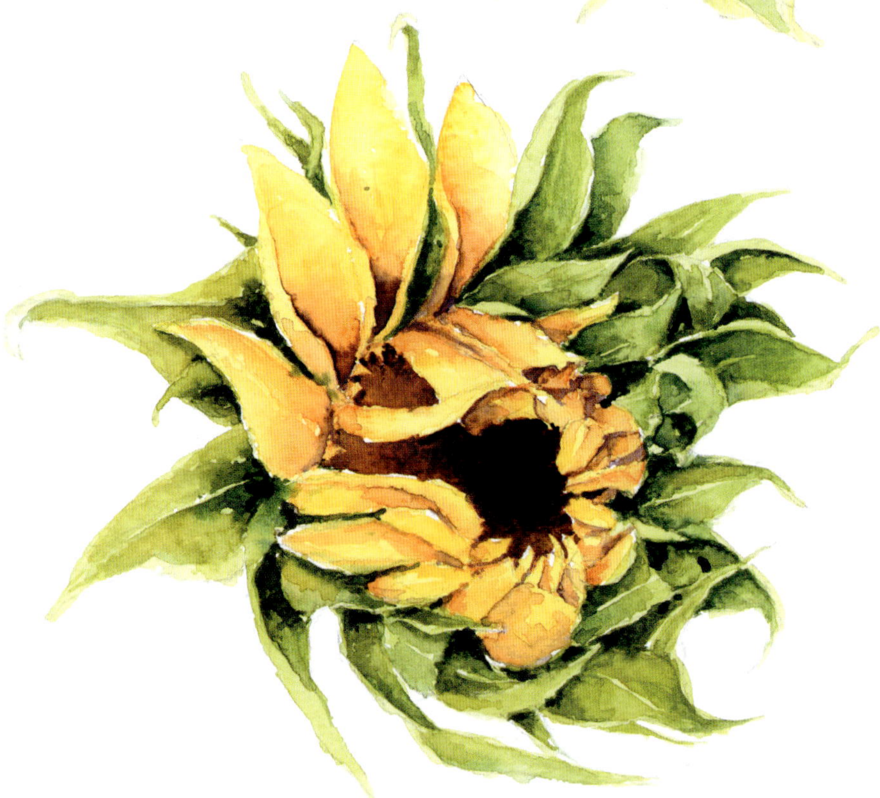

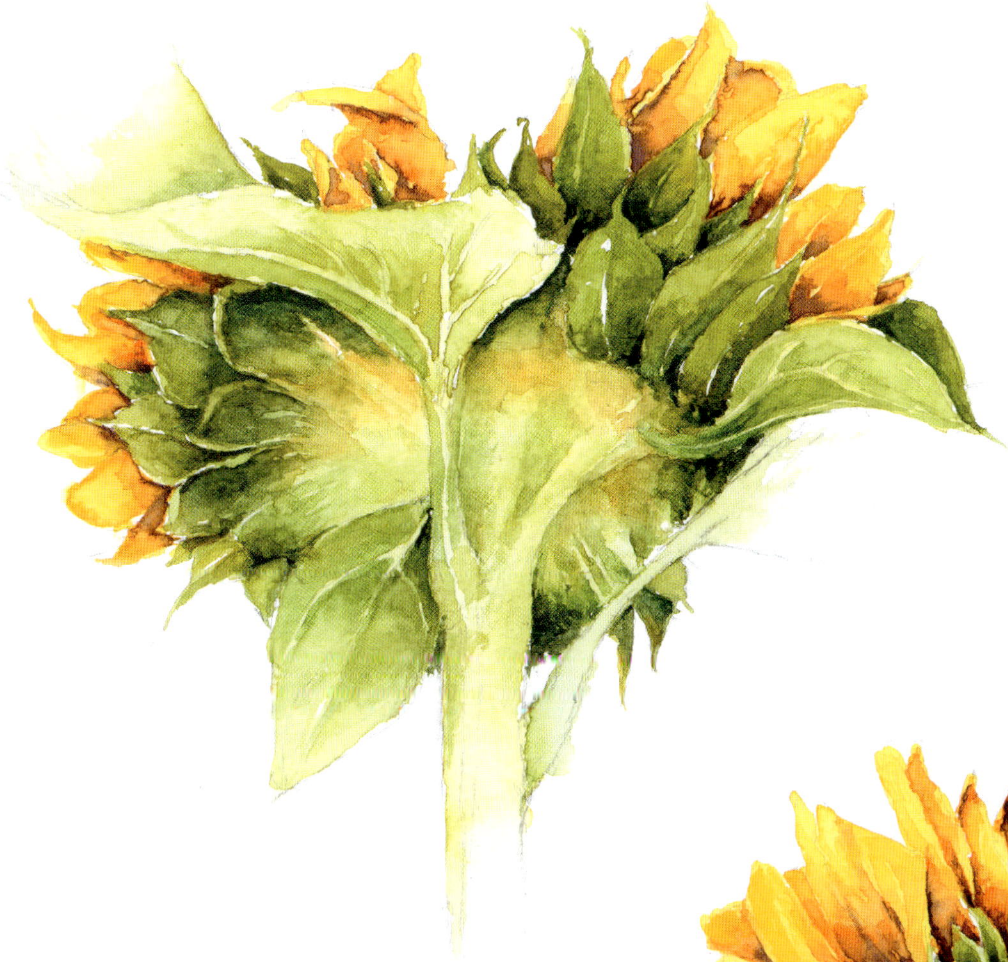

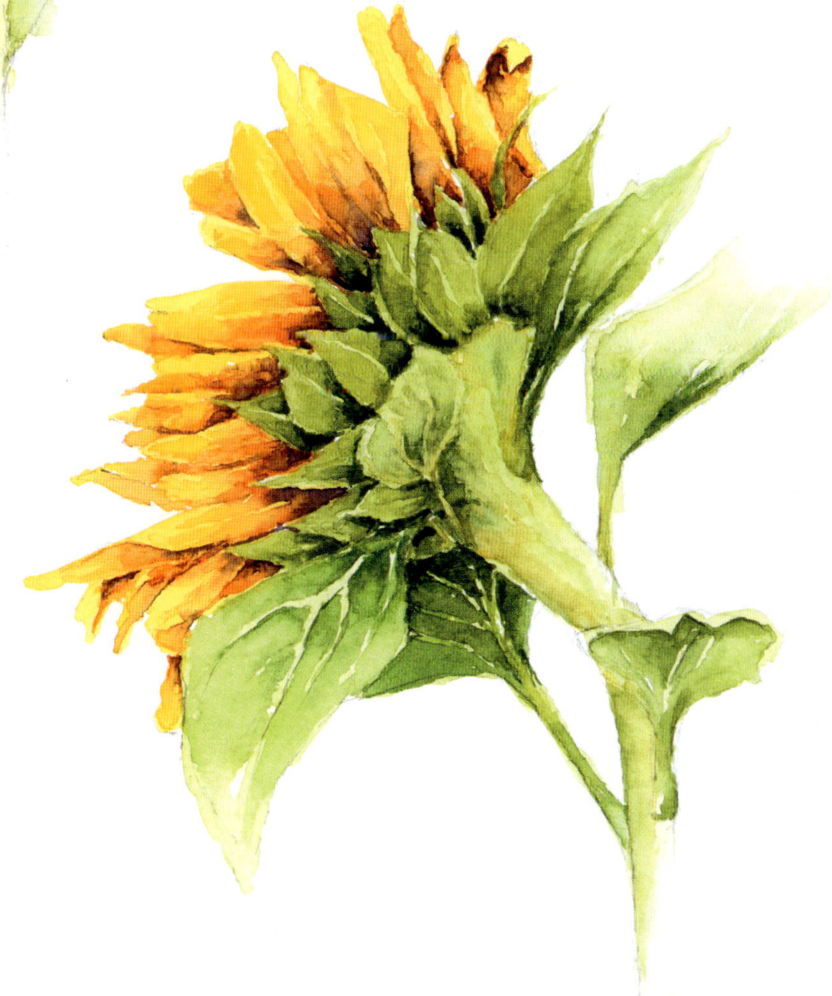

**NOTE:** It can be helpful to choose a sketchbook that contains the same type of watercolor paper that you plan to paint your larger work onto – if you do, you will get a better understanding of how the paint reacts with the paper.

***The reason for making these initial studies was to confirm in my own mind the types of greens that would work well with the intense "heat" of the yellows and oranges of the sunflower heads.***

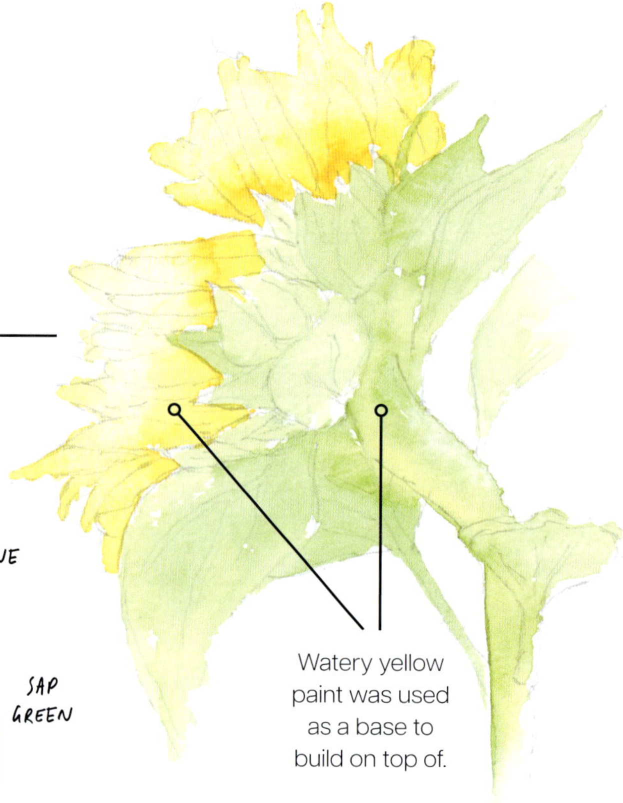
Watery yellow paint was used as a base to build on top of.

## STAGE 1

A thin yellow wash of Cadmium Yellow and Quinacridone Gold was created and used for both the flower petals and leaves, binding the tones together. Once dried, green was added to the mix to create the leaves.

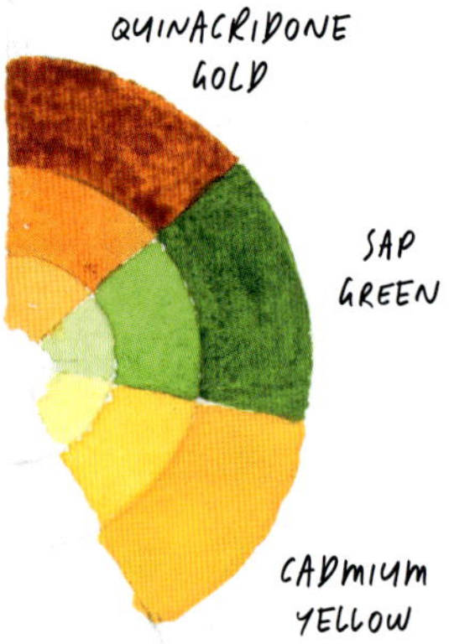
QUINACRIDONE GOLD
SAP GREEN
CADMIUM YELLOW

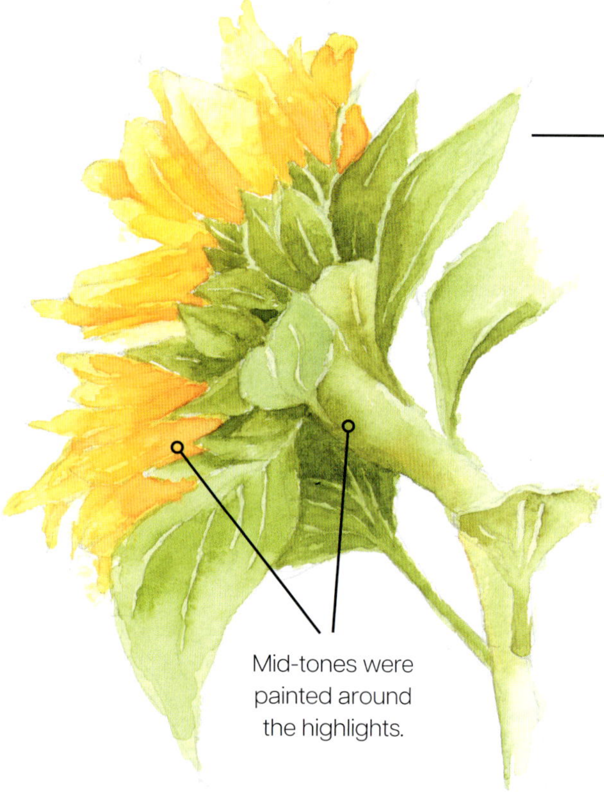
Mid-tones were painted around the highlights.

## STAGE 2

Next, blue was added to the green mix, painting around the highlights. A touch of orange was then added to the petal mix to push the highlights forward.

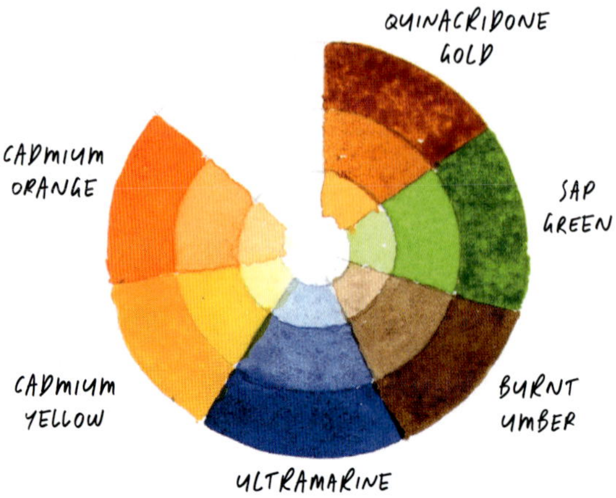
QUINACRIDONE GOLD
CADMIUM ORANGE
SAP GREEN
CADMIUM YELLOW
BURNT UMBER
ULTRAMARINE

STAGE 3

Finally, a touch of purple was added to the yellow petals to help make sense of the shapes. A touch of purple – for the sake of tonal continuity – was added to the deepest green tones.

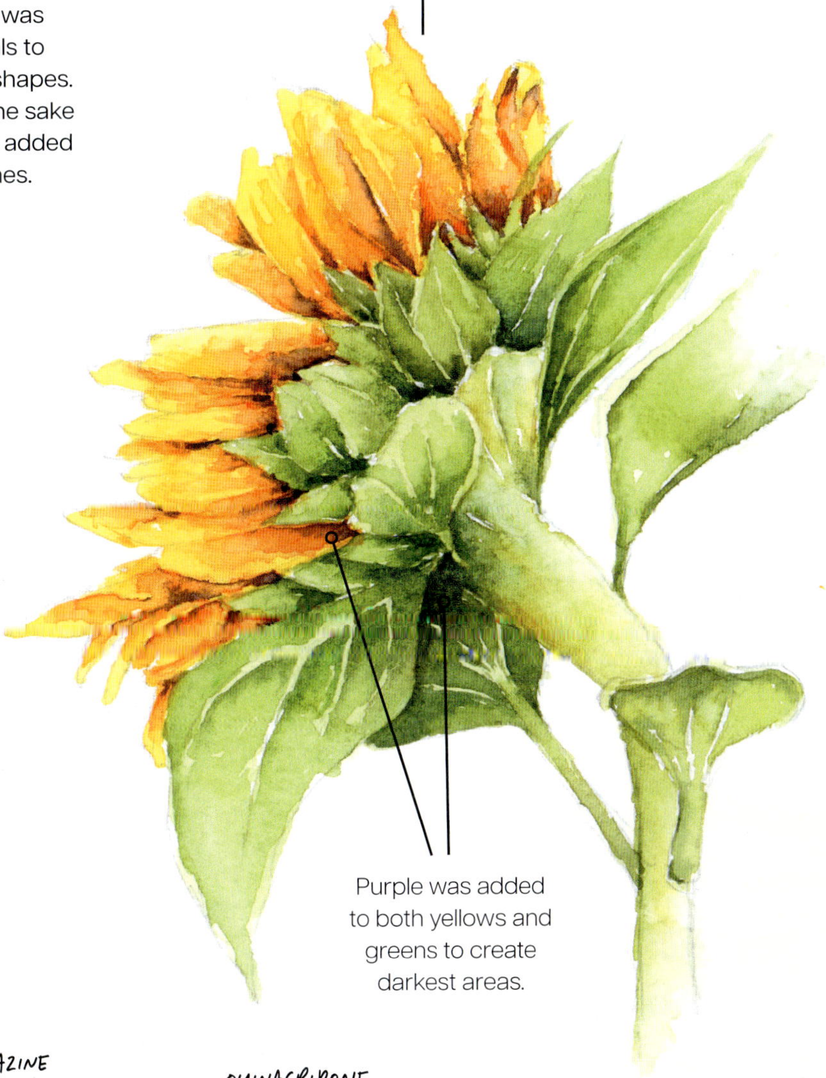

Purple was added to both yellows and greens to create darkest areas.

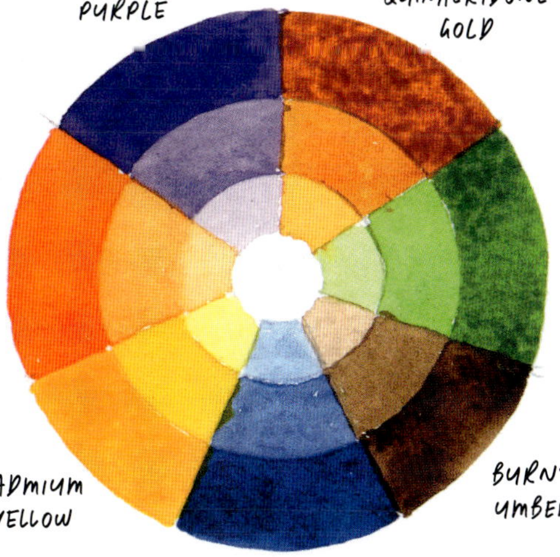
DIOXAZINE PURPLE
QUINACRIDONE GOLD
CADMIUM ORANGE
SAP GREEN
CADMIUM YELLOW
BURNT UMBER
ULTRAMARINE

***The studies on this page were, again, made in preparation for a large composition. My intention was to recreate the heat of the environments in which sunflowers grow, so oranges and yellows were crucial.***

### STAGE 1

The initial wash used a selection of yellows and oranges, using the darkest combinations of Burnt Sienna and Quinacridone Gold for the center.

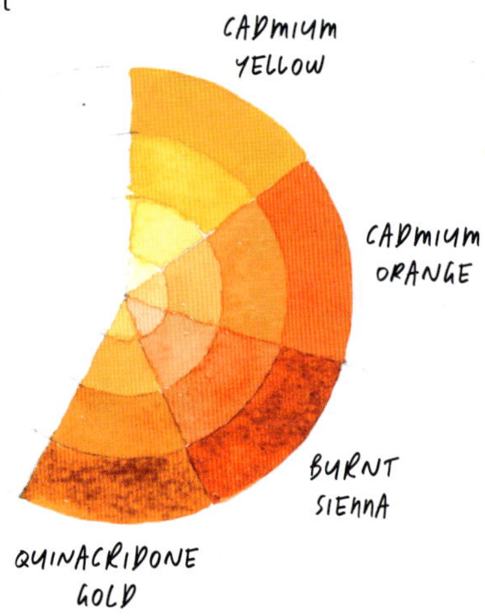
CADMIUM YELLOW
CADMIUM ORANGE
BURNT SIENNA
QUINACRIDONE GOLD

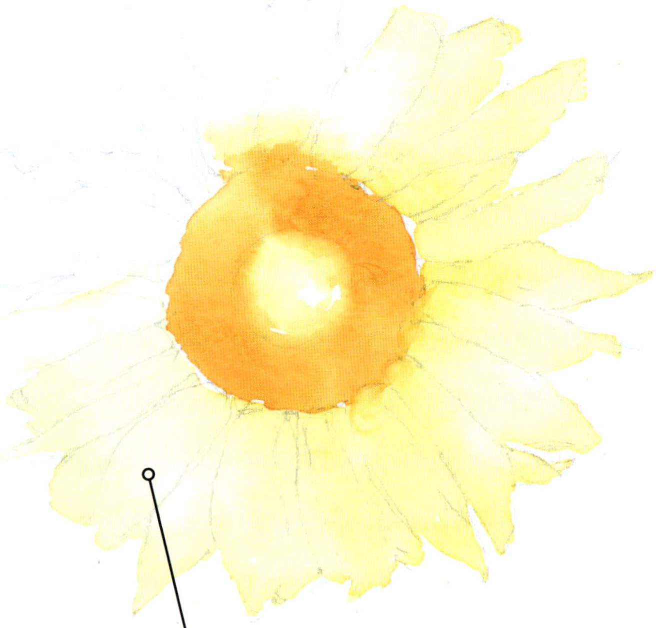

Lightest tones were painted with very watery paint.

### STAGE 2

Next, the darker oranges were applied to make some sense of the jumble of petals surrounding the sunflower head. A mixture of Burnt Umber and Ultramarine was applied to the very center.

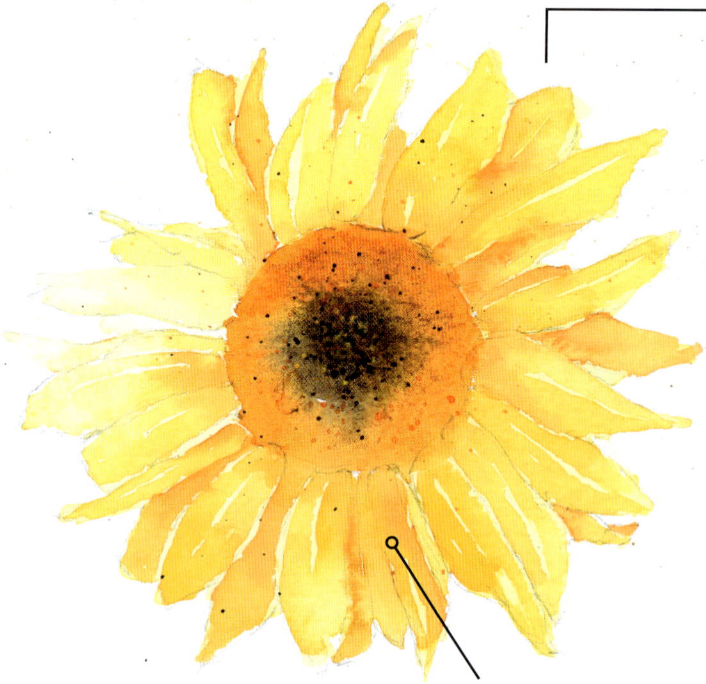

Mid-tone oranges were used to establish shapes of petals.

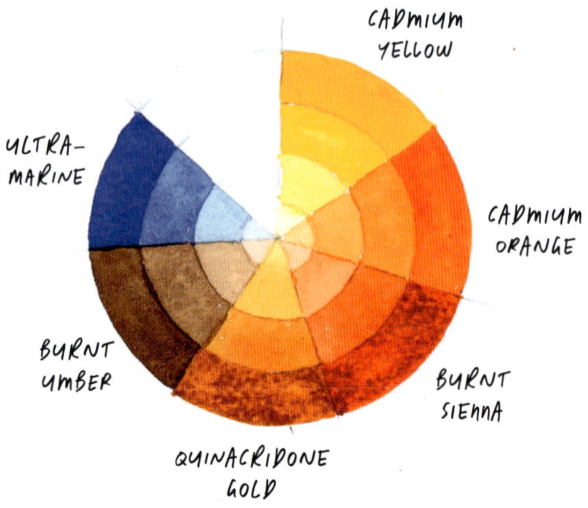
CADMIUM YELLOW
ULTRA-MARINE
CADMIUM ORANGE
BURNT UMBER
BURNT SIENNA
QUINACRIDONE GOLD

## STAGE 3

Finally, a little purple – yellow's complementary color – was dropped onto the sections where the petals meet the flower head to create the deepest tones.

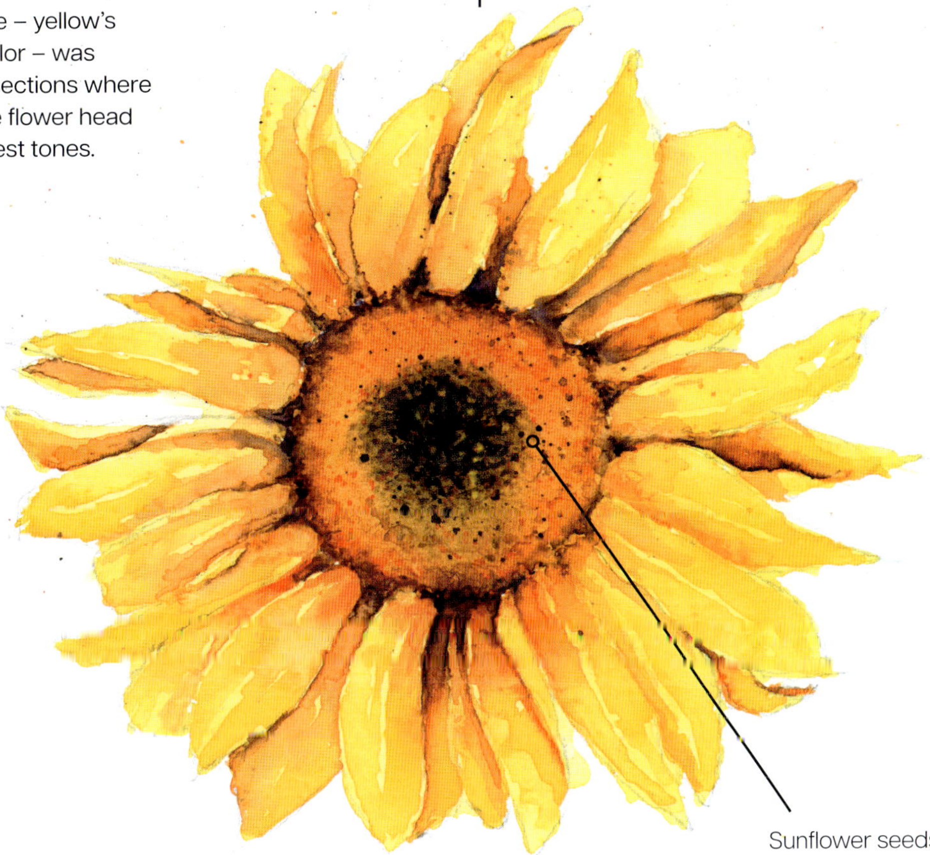

Sunflower seeds were suggested by flicking wet paint onto dry paper.

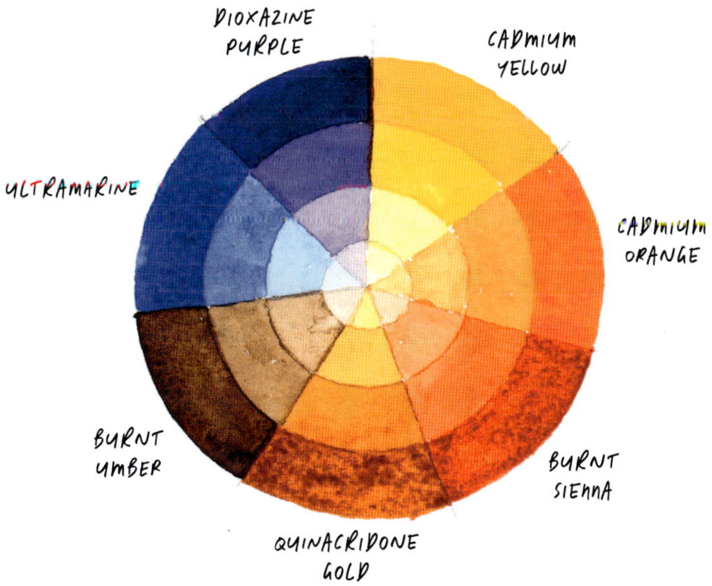
DIOXAZINE PURPLE
CADMIUM YELLOW
ULTRAMARINE
CADMIUM ORANGE
BURNT UMBER
BURNT SIENNA
QUINACRIDONE GOLD

***This set of step-by-step illustrations explores the ways in which color combinations, gained from the previous studies, are built up to create a composition.***

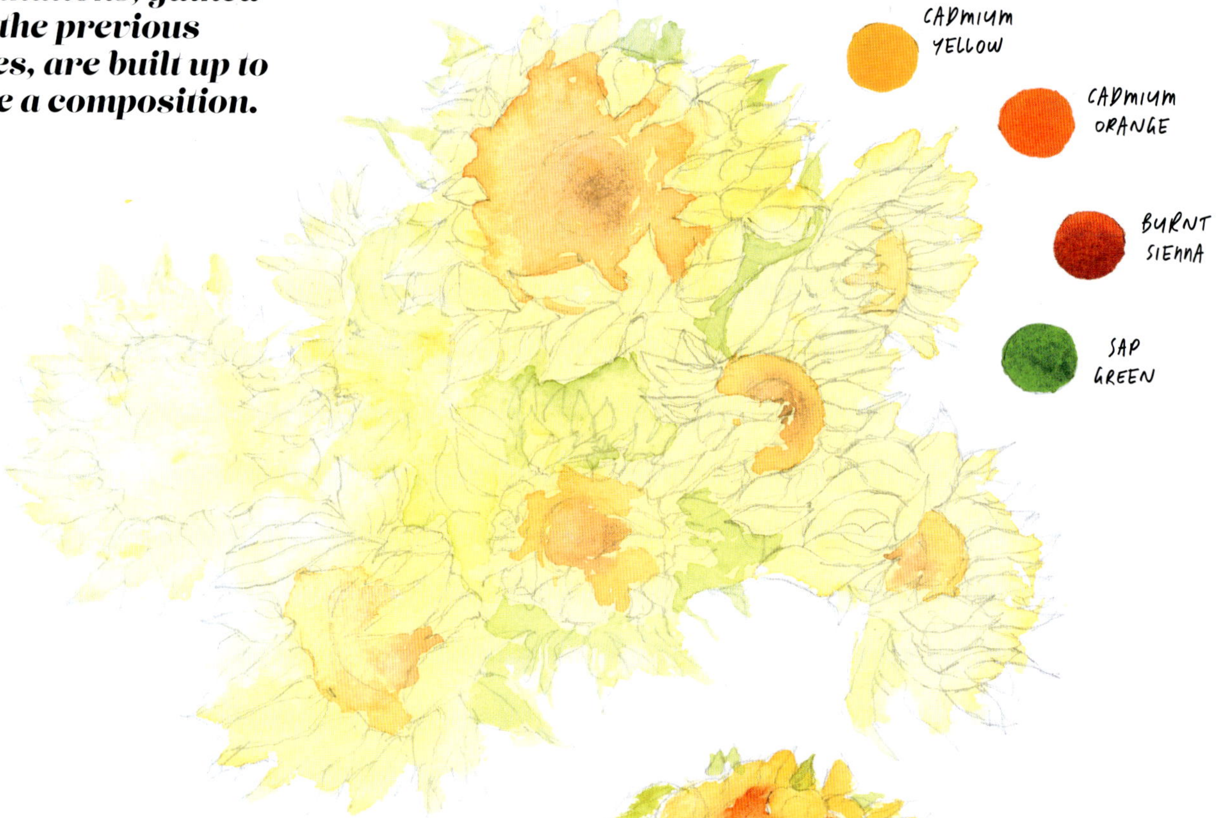

CADMIUM YELLOW
CADMIUM ORANGE
BURNT SIENNA
SAP GREEN


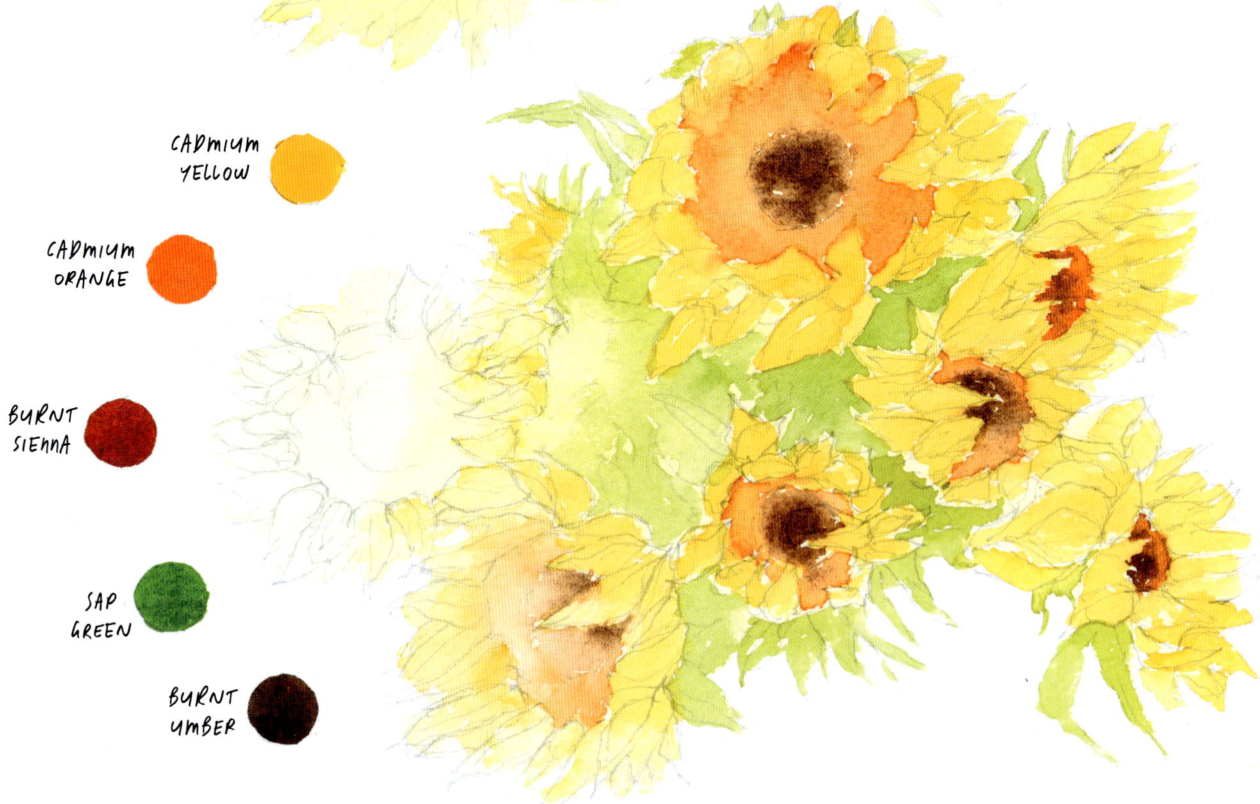

CADMIUM YELLOW
CADMIUM ORANGE
BURNT SIENNA
SAP GREEN
BURNT UMBER

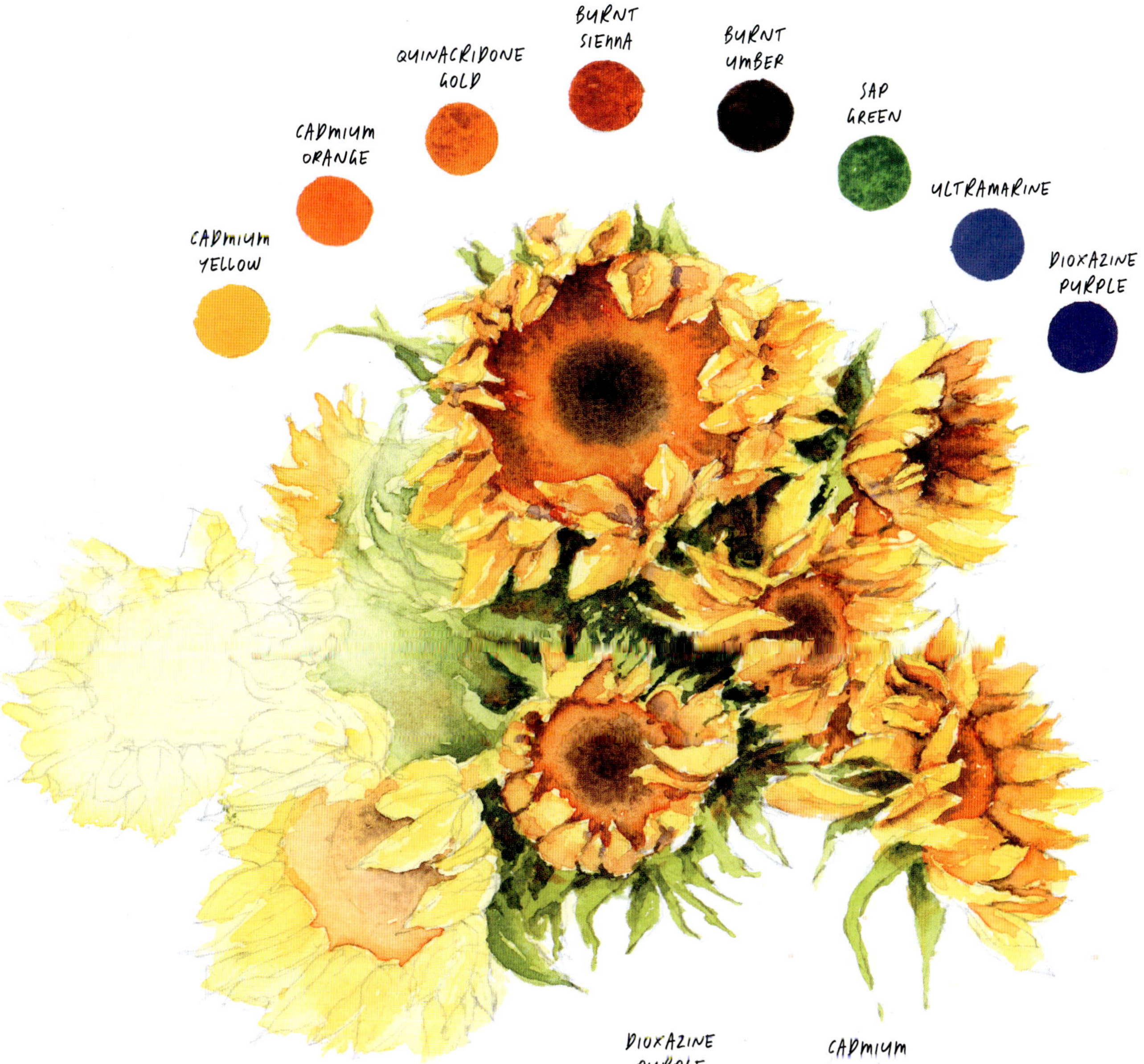
CADMIUM YELLOW
CADMIUM ORANGE
QUINACRIDONE GOLD
BURNT SIENNA
BURNT UMBER
SAP GREEN
ULTRAMARINE
DIOXAZINE PURPLE

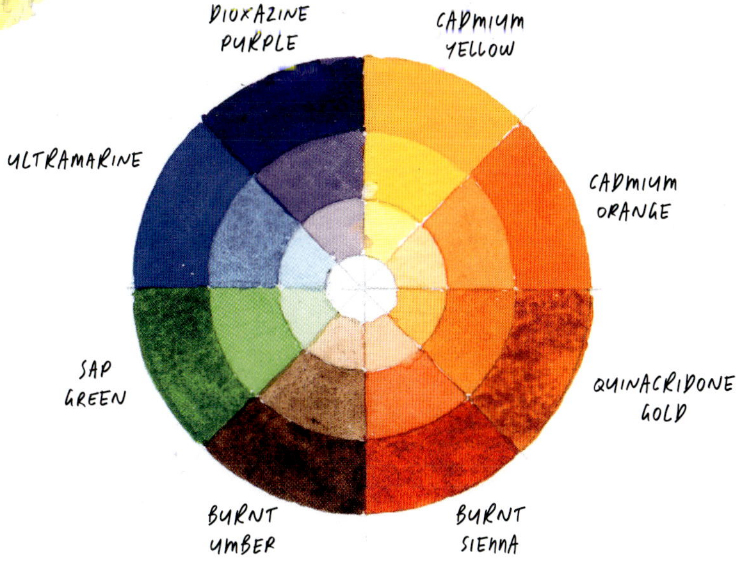
DIOXAZINE PURPLE
CADMIUM YELLOW
ULTRAMARINE
CADMIUM ORANGE
SAP GREEN
QUINACRIDONE GOLD
BURNT UMBER
BURNT SIENNA

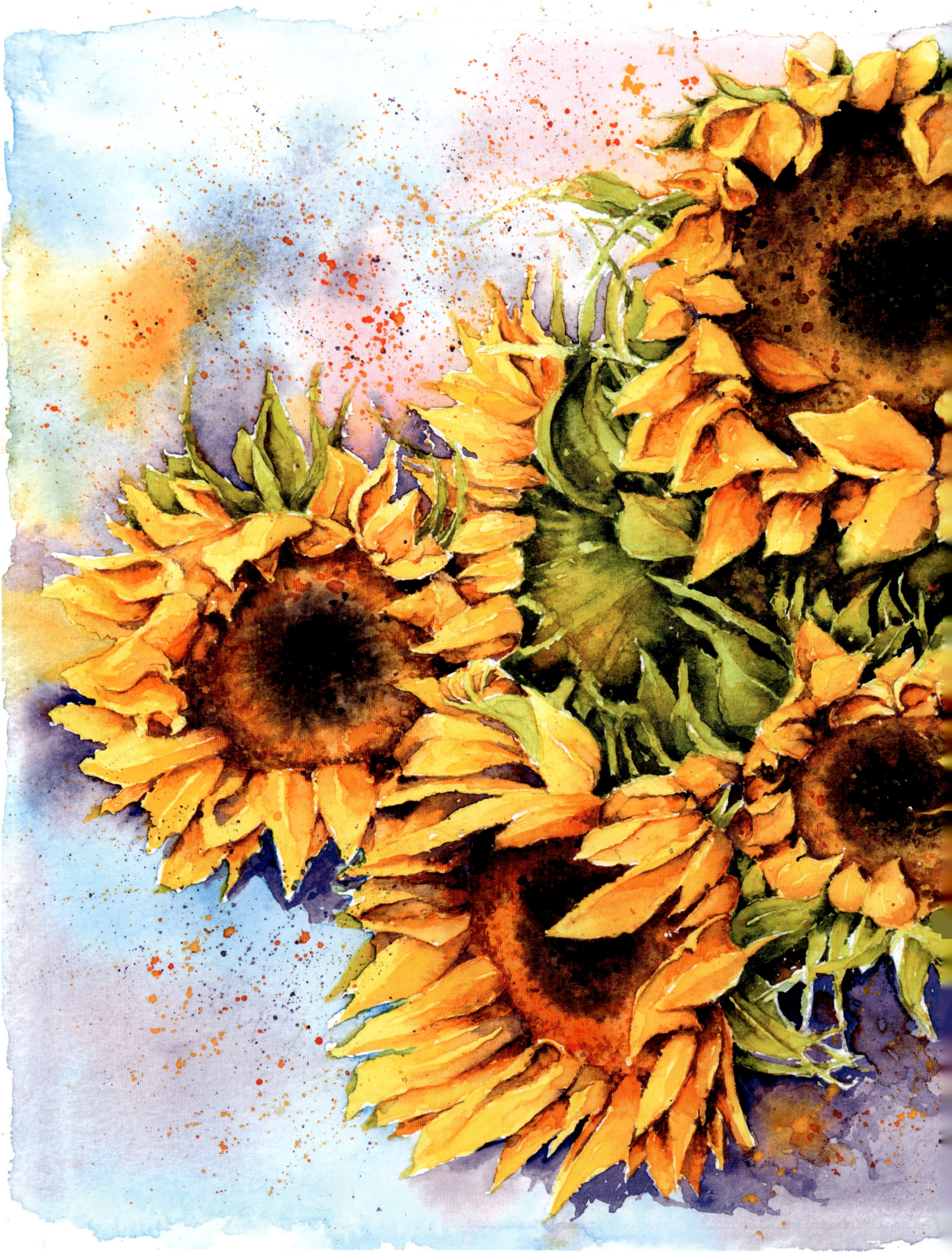

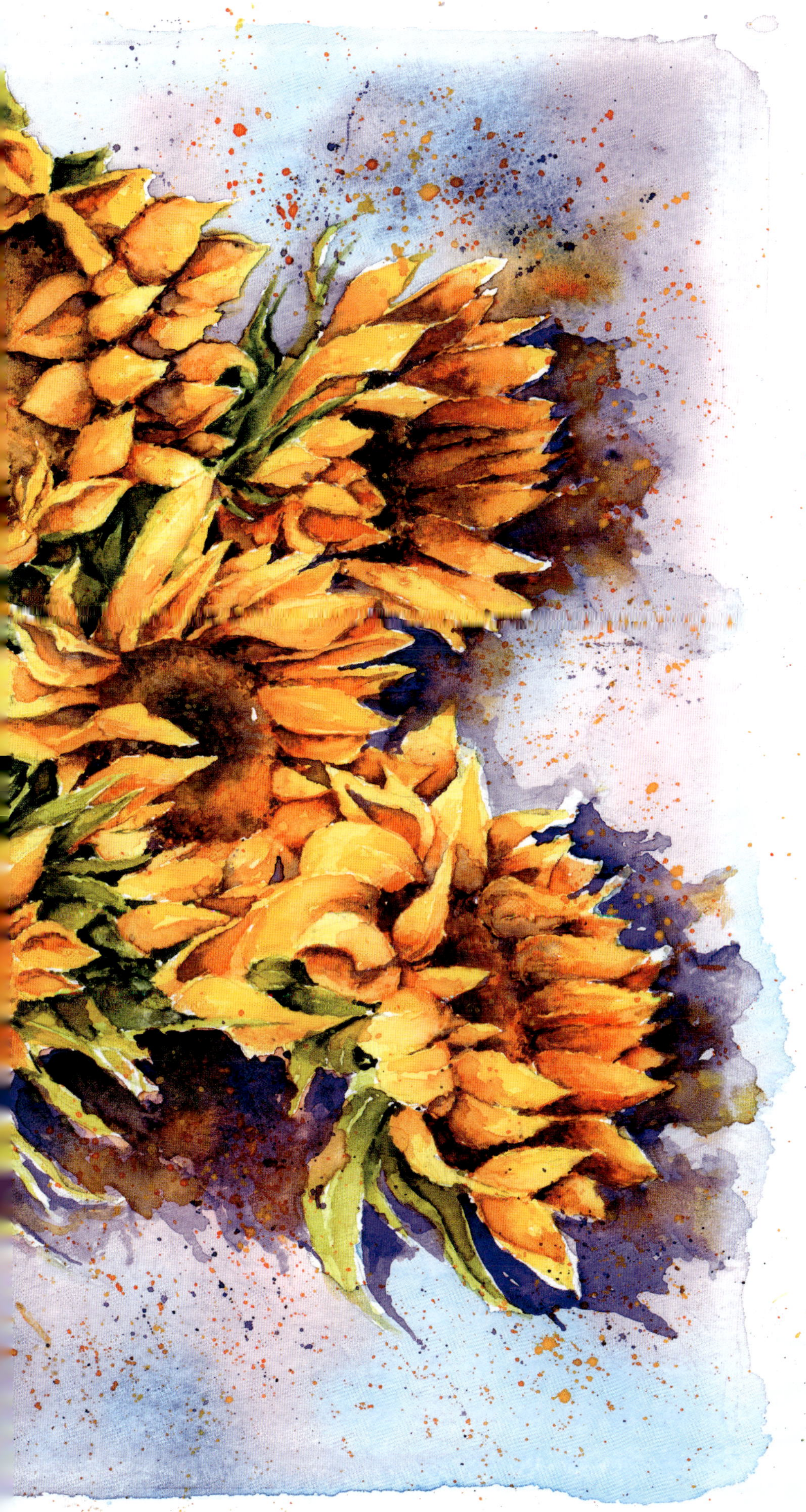

FINAL PAINTING

I felt that this composition needed to be "lifted" from the background by intensifying the surrounding shadow washes. The aerial viewpoint that I took here could have resulted in a "flat" feel so I employed strong mixes of purple and blue, breaking up the solidity of these by freely flicking their complementary colored paints at them.

# Final Thoughts

So, after many adventures along the way, we have finally come to the end of our journey together into color. I do, however, hope that it will not be the end of your own personal journey and that you will carry on to explore, experiment and eventually grow to enjoy using color in your painting as I have always done.

One of the key purposes of this book has always been to inspire you to delve further into the world of color on your own and enable you to make independent choices and decisions about your own painting.

All of the artwork used on these pages has come directly from the teaching materials that I have produced over several years for the courses that I run. Most double-page spreads were originally A2 watercolor sheets, created as a permanent visual aid for students during my classes. My hope is always that, on leaving my classes, students will feel considerably more empowered in their ability to choose and use color with confidence and, eventually, in a more creative way.

I usually start my classes with a statement that I believe to be true: No one, to my knowledge, has ever come to any physical harm by using colored paint on watercolor paper. The worst that can happen is that you will make some wrong choices, or the colors won't work as you had planned once they have dried. Should this happen to you, then consider what may have gone wrong, turn the paper over, and start again using your knowledge gained through these pages. So, don't be afraid of applying a hot, glowing Scarlet Lake to shining and simmering Sap Green. It won't hurt. Yes, I do understand the intimidating effect of a large sheet of pristine, white watercolor paper, knowing that the only marks made on it will eventually be ones that you will make yourself. If this is too scary, then choose a smaller sheet of paper to start off with.

Now, a parting word about the paints that you will encounter on the art store shelves. There are many paint manufacturers who produce a vast array of watercolor paints. As with many products there are affordable ranges and the high end products. Artists' paints are no different. It would be inappropriate for me to use these pages to recommend any one brand. In fact, I'm not really sure that I could as I tend to buy the colors that I need, regardless of brand or company loyalties. My suggestion to you would be to buy the most expensive that you can afford for the best results. The cheaper paints are more likely to contain a filler to "pad-out" the pigment. This will not produce quite the same level of luminosity as the paints with pure pigment and an additive to aid the flow of paint will provide. They are, however, perfectly acceptable and, indeed, useful for experimenting and taking your first steps.

*"I usually start my classes with a statement that I believe to be true: No one, to my knowledge, has ever come to any physical harm by using colored paint on watercolor paper. The worst that can happen is that you will make some wrong choices, or the colors won't work as you had planned once they have dried."*

As this book is all about color – where it comes from, how it works, and why it works as it does in watercolor form – I haven't dwelt too long on watercolor painting technique. Many different terms are used for the act of applying watercolor paint to paper using a brush: wet into wet, dry painting, layering paints, scrumbling and so on. Whichever technique you choose to use, understanding which colors work best together will remain much the same. No matter how skilled you may become with any one technique, if the colors are not right, then the picture won't work.

My last piece of advice to you would be to try to see the visual world as an artist, all day, every day. It is through seeing and observing that a greater understanding and awareness of color will develop. Look for color wherever you are. Notice it and, if you can't record it there and then, remember it. Try to see colors in shadows both indoors and outdoors. We are surrounded by it. But, most of all, enjoy it!

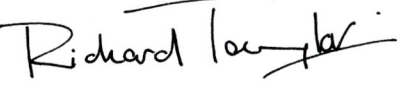

# ABOUT THE AUTHOR

It was the gift of a painting-by-numbers kit to the ten-year-old Richard that sparked the realization in him that he understood color much better than the emerging technologies and sciences of the post-war years. Sitting at the table in front of this pre-drawn canvas at his home in the leafy north London suburb of Enfield, it became clear that the mixing sequences were obvious – but what happened if you tried to change them?

The traditional education that followed offered little to satisfy his interest in paint and color, and before too long his passion for art took him to the East Coast of England where he trained as an art teacher – a qualification that was later to be supplemented by a Bachelor's degree in Art History and a Master's degree in Fine Art Authorship.

Since then, Richard has run courses in almost every type of school and educational institute imaginable, including teaching a watercolor summer school at The Heatherley School of Fine Art, Chelsea, and a period training teachers as an Associate University Lecturer. He has also worked as an art teaching advisor to Essex Education Authority, visiting schools and colleges to help establish specialist courses and to develop art teachers' skills. Richard has written articles for an assortment of instructional art publications and worked as consultant to *The Art Course* magazine.

For the past 20 years Richard has taught specialist watercolor courses at the Watershed Studio in the small village of St Osyth, Essex, near his home on the coast, as well as running workshops for art groups and societies.

*The Watercolor Artist's Guide to Color* is Richard's nineteenth instructional book.

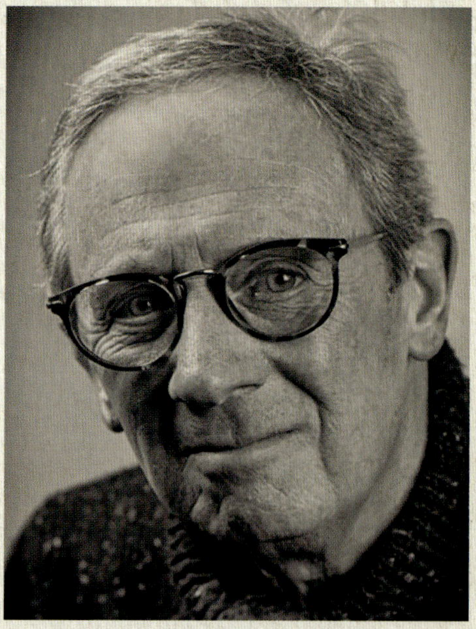

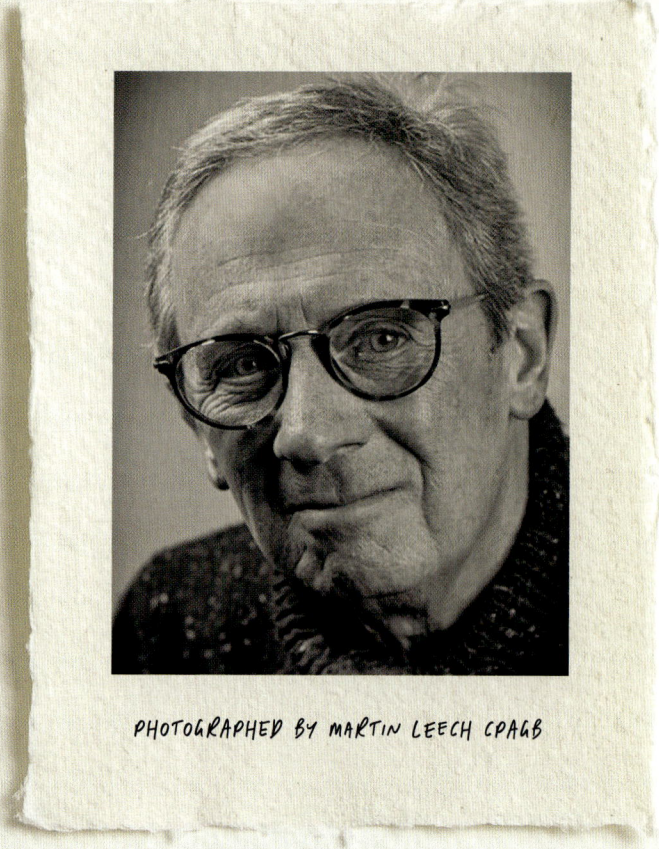

PHOTOGRAPHED BY MARTIN LEECH CPAGB


### THANKS

Thanks, as always, are due to my wife Debbie for her constant support in all things and at all times.


### DEDICATION

This book is dedicated to our grandson Austin. May your world be forever full of color.

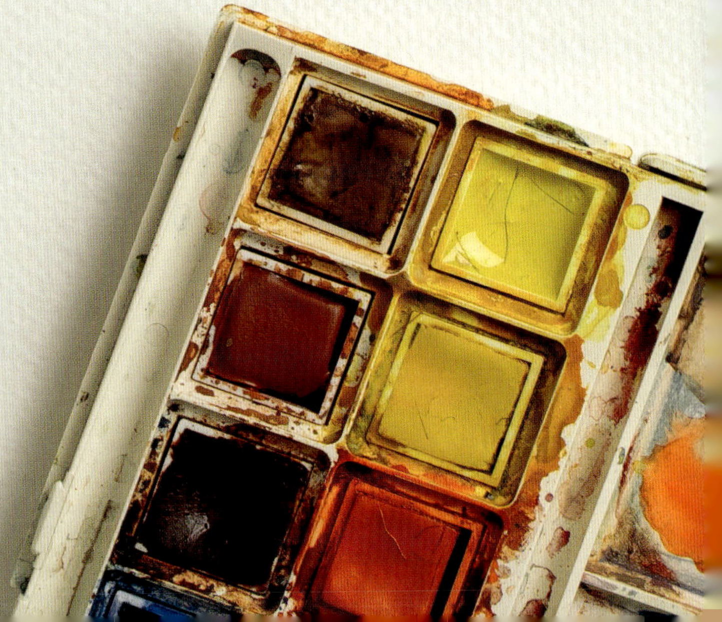

# INDEX

bleeding colors 11, 61, 74, 80, 84–6, 88, 105
blues 28, 30–2, 44–7, 62–75
- darkening 66–7, 79
- and purple 54–9, 60
- sketchbook studies 109–12, 116–19, 121
- temperature 90, 92–3, 97–101
- and the three-stage approach 79, 82, 86–9

cadmiums 17
color families 28–33, 86, 88
- *see also specific color families*

color mixing 24, 29, 88
- greens 68–71
- with a limited palette 87
- oranges 40–3
- purples 54–7
- shadows 81

color temperature 90–101
color values, graduated 89
color wheels 9, 16, 18
complementary colors 9, 23, 29, 32–3, 38, 45, 52, 66, 78–9
cool colors 90–101
cubes 79–81
curvature 10–13

darkening tones 36, 38, 79
- blues 66–7, 79
- greens 72–3, 79
- oranges 44–5, 79
- purples 58–9, 79
- reds 52–3, 79

dilution 8–9
dimension, creation 10–13
dioxazines 5, 17
dyes 4, 17

fish 96–7
fruit 49, 61, 63, 86–8

granulation 20
grays 22–7, 108–9
greens 33, 52–3, 68–75
- color mixing 68–71
- color temperature 92, 98–9
- darkening 72–3, 79
- sketchbook studies 108–9, 112, 116–17, 120–1
- and the three-stage approach 79, 82–3, 87–9

gum arabic 8

highlights 10–13, 36, 46, 74–5, 105, 110, 116

Industrial Revolution 4–5
integrity 23
iris 95, 105, 106–13

light 36, 38, 52–3, 66–7, 76–89
light sources 10

mid-tones 10, 11–12
modern synthetic colors 16–18

natural earth colours 18–21
natural organic paints 18, 19
neutrals 22–7

oranges 33, 40–7, 66–7
- color temperature 92, 98–9
- darkening 44–5, 79
- sketchbook studies 111, 116–21
- and the three-stage approach 79, 86–9

paints 5, 8, 14–33
- dilution 8–9

palettes, limited 87
phthalocyanines 17
pigments 4–5, 8, 16–17
primary colors 9, 28–33, 78
- *see also* blues; reds; yellows

purples 32, 38–9, 54–61, 74–5, 100
- darkening 58–9, 79
- sketchbook studies 108–12, 119, 121
- and the three-stage approach 79, 86–7, 89

'push-pull' theory 10, 12

quinacridones 17

reds 28, 31, 32, 40–7, 48–61, 72–3
- darkening 52–3, 79
- temperature 90, 92–3, 100–1
- and the three-stage approach 79, 82–3, 87–9
- types 51

reflected colors 80–1

secondary colors 9, 29, 32–3, 78
shade 76–89
shadows 10, 11, 13, 78–9, 81, 82–3
sketchbook studies 104–23
spheres 10–3, 24
still life studies 46–7, 60–1, 74–5, 82–9, 93–101, 104–23
sunflowers 34–5, 83, 105, 114–23

temperature circles 92–3
texture 20–1
three-stage approach 78–89
tints 27
tonal diagrams 8–9, 86
tonal range 21, 23, 24, 39, 42, 51–3, 67, 112
tones 9, 70–1
- darkening 36, 38, 44–5, 52–3, 58–9, 66–7, 72–3, 79

tulips 74–5, 84–5, 93

vegetables 46–7, 89

warm colors 90–101
Winsors 17

yellows 10–11, 28, 30, 33, 34–47, 58–61
- color temperature 92–5, 98–101
- and greens 68–75
- sketchbook studies 108–9, 111–12, 116–21
- and the three-stage approach 79, 82–3, 86–9

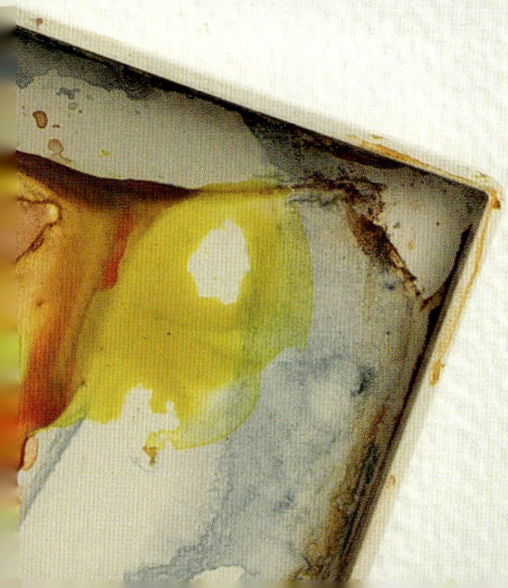

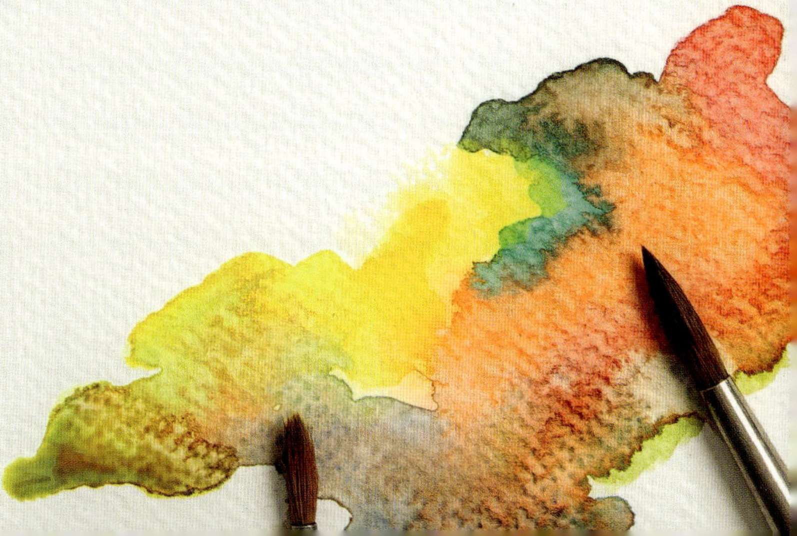

A DAVID AND CHARLES BOOK


David and Charles is an imprint
of David and Charles, Ltd
Suite A, Tourism House, Pynes Hill, Exeter,
EX2 5WS



First published in the UK and USA in 2024



A catalogue record for this book is available from the British Library.

ISBN-13: 9781446313473 paperback
ISBN-13: 9781446313497 EPUB
ISBN-13: 9781446313480 PDF

This book has been printed on paper from approved suppliers and made from pulp from sustainable sources.

MIX
Paper | Supporting responsible forestry
FSC® C136333

Printed in China through Asia Pacific Offset for:
David and Charles, Ltd
Suite A, Tourism House, Pynes Hill, Exeter, EX2 5WS

10 9 8 7 6 5 4 3 2 1

Publishing Director: Ame Verso
Managing Editor: Jeni Chown
Editor: Jessica Cropper
Project Editors: Jenny Fox-Proverbs and Cheryl Brown
Head of Design: Anna Wade
Design: Anna Wade and Nikki Ellis
Pre-press Designer: Susan Reansbury
Art Direction: Jess Pearson
Photography: Tom Hargreaves
Production Manager: Beverley Richardson



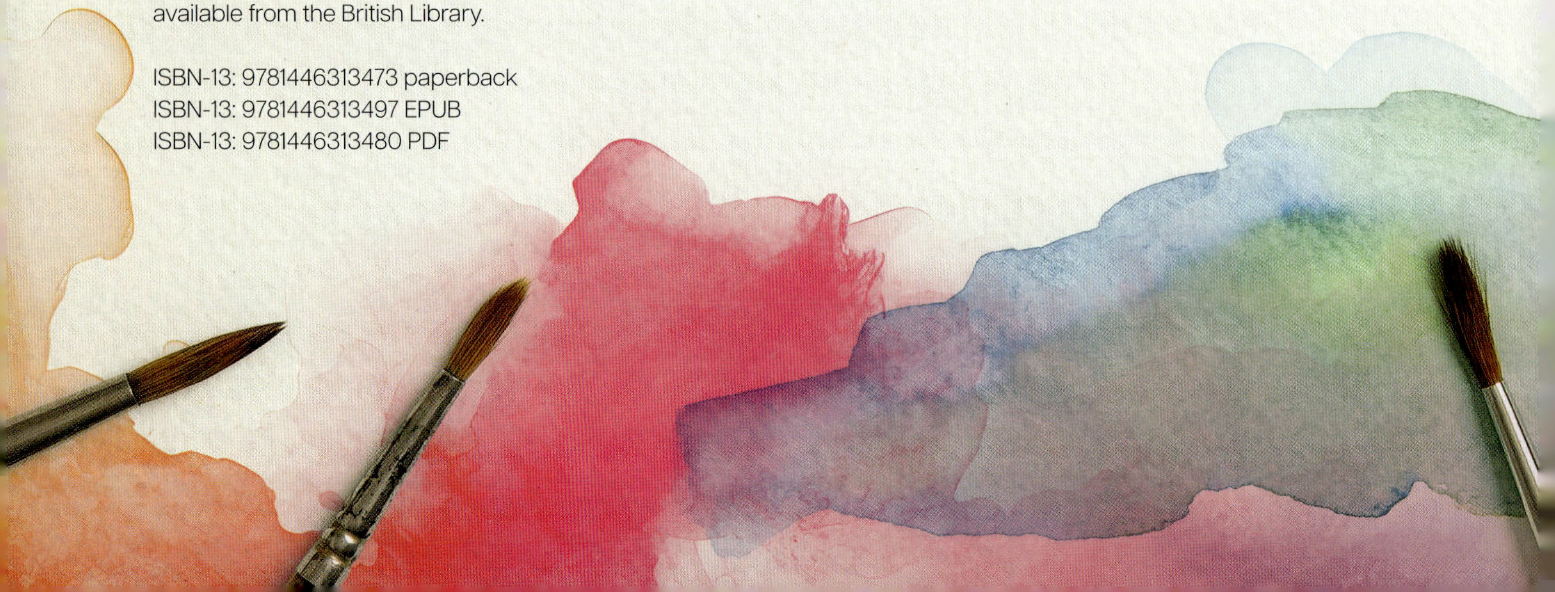